DEDICATION: LOREN AND MILDRED PUTNAM,
with the Stone Laboratory Classroom Building on Gibraltar Island in the background, Summer 1996.

Lost Stories: Yesterday and Today at Put-in-Bay

Including Theresa Thorndale's "Island Jottings" of the 1890's

2002

Ronald L. Stuckey

Lost Stories: Yesterday and Today at Put-in-Bay

Including Theresa Thorndale's "Island Jottings" of the 1890's

Volume Two of a Series: Stuckey's Contributions to the Lake Erie Area of Northern Ohio.

Volume One in this Series (although not identified) is *Edwin Lincoln Moseley (1865-1948), Naturalist, Scientist, Educator*, published in 1998 by RLS Creations.

Citation: Ronald L. Stuckey. 2002. Lost Stories: Yesterday and Today at Put-in-Bay, Including Theresa Thorndale's "Island Jottings" of the 1890's. RLS Creations, Columbus, Ohio. xvi, 224 pp.

Written, Compiled, Designed, Edited, and Published by:
Ronald L. Stuckey
RLS Creations
Box 12455 Columbus, Ohio 43212-0455

Computer page layout by Ricki C. Herdendorf, EcoSphere Associates
Garfield Farms, 4921 Detroit Road, Sheffield Village, Ohio 44054

Printed by Thomson-Shore, Inc.
7300 West Joy Road, Dexter, Michigan 48130

ISBN 0-9668034-5-0

Foreword

This delightful book of "Lost Stories" from the Lake Erie Islands has two heroes. The first is the subject of the book - Theresa Thorndale, a pioneering woman journalist on a remote isle in western Lake Erie. The second is the author of the book - Professor Ronald L. Stuckey, a scientist whose devotion to the Lake Erie Islands led him to rediscover Thorndale's writings of island life that happened a century ago.

Other than her writings of the islands, little is known about Theresa Thorndale. In fact Theresa Thorndale never really existed. That name was simply a pen name taken by Miss Lydia Jane Ryall as a news correspondent to the *Sandusky Register*. Her articles and books about Put-in-Bay and the surrounding islands are a romantic mixture of fact and fancy, in the late nineteenth century style. They are made more charming by alluding to the arts and classics and references to music, poetry, and even mythology. Although written during the "Gay '90s" when Put-in-Bay was a bustling summer resort, some of her works contain an element of loneliness and depression. However, Lydia was not one to spare an adjective which added a uniquely descriptive flavor to her writing. She was the reporter who chronicled the news events.

Sadly, Ryall's books are long out of print and the newspapers which contained her writings are yellowed with age, but their content still exists on microfilm. Indeed, her stories-the stories of the islands-were lost to the general public. Tales of grape harvests and wine making, the grand resort hotels, commercial fishing and the hatcheries, the ice company, the building of the lighthouse and the opening of the Oak Point House, along with many other topics, were all lost. Starting in 1971, Stuckey faithfully handcopied many of her articles from microfilm, and at the same time, he resurrected "Lost Stories" of other local writers to aid in rounding out the histories.

In 1959, Ronald L. Stuckey was a student at the Franz Theodore Stone Laboratory, The Ohio State University's biological research station at Put-in-Bay. He caught "island fever," an affliction which can never be cured, only soothed by frequent visits to South Bass Island. In 1966 he returned as an Assistant Professor of Botany, and he continued to spend most of his summers teaching about plants at the Lake Laboratory until retirement in 1991.

But Dr. Stuckey has done much more than reproduce Thorndale's writings. He has lavishly illustrated the book with historic photographs collected from many sources. To these he has added more recent photographs to demonstrate the changes that have occurred at South Bass Island in the past 100 years. Even more enlightening are the narrative sections written by Dr. Stuckey. In each chapter he brings the reader "up to date." We are able to trace, for instance the Hotel Victory from its heyday to its foundations now in the State Park and the Federal Fish Hatchery from its original design for raising whitefish to its present use as a university research laboratory.

I think you will be as fascinated, amused, and at times moved as I was in reading the accounts of Miss Ryall and of others and the retrospective writings of Dr. Stuckey. I believe we owe both of our heroes a debt of gratitude-one for capturing the flavor of the island life a century ago and the other for rescuing those pages of history from oblivion. Both of them faithfully recorded the stories of "Yesterday and Today at Put-in-Bay."

Charles E. Herdendorf, Director Emeritus
Franz Theodore Stone Laboratory

Dedication

Loren and Mildred Putnam

Loren and Mildred Putnam were summer residents of Peach Point at Put-in-Bay during 18 years, from 1956 to 1973, while he was Director of the Franz Theodore Stone Laboratory. Known fondly as "Puttie" and "Millie" to the students and faculty at the Laboratory, they were common folks from small town communities in western Kentucky. There, they began secondary school teaching careers following the receipt of Bachelor Degrees in 1935 from Murray State Teachers College in Murray, Kentucky. During the next six years, Puttie's principal classes were general science, biology, physics, mathematics, and music including being director of the school band; while during five years, Millie taught classes in English, theatre, and health science.

"Millie" and "Puttie"

Puttie had intentions of entering medical school, and during the summers of 1937 and 1938, he had begun a graduate program in physiology and endocrinology at the University of Wisconsin. A high school teaching companion, who had attended the Stone Laboratory, told Puttie about the graduate program in zoology at the Stone Laboratory of The Ohio State University. Putnam was attracted to this program because one could earn more credit hours there during the summer quarter than at the University of Wisconsin. For Putnam, who was seeking an advanced degree in an expeditious manner, the OSU Laboratory certainly had an appealing program, if one were to continue in the teaching profession.

Puttie first attended the Stone Laboratory in the summer of 1939, when he took courses in entomology, ornithology, and conducted research on the behavior of the cedar waxwing bird. The following summer on 13 June 1940 Loren S. Putnam (born 20 October 1913 in Morrison, Illinois) and Mildred E. Miller (born 26 February 1915 in Hazel, Kentucky) were married in Bowling Green, Kentucky. Immediately after the wedding, they left for the Laboratory where Puttie continued his graduate research on the cedar waxwing. During the winter, Laboratory Director Thomas H. Langlois met with the Putnams in the their apartment at Bowling Green, Kentucky, and later that winter he hired Millie to be his executive secretary beginning in the summer of 1941. At the same time, he offered Puttie a graduate assistantship in charge of equipment, supplies, and coordinator of connections between the Columbus campus and the Laboratory. Considerable time was available for Puttie to continue his graduate degree research on the cedar waxwing, and he completed his M. S. Degree in the summer of 1941. Millie worked as Langlois' executive secretary through the summer of 1941 until December 1942.

Prior to the conclusion of World War II, Putnam was a civilian instructor for the United States Navy teaching Air Navigational Physics in the V5 Program from 1943 to early 1944 at Murray State College. He then returned to high school teaching for a year in Shelbyville, Illinois, before resuming his studies on the behavior of the cedar waxwing at the Stone Laboratory in the summer of 1945. He completed this project for the Ph.D. Degree in Zoology in 1947. While at the Laboratory in 1945, newly appointed Chairman Lawrence Snyder of the Department of Zoology and Entomology on the OSU Columbus campus invited Putnam to be a full-time instructor. He accepted and began teaching courses in general zoology and later developed courses in basic ornithology and an advanced course in the physiology and anatomy of birds. Putnam completed his entire University teaching career at The Ohio State University, advancing through the ranks as an instructor (1945-1947), assistant professor (1948-1952), associate professor (1953-1960), professor (1961-1983), and professor emeritus of zoology (1984-present).

Dr. Loren S. Putnam served as the sixth Director of the Franz Theodore Stone Laboratory from 1955 to 1973, while Millie served as the Laboratory's librarian during that same time. He came to this position at one of the most difficult times in the history of the Laboratory. Based on an extensive review by the OSU Board of Trustees, followed by their action of 13 June 1955, the year-round program of biological research by faculty and graduate students and the summer teaching programs, all of which had been in operation since 1936, were discontinued at the close of the 1955 summer session. Former Stone

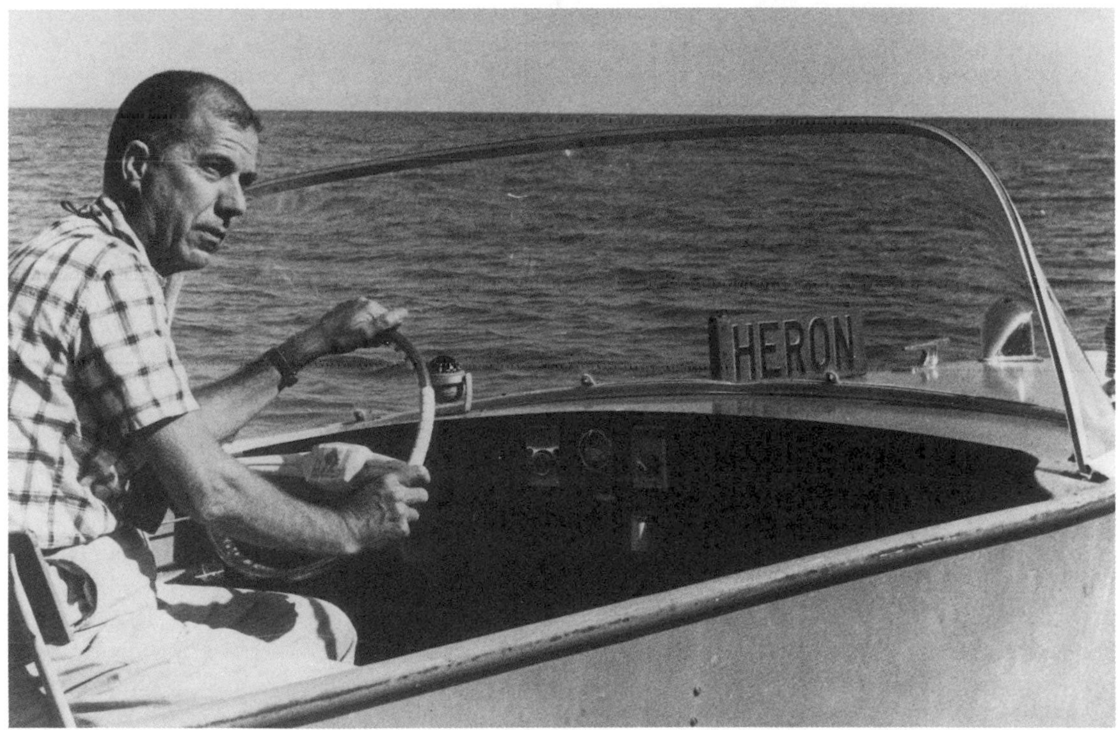

Loren S. Putnam, Stone Laboratory Director for 18 Years (1955-1973).

Laboratory faculty and students, principally of the Departments of Zoology and Entomology and of Botany and Plant Pathology, wanted summer field classes in these subjects available for their students, and they wanted them continued at the Stone Laboratory. Although, Frederic W. Heimburger, Vice President for Instruction and Research, was reluctant to reinstate a summer teaching program, he convinced the Trustees to allow for the Laboratory under certain restrictions to offer four courses during the first term, problem courses only for research students during the second term, and no research investigations by non-teaching faculty.

In October 1955, Loren S. Putnam, upon recommendation by the Chairmen of both the Zoology and Botany Departments, was asked to become the academic director of the Stone Laboratory. He accepted and immediately began preparations for classes in the summer of 1956. Under Putnam's directorship, with 25 students in attendance that summer, the enrollment continued to increase and eventually soared to a capacity of 88 students in the summer of 1967 with a full curriculum of twenty courses for upper level undergraduate and graduate students. At the 11 July 1958 meeting of the OSU Board of Trustees, Director Putnam unanimously was commended for his "administrative . . . leadership demonstrated in developing the 1958 program at the Franz Theodore Stone Laboratory."

Director Putnam slowly and quietly returned aquatic biological research on Lake Erie to the Laboratory, and by 1971, he was instrumental in the creation by The Ohio State University of a new research organization, the Center for Lake Erie Area Research (CLEAR), with headquarters for its research program at the Laboratory. The Center, under the energetic directorship of Charles E. Herdendorf, had by 1983 conducted over $10 million worth of sponsored research on the ecology and environmental problems of Lake Erie. Following Puttie's retirement from the Laboratory Directorship in October 1973, he taught his Advanced Ornithology course at the Stone Laboratory for three summers, including 1983, the year prior to his final retirement from the University. At that time, his successor Laboratory Director Charles E. Herdendorf wrote: "Putnam's contribution over the years to excellence in teaching, student guidance, and sound management have allowed Stone Laboratory to flourish and maintain its position as an outstanding field station." In 1973, Putnam was chosen President of the Organization of Inland Field Biology Stations, an organization representing 50 of the major field biology stations in the United States and Canada. At that time, the educational program at the Stone Laboratory was considered one of the best field stations for teaching excellence, as judged by the Field Biology Station Organization. In his own quiet, modest way during an interview in 1967, Puttie summed his role as Laboratory Director with the following statement: "My days are hardly predictable. I may find myself driving the bus, greeting guests, carting groceries, ordering equipment, or planning curriculum. I just handle all the weird little problems and see that everybody is happy."

During the Centennial Celebration of the Stone Laboratory in 1995 and 1996, Laboratory Director Jeffrey M. Reutter honored Loren S. Putnam with a Distinguished Service Award for "superior leadership and guidance of the programs, students, and staff of Stone Laboratory," and he was inducted into the Laboratory's Hall of Fame for "a lifetime of superior leadership and service to the Laboratory as its director (1955-1973), teacher, researcher, and mentor for hundreds of students." Mildred Putnam received the Laboratory Director's Award for her "quiet and selfless dedication to and support of the faculty, staff, and students of Stone Laboratory."

Ronald L. Stuckey
August 2001

Table of Contents

Introductory Commentary

"Lost Stories" is a collection of previously printed accounts revealing past happenings, for the most part, on those properties now owned by the State of Ohio at the village of Put-in-Bay on South Bass Island. These articles, printed here from their original source, appeared as early as 150 years ago in newspapers published in Sandusky, Ohio. The principal source is the *Sandusky Register*, a daily and weekly newspaper that has appeared under various other names since its establishment in 1822. The majority of the articles are from the 1890's when Miss Lydia Jane Ryall was Put-in-Bay's news correspondent to that paper. Miss Ryall's articles were written under her pseudonym, Theresa Thorndale.

Contents of Chapters

Chapter one introduces Miss Ryall, and is based on fragmentary information gathered through historical and genealogical research on her life. The two stories in chapter twelve written by Theresa Thorndale are considered to be autobiographical. Both stories are adventures in which Miss Thorndale could have participated at sometime during her time at Put-in-Bay. The second, thirteenth, and fourteenth chapters are comprised of articles about the village of Put-in-Bay and in general about South Bass Island. The remaining nine chapters constitute the major theme of the book, being historical happenings and activities on state properties belonging either to The Ohio State University or the State of Ohio Department of Natural Resources. With the exception of the first chapter on Gibraltar Island (No. Ten), one or more of Miss Thorndale's stories comprise the introductory or main component of each chapter. Her vivid, picturesque descriptions of landscapes, buildings, and activities give her stories a unique charm that characterizes first hand these historic places on South Bass Island. Her news stories, and those of other authors, during the "Gay Nineties" were written when activities on the Island were expanding, and tourism was becoming prevalent. Some of these enterprising activities were the building of Hotel Victory (1889-1892) at Stone's Cove and Victory Park, the United States Lighthouse (1897) on Parker Point, the Clubhouse for the Cincinnati Fishing Club (1893) on Oak Point, the United States Fish Hatchery (1889-1890), and the large Ice House of the Forest City Ice Company (1894) on Peach Point.

Theresa Thorndale and Island History

Theresa Thorndale's articles described activities at the Hotel Victory, the Lighthouse, the Cincinnati Fishing Club, the United States Fish Hatchery, and the Forest City Ice Company. Through the years these properties gradually were acquired by the State of Ohio. The Ohio State University received Gibraltar Island with Cooke's Castle and other buildings (1925), the United States Fish Hatchery and Superintendent's House on Peach Point (1940), and the Lighthouse on Parker Point (1967). The Division of Conservation, later named the Department of Natural Resources, acquired some of the Forest City Ice Company property on Peach Point for a State Fish Hatchery (1907), Victory Park with its ruins of Hotel Victory for a State Park (1946), and Oak Point with the Clubhouse of the Cincinnati Fishing Club (1938) which was leased to The Ohio State University until 1956 when the building was razed and the site became the Oak Point Picnic Area. Miss Thorndale also wrote on the activities of the first biological survey of plants and animals in Lake Erie waters, which was conducted from the United States Fish Hatchery, and gave a vivid description of Peach Point after taking a tour of that peninsula in 1894.

Theresa Thorndale is no stranger to the written history of the islands in western Lake Erie. Long out of print, her two charming, classic books, *Sketches and Stories of the Lake Erie Islands*, are important base-line references for insights of what happened on these islands. The first, labeled *Souvenir Volume* (1898), appeared under her pseudonym, Theresa Thorndale. It represents a contemporary account of the situations and life on the Islands during the "Gay Nineties." The second, called the *Perry Centennial Edition* (1913), was an expanded version published under her legal name, Lydia J. Ryall. In these books she had chapters on the Hotel Victory, the Fish Hatcheries, and Gibraltar Island. Most of her stories reproduced here are originals from her pen as published in the *Sandusky Register*. For Gibraltar Island, however, her account is taken from descriptive selections of that Island's chapter in each book. Her newspaper stories constitute "new" first hand historical data and descriptions of a part of South Bass Island not previously available in book-form to the general public.

Aside from Miss Ryall's two books, South Bass Island history has been told in a number of places. These histories are *South Bass Island and Islanders* (1948) by Thomas Huxley Langlois and Marina Holmes Langlois, *Enchanting Isles of Erie* (1949) by Harry H. Ross, *Now and Then at Put-in-Bay, Sesquicentennial 1813-1963* (1963), anonymously written, and *The Put-in-Bay Story Told from the Top-of-the-Rock* (1968) by Ruth Dickerman Moizuk. The two most recent documented histories with numerous photographs and cited references are *Put-in-Bay: Its History* (1971) by Charles E. Frohman and *Isolated Splendor: Put-in-Bay and South Bass Island* (1975) by Robert J. Dodge.

Stuckey's Interest in the Erie Islands

My first acquaintance with South Bass Island came in 1959, when as an undergraduate at The Franz Theodore Stone Laboratory, I was initiated into the study of the flora of the Erie Islands. At that time I took the course in Field Botany taught by the late T. Richard Fisher of The Ohio State University. Returning in 1966 as an Assistant Professor of Botany in The Ohio State University, I taught Field Botany and the next year I taught Higher Aquatic Plants. From these experiences, I solidified my interest in this flora and continued to teach these courses at the Laboratory until the summer of 1991. At that time also, my career in teaching, research, and administration at the Laboratory had its beginning, as did my sincere interest in the history of South Bass Island. It was then that I began collecting postcards, published papers, and books on the subject. This history initially provided background information and data upon which I was able to access some of the changes in the Island's terrestrial and aquatic flora. Human history was not neglected, and with the documented publication of Charles E. Frohman's book, *Put-in-Bay: Its History* (1971), I now had an index to many of the original news articles that appeared in the Sandusky newspapers which he cited at the end of the chapters in his book. In September 1971, I faithfully hand-copied many of these newsworthy stories from microfilms of the original papers retained in the Sandusky Library, Sandusky, Ohio. These articles were initially assembled into the present sequence in the winter of 1983 and were subsequently typewritten by Ms. Andrea Wilson, the Stone Laboratory secretary.

Guide for the Reader

For the most part, the newspaper articles selected for this book are reproduced much like they appeared in the printed newspaper. Some stories, however, have had to be shortened or edited to be accommodated in the available space in this book. In the original newspaper articles where mistakes had been made or incomplete information given with respect to names of people, places, and/or dates, these items have been corrected without comment when discovered. Sentence structure and punctuation have at times been changed to clarify the original or to correct obvious errors. Some information is of necessity repeated in two or more articles; however, in many instances extensive repetitious material has been eliminated. The reader, however, will notice considerable wordiness in the articles, which is largely retained to keep the writing style of that time period. Most of Theresa Thorndale's columns appeared under the headings "Put-in-Bay" or "Island Jottings." These headings for her stories in this book have been replaced by new headings to reflect more accurately the contents of the article, rather than using her more general column heading. Special feature stories may bear their own descriptive titles and have been retained in many instances.

Throughout this book, the reader will notice two styles of type. The small size type (Times) is identified with that text placed in two columns on a page; whereas the large size type (Helvetica) pertains to that text which extends across the page. Each type size signals its author. The stories from the Sandusky newspapers written by Theresa Thorndale and other authors are in the small-size type, in two columns, thus resembling their newspaper origin. As the compiler of this book, I wrote all the text in the larger-size type that spreads across the page. This information introduces the reproduced "Lost Stories" of Theresa Thorndale that follow in the two-column format, or it summarizes the situation at each State owned site on South Bass Island during the past ten or more years.

In the "Table of Contents," the titles of all the "Lost Stories" and the subtitles appearing throughout the text written by Stuckey are identified by each author's initials in parentheses following each story title. The authors' full names corresponding to these initials and the page numbers to where their stories appear in the book are on page 206.

Reading stories from century-old newspapers can be fun, interesting, and informative. It is anticipated that these "lost" stories will bring back memories from past eras and provide a contemporary and factual account of what happened at various points in time at these selected sites on South Bass Island. These stories of yesterday are reprinted here in order that they may live with us today and no longer be lost from us or future generations. These selections of South Bass Island history are only a part of the entire glorious history that has been the attraction of this Island to its few pioneer and permanent settlers, its frequent summer residents, and its numerous sightseers and tourists. Accounts of what is happening now, if not recorded or published, will also become lost in the future. In reality, this book comprises the "Lost Stories" of *Yesterday and Today at Put-in-Bay*.

Ronald L. Stuckey
September 2001

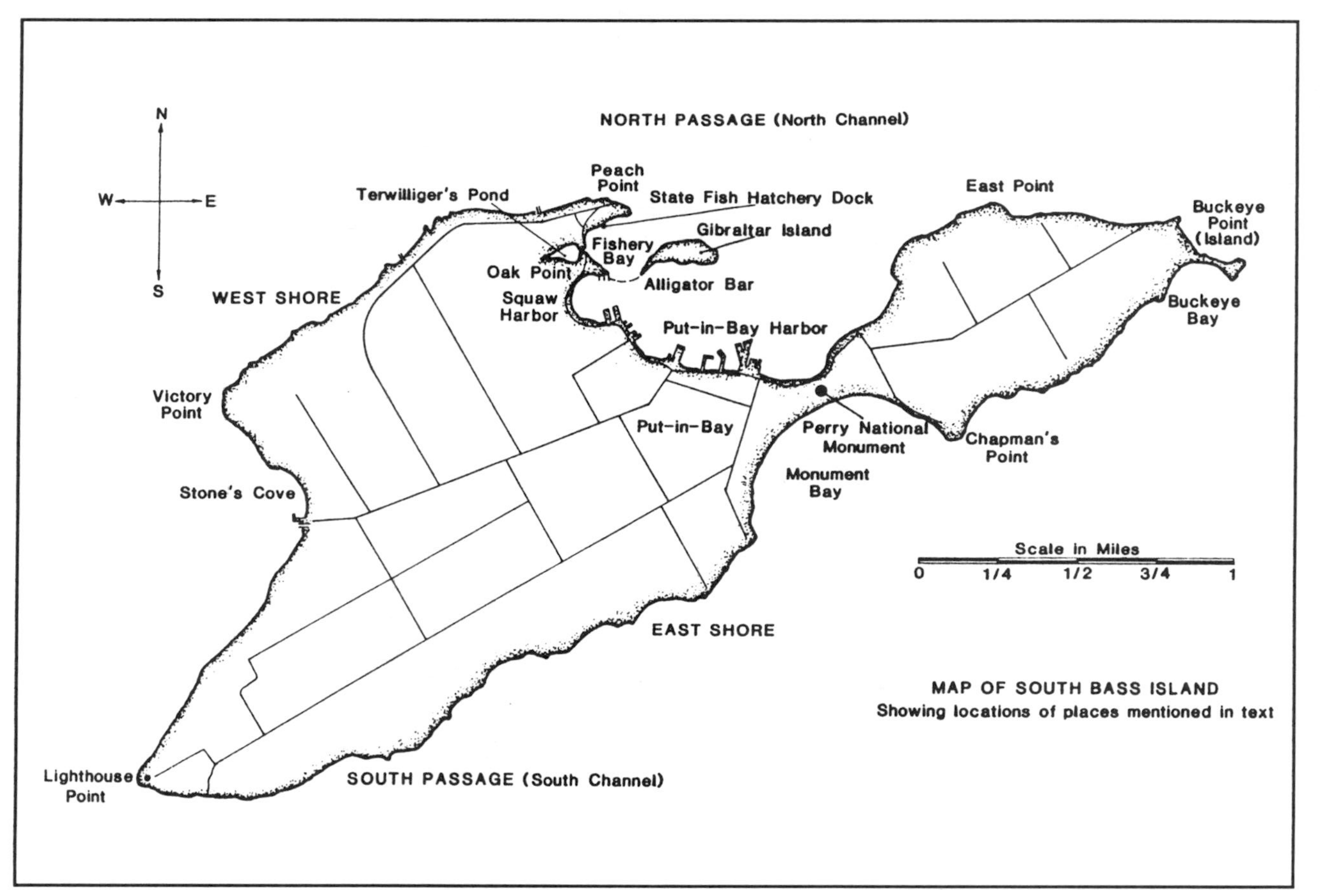

Map of South Bass Island with names of many places referred to in this book.

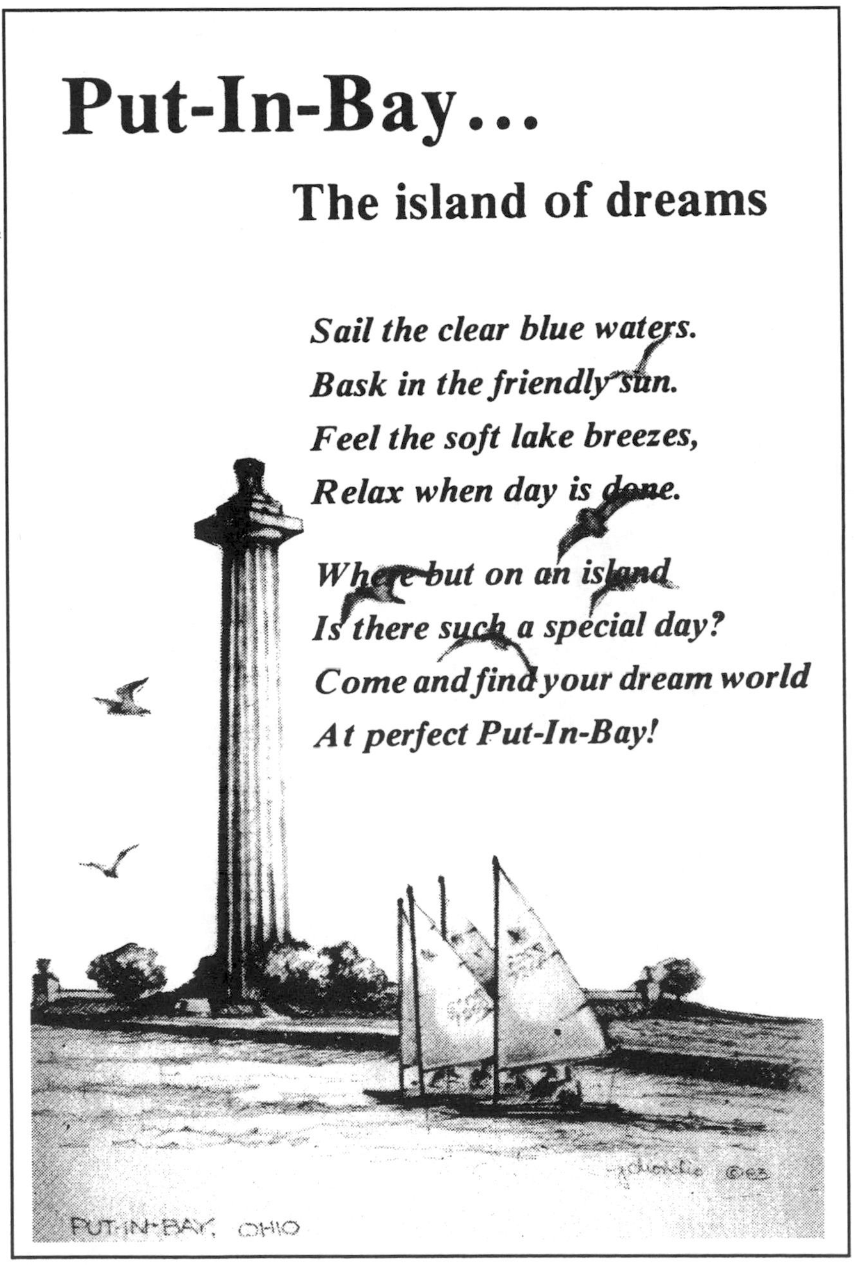

Put-In-Bay...
The island of dreams
Sail the clear blue waters.
Bask in the friendly sun.
Feel the soft lake breezes,
Relax when day is done.
Where but on an island
Is there such a special day?
Come and find your dream world
At perfect Put-In-Bay!
PUT-IN-BAY, OHIO

Perry's Victory and International Peace Memorial.

SKETCHES AND STORIES

OF THE

LAKE ERIE ISLANDS

BY

THERESA THORNDALE.

SOUVENIR VOLUME

SANDUSKY, OHIO:
I. F. Mack & Brother, Publishers.
1898.

Title Page of Theresa Thorndale's Book, *Sketches and Stories of the Lake Erie Islands* (1898), with illustration believed to be Miss Thorndale.

Introducing Lydia J. Ryall (Theresa Thorndale)

Who was Miss Lydia Jane Flint Ryall (1850-1920), known as Theresa Thorndale? To islanders familiar with local history, she should be recalled as the author of the first and most extensive book on *Sketches and Stories of the Lake Erie Islands*. It was published in 1898, and authored under her pseudonym, Theresa Thorndale, followed by a second expanded edition in 1913 under her legal name, Lydia J. Ryall. Little is known of this lady, an enigmatic writer of especial talent who mixed fact, fiction, and romance, peppered with references to mythology, poetry, music, novels, and classic historic writings. Loaded with strange and overly descriptive adjectives, her stories possess a uniqueness not attained by many other authors. Perhaps largely self-educated, Miss Ryall's stories reflect an apparent lonely and sometimes depressed life written during the happy gay-ninety period when she lived and wrote at the village of Put-in-Bay.

Professional and Personal Life

Lydia Jane Flint Ryall, while writing under the pseudonym of Theresa Thorndale, considered herself a journalist and served as Put-in-Bay's news correspondent to the *Sandusky Register* during the 1890's. Of her professional life as a writer here, or elsewhere, little is known, but internal evidence from her book, newspaper articles, and other standard genealogical sources suggest that she lived at Put-in-Bay throughout the 1890's and beyond, perhaps until about 1915. Her news columns and feature stories in the *Register* are known to have appeared nearly continuously for twelve years, from 1889 to 1901. Most of her articles can be located under the headings, "Put-in-Bay" or "Island Jottings." Special feature stories usually bore their own descriptive titles.

Of Miss Ryall's personal life, again, only fragmentary information is available and it in itself represents a "lost story." Born in August 1850 in Carlisle Township, Lorain County, Ohio, she was the daughter of David Flint and Susan Halle. However, as of the 1860 census, this Lydia J. Flint, aged 10, was residing in the household of George W. Ryall (1831-1900), there recorded as aged 28, in Milton Township adjacent to the southwestern portion of the town of Ashland in Ashland County, Ohio. Mr. Ryall, who was engaged in farming and served as a county surveyor from 1861-1864, is believed to have been a single individual who was living with his mother, Phoebe J. Ryall (1793-1869), recorded as aged 68. It has not been learned why Lydia was residing with this family, but she evidently used their last name as hers. No records of adoption have been discovered. As of the 1870 census, Lydia Flint was still living with George W. Ryall in Milton Township. By this time he had become a well-to-do farmer, his real estate being valued at $17,600 and his personal property at $3,000. Neither of their names are known to appear in the 1880 census records for Ohio. George W. Ryall (1831-1900) died in September 1900, and Lydia received $1,000 from his estate. The year of Miss Ryall's arrival on South Bass Island as a resident is not known, but evidence from her book would place her arrival sometime before 1882. As noted above she had begun her newspaper column of the Island's news as early as 1889. In the 1900 census, Miss Ryall was residing alone in rented quarters at Put-in-Bay, where she called herself an "authoress." Her occupation, according to the 1910 census, was a "book agent," travelling "house to house" evidently selling and/or distributing books.

For a number of years at Put-in-Bay, Miss Ryall lived near the home of Capt. John Brown, Jr. (1825-1895) on or near the south shore of the Island. Brown, whom she "knew. . .personally and well," was self-educated in geology, phrenology, metaphysical science, and geometry. He came to the Island in 1862 and became recognized as a community leader. Frequently, the Captain was called upon to head enterprises of various kinds, for example, conducting the land survey necessary for the location of the United States Fish Hatchery on Peach Point. Capt. Brown, Jr., of course, was the son of the famed abolitionist John Brown, Sr. who figured prominently in the Civil War affair in Kansas and who died a tragic death at Harper's Ferry, Virginia. Miss Ryall obviously admired the educated, influential, and heroic heritage of Capt. Brown, Jr. , and wrote his biography in the *Sandusky Weekly Register* after his death of 2 May 1895. She revised the column for inclusion as part of a chapter in the 1898 edition of her book. The latter contains a note about the burial service by the Masonic Order in Crown Hill Cemetery on South Bass Island, and the reproduction of a lengthy poem commemorating the impressive occasion by Prof. C. S. Coler of Sandusky.

Tombstone of John Brown, Jr. (1825-1895) at left and his sister at right, Crown Hill Cemetery, South Bass Island.

While at Put-in-Bay, Miss Ryall also lived in the house now owned and occupied by the late Island historian, Robert J. Dodge. Miss Ryall often visited her home area in Ashland County, where she retained acquaintances, and in the latter years of her life, spent winters in Florida. At Put-in-Bay she kept house for herself in a portion of her Aunt Emmaline's house, although the two ladies often disagreed and did not "get along" very well. After the latter's death, Lydia, who had become quite deaf, left the Island, probably to Cleveland, Ohio, where she lived with her cousin, Mrs. Alice Adams and her husband, Robert.In the last four months of her life, Lydia suffered from manic depression psychosis, which may have plagued her to a less severe degree throughout portions of her life. She died of an acute cardiac dilation, 30 June 1920, at the Adam's house, 1776 Avalon Road, Cleveland. Funeral services were held in Cleveland, 1 July, with burial the next day at Put-in-Bay, where she now lies in an unmarked grave next to the Burgraff lot in Crown Hill Cemetery. The site, seen in the photograph on page 4, shows the Burgraff lot to the right marked by the large tombstome. The name on the low markers in the lower left is Holly, the maiden name of Miss Ryall's mother. The family name was originally spelled Halle.

Believed to be the unmarked burial site for Lydia J. Ryall (Theresa Thorndale) in Crown Hill Cemetery, South Bass Island.

Her Books and Other Writings

Having lived inland on a farm in Ohio during early life, Miss Ryall had not seen a body of water any larger than a creek or millpond. She obviously was astounded when seeing Lake Erie for the first time, as she described in the ninth Chapter of her 1898 book.

> I experienced then a rapture inexpressible when I first sighted Lake Erie, wide rolling in all the reflected blue and golden glory of summer skies. And when in amongst the sleeping islands, emerald dotting her broad bosom, I was borne and sighted the shifting sails, grey and white, of cruising vessels, and the pretty painted pleasure craft gently rocking the Bay, the scene impressed me like a dream.

From her personal experiences of island life and her endeavors as a writer and news correspondent for the village of Put-in-Bay, Miss Ryall had the opportunity of becoming thoroughly acquainted with each individual island in western Lake Erie. That information was collected into a 5 by 8 inch compact book, *Sketches and Stories of*

The Lake Erie Islands, published as a *Souvenir Volume* in 1898 by I. F. Mack and Brother of the Sandusky Register Press. From her own statements in the Introduction, Miss Thorndale's scope and intentions can be learned for this compilation. It includes a collection of

> interesting and hitherto unutilized material;historical and reminiscent, legendary, combined with story and romance, tales of adventure and matter descriptive of the picturesque and striking scenes in which the Islands abound. Though appearing in fictitious garniture, most of the stories herein transcribed are founded upon fact; and are true to life and conditions as they exist in the archipelago.

Descriptions of Theresa Thorndale's book appeared several times in the *Sandusky Register*, and on some occasions was contained in an advertisement with large size words utilizing two full columns of a page. Excerpts from these advertisements, along with comments by Jay Cooke and a review printed from the *Toledo Blade*, constitute this material. Some of the text for these articles appears to have been written by Miss Thorndale. The following stories are about Miss Thorndale's book.

Sketches and Stories of the Lake Erie Islands

[Theresa Thorndale]

Sandusky Weekly Register,
29 June 1898, p. 5.

The attention of the reading public is called to a book soon to be issued from the Sandusky Register Press, entitled *Sketches and Stories of the Lake Erie Islands.* The book is intended to be a souvenir volume and will contain about 350 pages of printed matter, and between 75 and 100 illustrations, large and small, giving true to life views of objects, places, and characters historic; of summer life at the resorts; of the islands amid both summer and winter environments; views on lake and land, in the vineyards and among the fisheries; with some leading curiosities of geological structure seen in the archipelago. Each sketch, article, and story is complete in itself; the whole appearing within a neat binding with a pictured representation of "Perry's Lone Willow" stamped upon the front outer cover.

As a journalist and literary contributor, resident for several years at Put-in-Bay, and a writer of marked ability, the author, Miss Lydia J. Ryall—better known as "Theresa Thorndale"—has taken advantage of the exceptional opportunities afforded her for becoming familiar with each individual island of the Lake Erie group. The object of her work, therefore, is the presentation of a collection of interesting material—historical, biographic, reminiscent, legendary; combined with story and romance, tales of adventure and matter descriptive of the picturesque and striking scenes for which the Lake Erie Islands are so widely noted.

The book is designed to supply a long recognized and oft expressed demand, nothing of a similar character having ever been attempted. The information which it will contain is reliable, and its pages throughout are intended to interest readers of all classes both young and old. The illustrations, numbering nearly one hundred, will alone be worth more than the price of the book. They are to be fine half-tones, many of them full pages, . . .The many. . .pictures. . .indicate the high character of the work as a volume especially interesting. The book is being sold on subscription at $1, and already over 300 copies have been ordered. It will be ready for delivery in July and orders for copies can be left at the Register counters, or mailed direct to the authoress, Miss L. J. Ryall, Put-in-Bay.

Sandusky Weekly Register,
14 September 1898, p. 10.

Mr. Jay Cooke, the great financier, subscribed for ten copies at first, but after seeing the book, he ordered 25. In a letter to the author at Put-in-Bay recently, he said: "I am so well pleased with the beautiful work the Register has turned out. The illustrations and your tact as an authoress, induce me to take 25 copies instead of 10. I will distribute these among friends and perhaps take still more."

In a letter to the publisher he says: "The Register Press has in my opinion done itself great credit in producing such satisfactory work, and the authoress' volume is unusually worthy and interesting. Several who have read my first copy expressed their pleasure in warm terms. I do hope the sales will be large as they should be."

Sandusky Weekly Register,
19 October 1898, p. 2; 27 October 1898, p. 5; 2 November 1898, p. 7; 14 December 1898, p. 8; 28 December 1898, p. 8.

The *Toledo Blade's* book reviewer recently said: "I looked over with a good deal of interest an illustrated volume entitled *Sketches and Stories of the Lake Erie Islands*, by Theresa Thorndale. It is made up, as the name denotes, of short articles about these historic scenes, opening with a description of the group, which seems to one who first glimpses it *a veritable emerald cluster in a setting of sapphire*. Then follows Perry's Victory in the light of local reminiscence, containing memories of those who were witnesses of the battle, and the story of the Lone Willow. There is also a short account of the capture of the two steamers, *Philo Parsons* and *Island Queen* during the Civil War, it being a part of the defeated conspiracy to liberate the Confederate officers upon Johnson's Island and to capture Sandusky and other lake towns."

"The different islands are described; bits of local history and romance given; pen sketches of historical characters made; an account of the various resources and attractions of the whole group mentioned. The writer's familiarity with the localities through her long residence at Put-in-Bay and the searching for diverse matter for newspaper correspondence has given a wide variety of interesting matter. As a souvenir volume it ought to command no inconsiderable circulation. It came from the Sandusky Register Press, Sandusky, O."

The second edition of Miss Ryall's *Sketches and Stories of the Lake Erie Islands* appeared in 1913. It was published for the "Perry Memorial Centennial" (1813-1913) by the American Publishers Company, Norwalk, Ohio. It too was a work "constructed at random from the large amount of legendary, reminiscent, and historic lore connected with the most romantic and interesting locality—the Lake Erie islands." Compared to the first edition, it was of larger size, and contained new information and many new illustrations; while at the same time included previously historic and descriptive passages "that could not be excluded, [but] has been carefully brushed of cobwebs." Miss Ryall is reputed to have contributed articles for magazines and books, but only one item has been located, "Life in Lake Erie Lighthouses" printed in *Ohio Magazine*, 1907. Much of the information in this article is reproduced in her 1913 book. Reference to "The Daisy Her Favorite" which was published in *Household Realm* and reprinted in the *Sandusky Weekly Register* for 19 December 1894, has eluded all efforts to locate it in the original.

From questions raised in this short incomplete biography of Lydia Jane Ryall, one wishes more details would emerge to fill in the many gaps of her life. Certainly other items of hers are lurking away in newspapers and magazines that surely someday will come to the surface, but until then it will be necessary to wait. However, do not stop here, but read the other chapters in this book, and find out what news and features she wrote under the name Theresa Thorndale in the *Sandusky Register*.

According to the OCLC On Line Computer Library Center bibliographic database (Worldcat) in the year 2001, Theresa Thorndale's book, *Sketches and Stories* (1898) is available at 40 locations in the United States and Canada, with 18 of them in the State of Ohio. The book is also reproduced in two microfiche editions: The 1982 reproduction is held by nine libraries in Canada and other foreign countries, while the 1988 reproduction is in 13 libraries in the United States. Lydia Ryall's book, *Sketches and Stories* (1913) is recorded for 55 locations in the United States, with 27 of them in the State of Ohio.

During the thirty-year period that Ronald L. Stuckey worked on the preparation of *Lost Stories*, he acquired through purchase both of the *Sketches and Stories* books. During the summer of 2000 he learned that the local library-archives at Lakeside, Ohio, did not have these books. On 11 July 2001, Stuckey presented his copies as gifts to the Lakeside Heritage Society. As part of the short presentation event, archivist Janet

SKETCHES AND STORIES

OF THE

LAKE ERIE ISLANDS

BY
LYDIA J. RYALL

PERRY CENTENNIAL EDITION
1813—1913

NORWALK, OHIO
THE AMERICAN PUBLISHERS CO.
1913

Title page of Lydia Ryall's book, *Sketches and Stories of the Lake Erie Islands* (1913).

Stephenson told about Stuckey's interest in the Lake Erie Island region; when as an undergraduate student he first attended the Stone Laboratory on Gibraltar Island (1959), and later as a faculty member taught courses in field botany and vascular aquatic plants (1966-1991) and served as the associate director for the academic program (1977-1985). Stuckey also vacationed for two to three weeks in September from 1970-1990 on the Marblehead Peninsula, where he stayed at Taylor's Resort and worked on his book, *Lost Stories*.

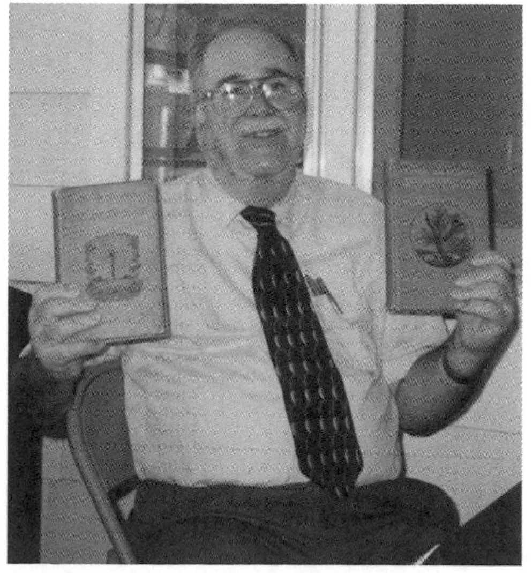

R. L. Stuckey holding his copies of *Sketches and Stories* at the 11 July 2001 presentation event.

References:

Chapter One, Introducing Lydia J. Ryall

Durr, Eleanor. 1985. "Heritage Notes: Lydia Jane Ryall." *Peninsular News*, Marblehead, Ohio, 12 December, p. 3.

Ryall, Lydia J. 1907. "Life in Lake Erie Lighthouses." *Ohio Magazine* 2: 204-208.

Ryall, Lydia J. 1913. *Sketches and Stories of the Lake Erie Islands*. The American Publishers Co., Norwalk. vi, 546 pp. (Perry Centennial Edition 1813-1913). Introduction, pp. v-vi.

Thorndale, Theresa. 1895. "Capt. John Brown Jr.The everyday life of a noted man." *Sandusky Register*. 5 June, p. 4.

Thorndale, Theresa. 1898. *Sketches and Stories of the Lake Erie Islands*. I. F. Mack & Brother, The Sandusky Register Press, Sandusky, v. 379 pp. (Souvenir Volume). Introduction, p. v.

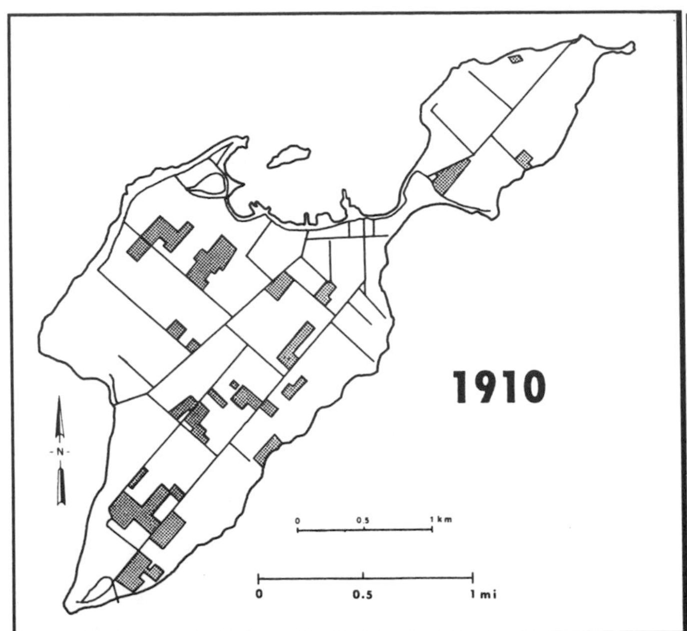

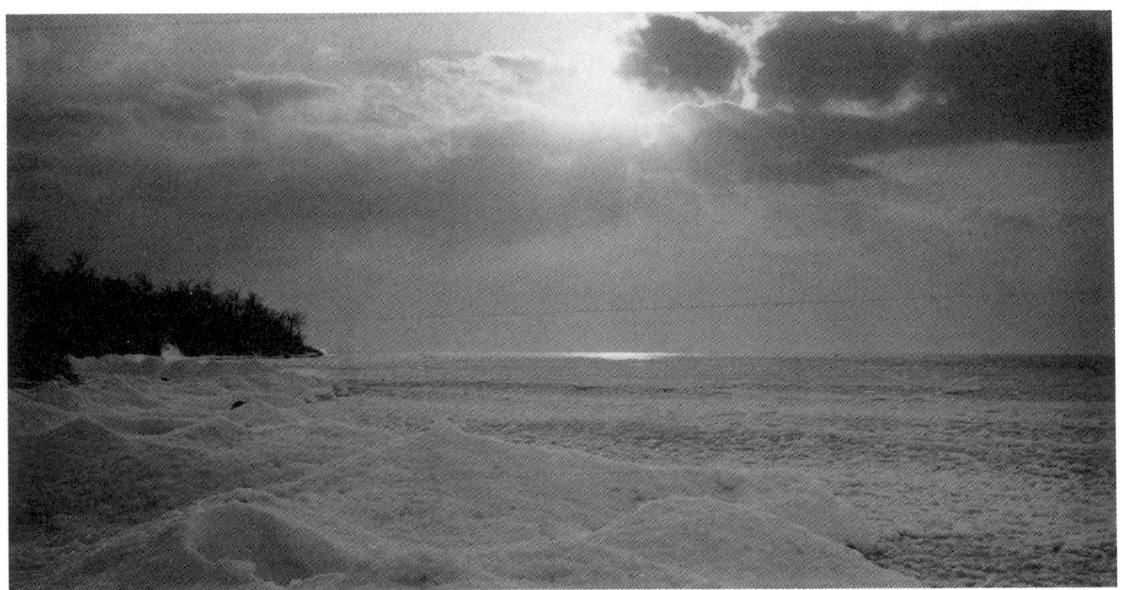

Commercial Fruit Orchards, in 1910, as shown by shaded areas on Map of South Bass Island. The Pear: A common fruit tree of the commercial orchard. A Storm approaches the Lake Erie Islands.

South Bass "Island Jottings"
I. Natural Products and Weather

"*The chief products of Put-in-Bay are fish, flirtations, limestone and Perry's victory.* Thus facetiously comments an observer after duly sizing up the Island. . .," according to Theresa Thorndale in her 1898 book. South Bass Island, or sometimes referred to as Put-in-Bay Island, is probably best known historically for Commodore Oliver Hazard Perry and the Battle of Lake Erie during the War of 1812. Perry's fleet laid anchor in the Bay at the Island prior to defeating Capt. Robert H. Barclay's British fleet on 10 September 1813. After victory, Perry sent a message to Gen. William H. Harrison, writing the now famous frequently repeated words, "We have met the enemy and they are ours."

Introducing the Island

Today, on the Island stands Perry's Victory and International Peace Memorial National Monument, a 352-foot high limestone Doric column, built between 1912 and 1915. This Doric Column is the tallest in the world, and is the third tallest national monument in the United States being shorter than the Washington Monument and the St. Louis Arch. The observation deck, reached by elevator, is 317 feet above the Lake, whence on an exceptionally clear day can be seen not only the battle site between Rattlesnake Island and West Sister Island, but also distances as far as Lorain, Toledo, and Leamington. Operated by the National Park Service on a 25-acre site, the Memorial was designated as a National Monument in 1936. The Monument, in addition to commemorating Perry's victory, honors the nearly two centuries of peaceful relationship between Canada and the United States. During 1986, 155,127 visitors viewed the Island Archipelago from atop the column.

The earliest settlers came to South Bass Island prior to the War of 1812, but abandoned it during the War. After the War, the Island was purchased by the wealthy Spaniard, Jose DeRivera St. Jurgo (1813-1889) of New York City. Initially he raised sheep, but upon realizing that the soil and climate were more conducive to the cultivation of grapes, he encouraged settlers to come and establish vineyards and build winduced about 1860 and by 1865, 450 acres were in vineyards. The Catawba and Concord were the most commonly cultivated varieties. By 1900, at peak production of the wine industry, over 600 acres were in vineyards supplying grapes to 17 active wineries on the Lake Erie Islands. The passage of the Prohibition Amendment in 1920 and the Great Depression of the 1930's were disastrous to the Island's wine industry, but a few establishments did survive until repeal of Prohibition and the nation's economy was restored in the 1940's. Today, the industry still prospers to a limited extent selling wines and grape juices almost exclusively to the tourist population in the summer. Only about 50 acres of vineyards remain on the Island, most of whose grapes are used by the Heineman Winery, founded in 1886 by Gustav Heineman. It is now operated by his grandson Louis Heineman and his great-grandson, Edward Heineman.

Tourism began in the 1850's on the Island when the steamboats began bringing visitors from the mainland to sample the wine and enjoy an excursion and holiday weekend away from work, home, and the toil of everyday life. As more tourists came and wanted to remain overnight, large hotels were built around the Park in the village. Prominent among them were the Beebe House, the first and second Put-in-Bay House, the Crescent, and the Park. The first three of these burned, the second closed in 1971, and the last is still in operation. The pinnacle of hotels came with the construction of Hotel Victory from 1888 to 1892 at Victory Bay, now called Stone's Cove on the west shore of South Bass Island. A wood-frame structure, said to be the largest summer resort hotel in North America, never attained the success in visitor business as envisioned, and it too met the same fate as several large former hotels—destroyed by fire, 14-15 August 1919. The tourist industry flourished during the 1890's, and thousands came to the Island for special ceremonies to celebrate the Centennial of Perry's Victory in 1913 and the dedication of the Monument when it was opened in 1915.

During the Great Depression and the years of World War II and following, the wine industry declined and excursions to the Island were not affordable for many families. The steamers that plied the Lake gradually disappeared, largely because of government regulations pertaining to numbers of crew members and passengers necessary, which made them unprofitable to operate. The coming of the automobile made families more mobile, and they could travel to other recreational areas. With tourism reaching its lowest level in Island history during the 1950's and 1960's, some of the remaining hotels closed, many of the shops sat empty, and even an adequate grocery store had no longer been maintained. Buildings were in need of paint and repair. The decline of tourism was in other respects related to the appearance of rowdy college students and the worldwide publicized statements that Lake Erie was polluted and dead, with fish contaminated with mercury and dying. The Island and the Lake's image had deteriorated immensely, but in the 1970's a number of island residents and businessmen worked together for improvement to bring back the tourist trade. This Island revival story is here interrupted, but is continued and further discussed in the introductory portion to Chapter 13, page 171.

In Chapter Two the stories to follow, other than the first one, are "Island Jottings" by Theresa Thorndale. They are concerned with yesterday's natural products and weather on South Bass Island.

Improvements in 1848 on Put-In-Bay Island

Detroit Free Press

Sandusky Clarion,
27 November 1848, p. 1.

Put-in-Bay Island is located in Lake Erie, nearly opposite Sandusky. A friend of ours who happened not long since to land there, gives us some information that will be interesting to our readers. The Island has now got into new hands. It contains some 1800 [1382] acres, on a strata of limestone. There are now five farmers upon it, who are enterprising and making rapid improvements. Last season, 4000 bushels of wheat was raised there, besides large quantities of vegetables, which were sold to boats and vessels that went into the Bay, which is a very excellent one, to shield themselves from storms. A wharf has been built, which has large quantities of wood upon it. Over 3000 cords were sold last season to steamers, at $1,50 to $1,75 per cord. There is an abundance of hickory timber on the Island. Near 800 cords have been taken in as ballast this season by vessels going to the upper lakes, and sold above us at a profit. This seems like "taking coal to Newcastle"--but such is the fact.

Frost is never known there, and one of the farmers is now engaged in raising peaches, to supply the lake country. One thousand trees are growing finely, and will be increased to 3000 this fall. There is much other fruit growing. Pears seem to do remarkably well.

The stone quarry keeps several at work. A company of gentlemen from Thomaston, Maine, are now erecting lime kilns. The stone of a superior quality abounds. They say they can furnish vessels another season, on the wharf, at 45 cents a barrel, which will make good ballast for the upper lakes. A ship yard will be erected the coming winter, and a vessel built. Excellent timber can be had.

Grapes, Fruits, and Other Vegetables

Theresa Thorndale

Sandusky Weekly Register,
18 June 1890, p. 2.

Being almost exclusively devoted to the cultivation of fruits, the islands of Lake Erie have little to exhibit in the line of farm products. No wheat or barley is grown on any of the islands excepting Kelley's and Pt. au Pelee. Rye, in small tracts, is raised by vineyard owners, the straw, cut green, being used for grape tying purposes. An occasional patch of oats is sown, and corn is frequently planted between grape rows. Though meager as to quantity, these samples of farm products are sufficient to show the capabilities of island soil. Rye exhibits an exuberant growth and full heading. Though planted late, corn is looking well. Oats stands thickly and heavily on the ground, while the most unavailable grass lands are covered with a rank product.

Potatoes are very generally planted on the Bass islands. The land being specially adapted to the production of a superior quality of the tuber, the vines are growing rapidly. London Purple or Paris Green in solution, is being used to some extent in the spraying of potato tops infested with bugs. The main production of island soil is the grape; and of the many varieties cultivated, the Catawba takes the precedence. At present it is impossible to form a conjecture as to the prospect of the crop. The vines appear thrifty and are prolific in clustering blossoms. No indications of mildew are yet reported, but there is still ample time for the development of this vineyard scourge. The spraying of vines with London Purple, as a preventative of mildew, is being experimented upon.

From the present indications the early variety of plums will produce largely. Cherries will be plentiful, and apples a medium crop. Of peaches, the early varieties show very light, but the smock, salway, and others of the later soils look promising. While not over loaded, there is enough healthy, young fruit to ripen well, and a valuable crop is anticipated. Pear trees of sound varieties are heavily laden, others will produce lightly. The strawberry, raspberry, and blackberry are cultivated to some extend on the islands. The red raspberry especially, is grown on a considerable scale at Put-in-Bay and Middle Bass, and at the present writing there is promise of an abundant crop.

Sandusky Daily Register,
22 October 1891, p. 3.

Grapes picked for wine are piled into boxes, barrels, and half barrels and carted to the steamboat wharves where they are shipped to Sandusky, Toledo, and various other points. Large quantities of grapes are being worked up by the island wine cellars. The great market for basketed grapes for table use is Detroit, and the steamers *Kirby* and *Remora*, on their daily home runs, carry wholesale quantities, together with cargoes of peaches from Catawba Island and the Marblehead Peninsula, Ohio's great peach center. The peach orchards of Put-in-Bay are also quite extensive and are yielding largely; and lots of pears, quinces and plums also contribute to swell the fruit exhibit in the warehouses at the Bay. The Island plum crop is especially large this season, the trees bending beneath heavy loads. A medium sized tree in the orchard of Matt Burgraff yielded 7 1/2 bushels of the product, while nine bushels were picked, it is said,. from a tree on the premises of H. Jackson Jones.

Active grape vineyard in 1974 along Mitchell Road on South Bass Island.

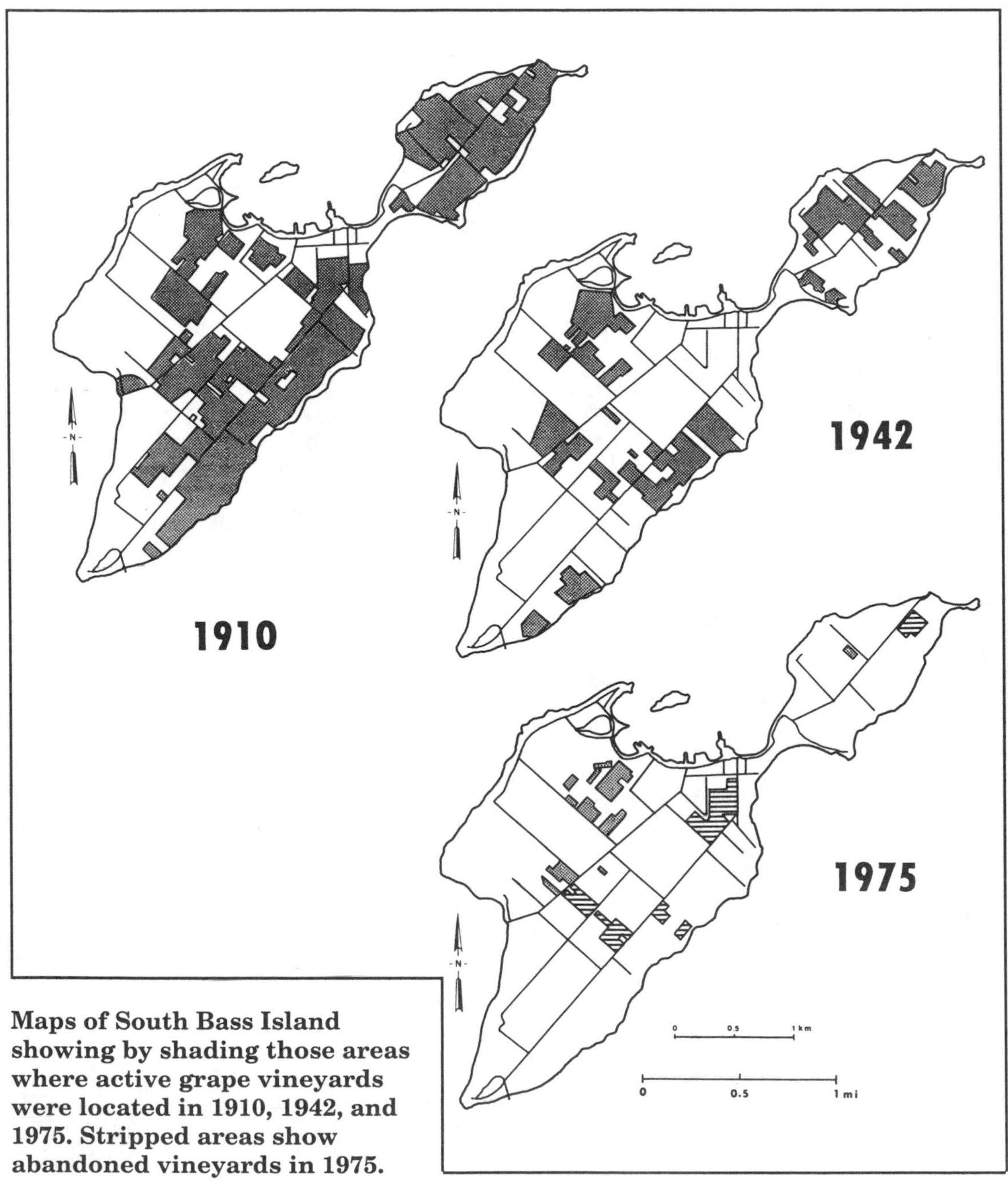

Maps of South Bass Island showing by shading those areas where active grape vineyards were located in 1910, 1942, and 1975. Stripped areas show abandoned vineyards in 1975.

Weather and the Changing Seasons; Island Life Affected

Theresa Thorndale

Sandusky Daily Register,
19; 27 March 1889, p. 1; p. 2.

The weather during the latter part of the week past was delightful. The days were bright and warm with sunshine, and gentle breezes wafted from the south lands. The nights were perfect with still air and cloudless skies, white with moon and starlight. In the warm afternoons, flies and insects awoke from their torpor and flitted hilariously about. Bees ventured forth into the open air, and the musical drone of their wings mingled with the buzz of fly and insect. The denizens of the poultry yard picnicked on the wood pile, having a jolly time burrowing in the moist, chippy mould, and sunning themselves complacently in the strong rays of golden light which slanted upon them. Water spiders crawled out of their dens in the loose gravel on the beach and ran scurrying before the footsteps of intruders. Robins, swamp [red-winged] blackbirds, and others of the feathered tribes of early spring piped, twittered, and warbled in the low tangles of marsh and thicket; while from the forest puffs of woody fragrance, faint yet subtle, filled the air. In slivered and shattered fragments the ice banged upon the shore, or, borne by wind and current, drifted away into hazy distances. All these familiar sights and sounds of nature seems fraught with promise, and instinct with prophesies of "The resurrection and the life" was yet to follow.

With the exception of a narrow fringe skirting the shores of the Bay the ice has all disappeared. This too will soon be gone, as it is broken and fragmentary. The weather still continues a delight.

Sandusky Daily Register,
28 August 1889, p. 2.

The continued warm, dry weather, and consequent salubrious atmosphere, renders the season delightful. The excessive dry weather prevalent among the islands throughout the summer is a matter of surprise to visitors from other localities, who report an abundance of rain and thrifty growing vegetation in the vicinity of Cleveland, Zanesville, Ashland, Mansfield, and at many other places throughout Ohio. So scant has been the rainfall at this place, that the turf has a brown, singed appearance, and pasturage is very short. The corn yield is principally nubbing, and potatoes are small, sunburnt and strong to the taste; while cucumber vines and other garden products are wilted and weakened, and look like hard times. . . . Heavy rains frequently pass to north or south of us, sometimes near enough to be seen; but like the Tantalus "cup," they tempt, but do not satisfy. Clouds fail to bring rain to thirsty Put-in-Bay. It has been suggested that possibly the great dispenser of benefits has withheld this minor blessing, under the impression that the islands would not appreciate water, when wine was so abundant.

Sandusky Daily Register,
4 September 1889, p. 1.

The drought at this place is becoming very severe. The sod is as brown and dead as in winter when bared of snow. The dust on the thoroughfares is fine and deep, and covers with grey the wayside trees and shrubbery. Vegetation is drooping sadly, and garden products are stunted and shrivelled. The cool breezes which blow across our shores almost daily, tempering the heated atmosphere, are a redeeming trait of the weather. Friday last was an exceptional day, however. The winds all died, the lake was a sea of glass, the sky brazen, and the heat oppressive. Smoke settled over lake and land as dense as if ten thousand furnaces had combined to produce it. So thick was the smoke on Friday night that the fog whistles of cruising steamers were constantly sounded. Orchards and vineyards are the only land products which do not materially suffer from the continued drought. Apples are plentiful; pears and plums are a prolific crop. In the orchard of D. L. Webster, East Point, on a branch 26 inches in length were counted 116 plums. A late variety of raspberries grown by L. R. Webster is at the present season loaded with fruit. A stem nine inches in length broken from the bush on Sept. 1 contained eighty-seven perfect berries.

Sandusky Daily Register,
18 September 1889, p. 2.

The afternoon of Sunday last afforded an occasion for general rejoicing. The long anticipated and long denied rain, for which the islands have languished, fell in copious showers.

How the thirsty leaves,
And arid earth drank in the welcome drops,
How merrily they pattered on the lake,
In haste to kiss their mother, and her cheek
Was dimpled with a thousand answering smiles.

Yes, and how they pattered on the shingles and cascaded into eave troughs, and galloped along spoutings, and whirled into empty cisterns filling them with tumult and with water. How the toads and tree frogs got them from their dry weather burrows to receive the shower bath vouchsafed them, how they opened their capacious throats to imbibe the refreshing draught poured from the clouds, and how they croaked and blubbered their satisfaction. A brief second spring time is now expected. A reanimating of the dun-brown sod, from which nearly all indications of life and freshness had departed; while in their stalls the hay fed horse and cow patiently await the first tempting mouthful of tender, springing blades.

Much of vegetation is past being helped by the rain, but cabbages, turnips, and other late products of the garden, together with the most kinds of fruit, will be materially benefited. Concord grapes and plums, it is feared, will be damaged to some extent, as the sudden accession of moisture will probably cause a bursting of the tender rinded fruit. The rain was accompanied by a fierce gale on Sunday night which passed through the Island orchards and shook down peaches, plums, and apples in extravagant quantities. In plowed orchards these windfalls have been muddied and soiled rendered, unfit for market, though otherwise undamaged. On Monday a misty drizzle continued all day at intervals, and the ground is now penetrated with moisture to a greater depth than at any time since the June rains. The picking and shipping of Concord and Delaware grapes is now at full tide. Catawbas which were girdled in the spring have a rich color and a fine flavor and are being put into market.

Sandusky Daily Register,
5 December 1889, p. 2.

After weeks of dull, yet mild and evenly tempered weather, the closing days of November brought to the island region a foretaste of the wintery days acoming. Driving gales swept lake and land bearing with them blinding flurries of snow, which covered the ground to the depth of an inch or two. The mercury fell several degrees and the first regularly commissioned cold snap, mailed and armored, charged down upon us. Frost appeared in wide patches upon the window panes. Showering spray covered with icing the boulders along the shore, and many with pendant, gleaming points, the overhanging rocks and gnarled cedars, while the winds, keen-edged, and wielded in the clutch of the storm demons, cut sharply the tender nosed individuals who dared defy them. Notwithstanding this flourish of trumpets on the part of the Winter King, and his retainers, however, December came to us--as His Majesty's courtier--with a smile of blandness and a nod of affability, beginning a message of amnesty and allowing us yet a short reprieve ere he fastens the clamps upon us. In this world of procrastination are always to be found individuals who, "like donkey's tail, are always behind" and even on the archipelago, where energy and forehandedness are characteristics of its inhabitants, there are some who never get quite ready for the closing in of the ice, though it should keep clear until the middle of February. Winter preparations on the islands are something like the island excursions--there's always somebody left. Among these unfortunates may be enumerated the timid Mrs. A. who intended "just as much as could be" to have made a visit abroad before the ice came. The procrastinating Mr. B. who had calculated on a load of produce to be procured from some adjacent port before the advance of freight rates. The belated Mr. C. who had got his heart set on a cargo of wood which failed to materialize in season; or mayhap the negligent fisherman whose pounds left in just a day too long have become inveigled in icy fetters. Many similar disappointments might be mentioned as due to the "nemesis of neglect," but numerous as they are, these cases are exceptional; for the average islander knowing the uncertainties of the weather, makes ample and seasonable provision for all contingencies, stocking his larger, cellar, coal-bin, granary, and hay loft with all necessary requirements for man and beast.

Sandusky Weekly Register,
21 February, 1894, p. 4.

The most terrific storm for year was the general report coming in from all over the country, and Put-in-Bay can echo with double emphasis. To dwellers upon exposed northerly and easterly shores commanding the unbroken sweep of Lake Erie, its fury seemed unprecedented. All night following its commencement was heard the war of elements, and when dawn came, there appeared a scene of chaotic confusion which might have suggested an event preceding the opening period of creation. The lake, partially open the day before, was now entirely broken up of ice. A sixty-mile-an-hour gale blew straight from the horizon with a lifting force irresistible to those obliged to face it. Snow drove through the air in horizontal lines, and despite the heavy ice adrift near and far, a tremendous sea set shoreward, lifting and flinging gigantic floes of ice. Broken and pulverized masses of ice accumulated to great heights upon the beach, forming vast, solid ridges from five to forty feet deep. Long tongues of wavelicked ice covered the faces of bold rock barriers, flinging over them like a froth of foam. The wind caught and carried forward these misty ice sheets, where they were falling upon crag, rock, stump, and overhanging cedar clump; heavily incrusting and crystallizing everything within the vicinity of the shores. The roar of wind and wave, and crash and grind of ice was terrific. The whirling snow sought every crack and crevice, sifting in through seemingly impossible entrances. Wide spaces of ground were swept clean, and the contents piled into immense drifts. Considered altogether the mid-winter storm upon these bleak shores presented a spectacle of sublime savagery such as is seldom seen.

Considerable uneasiness was felt for the safety of the steam yacht *Ina* which lay in the ice abreast of Gibraltar partially sheltered but still getting a strong brash of the storm. Captain Dodge had the boat tied up at Middle Bass, but on the day previous surprised the islanders by making a trip to Sandusky, returning with a cargo of sugar. From Middle Bass she steamed for the Bay, but found the ice too tough to permit her reaching a perfectly safe anchorage, and in this situation was struck a few hours later by the storm. Capt. Dodge dared not leave the boat unmanned, and he and Capt. Hugo Stirit accordingly remained on board of her until Thursday morning, though she drifted uneasily with the moving ice, and very many expected to see the little craft crunched in the jaws of the Feine Euroclydon.

Capt. Dodge, who possesses apparently a charmed life, or as many lives as the proverbial feline, and is not easily scared, emulated Ebza of Uncle Tom's Cabin fame, and performed the somewhat stagy exploit of crossing on foot from boat to shore and back again, with the broken ice singing, swinging, and bobbing up and down in the most threatening manner. As the gale became wilder and the rising water came awashing shoreward over the unbroken ice, the alarm increased. Men collected in great numbers upon the shore, and it was finally decided to send a line out to the *Ina*. Three men with a boat succeeded in reaching her, and the line, which was a long one, was made fast to the craft. It was impossible for her to wade through the heavy drift, nine feet deep in places, as the other end of the line was carried shoreward and fastened to the docks. Fortunately the main body of ice which clung in the Bay remained intact, and the little craft weathered the storm gallantly and in good shape, a bucket broken from her wheel being the only damage reported.

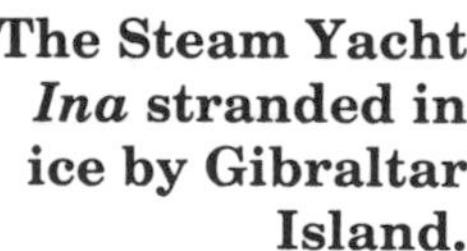

The Steam Yacht *Ina* stranded in ice by Gibraltar Island.

Sandusky Weekly Register,
11 April 1894, p. 1.

The willow copses of the Island bore enggestions of the harvest field during the past week. The little yellow twigs of last year's growth have been sickled and bound into generous sheaves and now only the stubble remains. The willow harvest is of no small interest in a locality where, as an industry, viniculture takes the lead as it does it here. Everybody uses the yellow willow for grape tying purposes and with each returning spring nearly every new tree and sprout thereof is regularly cropped. Rather discouraging for the willows one would surmise, but unabated they immediately send forth whole regiments and brigades of new shoots. By mid-summer they have covered their scars with a glory of tender green foliage and look very pretty. Thus they serve a double purpose, making themselves useful as well as ornamental. Grape tying has fairly begun, and women and girls in sun-bonnets with aprons full of willow cars, and men and boys with willow bandies swung from their girdles, are seen working up and down vineyard rows near and far.

The trailing arbutus has opened in the woods, and the aroma of dandelion greens and salads is wafted from the kitchen windows. The odd-time house wife, who sowed cabbage seed on Good Friday, is anxiously looking for the first appearance of her embryo kraut crop; but the cold winds recently prevalent have somewhat retarded vegetation. The too forward strides of the flag and lily were severely snubbed for their boldness by Jack Frost, though the turf grows brighter day by day. Lilac leaves are unfolding, and hyacinth and narcissus budding. Burning grape brush fills the air with the blue of curling smoke by day and fires by night, and ice yachts ashore at various points are about the only relics and reminders of the past winter.

Sandusky Weekly Register,
6 June 1894, p. 7.

Everybody seemed glad when the dreary days of driving mist and howling storms were ended. There is a rythmical cadence in the beat of rain drops during the first twenty-four hours, but the music grows monotonous in time, and breeds melancholia, sadness, and all that is blue and horrid. The graveyards of memory open wide their vaults and dead things come forth clothed in a semblance of that which once they were, but only to pain us by their presence for a time, then to slip away and dissolve with the mist wreaths.

Those who observed the new moon will remember how flatly upon its back it lay--a silver sheened argosy, low sailing in the West, full to the rim of rain showers for the thirsty earth. Somewhere in space this silvery sailor must have capsized and spilled out all her cargo, from the way the rain came down. Lake Erie was a great grey blur at times and 'twas hard to tell just where the water left off and the sky began. Storm birds whistled in the air and the sails of beating vessels flapped dimly into view through the driving rain. The lake churned itself white and licked, with frothing tongue, rock wall and gravel stretch, and cast upon the shore debris enough to have kindled a hundred "drift-wood fires." Nature seemed burdened with such an accumulation of griefs. She could do nothing but weep out her heart, with its aches and pains.

"A pleasant thing it is for the eyes to behold the sun," observed the Hebraic writer, and so when on Wednesday, the day God blinked blandly forth, people looked up with glad eyes and thankful hearts. There were more sun worshippers that day than usual. The world seemed fresher and sweeter for the rinsing it had got, vegetation had received a new impetus, life seemed a little less burdensome, and its duties less thankless and irksome.

The greatest diversion afforded perhaps during the long, wet storm, and one which made us smile wickedly, even through our tears, was the arrival of the Hocking Valley Editorial association members and friends, per moonlight excursion. They were "land-lubbers" the most of them evidently, had not much idea when they reached Sandusky what the weather was outside. The excursion materialized but the moon did not, nor even a star. They had a small margin of daylight but night closed in with tumbling cloud, rain, and driving storm, and when off the Marblehead Lighthouse the *City* nearly rolled her guards under, some of the editors thought they were rounding Cape Horn, where, on that "battle ground of the elements" contending seas and currents are said to meet in unending strife. They had really thought Lake Erie incapable of getting up such a splurge, but supposing it all designed for their especial entertainment accepted the doubtful compliment since they could not well do otherwise. Thoughts of John Howard Payne were suggested, and "Home Sweet Home," "Take Me Back to Home," and "Mother," and other pathetic melodies were touchingly sung. Most of them paid tribute to the fresh water Neptune, but did it under protest, and when at last Cedar Point was rounded, and through sheeted rain and midnight gloom the lights of Sandusky glimmered, overjoyed with the prospect of again reaching land, some of the editors for once in their lives, it is said, thanked the Lord.

Large quantities of grape buds and young fruit settings, were reported knocked off and destroyed by the storm. There still seems enough left however, to insure an abundant crop.

Sandusky Weekly Register,
20 June 1894, p. 5.

Just now Put-in-Bay is halting between seasons--the bass fishing, and guest and excursion seasons. The between interval is a slack, lazy time as far as outside stir is concerned, but those interested in the entertainment of later coming guests get a hustle on as soon as the last party of bass fishermen have boarded the outgoing steamer. Hotel, boarding house, and restaurant proprietors are especially busy. There is painting, plumbing, repairing to be done, and unfinished house cleaning--and the latter is a formidable affair by the way, when it includes the whole of a big hotel. Painters are handling brushes expeditiously about this time at Put-in-Bay for two reasons--first, to get the paint on and dry before the June fly visitation; fifty million June flies permanently paint stuck all over a building give a fantastic appearance; reason second, to get through in time for an early opening.

During the past week an extensive job of painting was done on the Beebe House. The color is between a cream and lavender, very delicate and showing handsomely amid the dark foliage of surrounding trees. The flat-roofed verandahs are edged with rows of bright green flower pots of fancy patterns, filled with choice exotics and tender, trailing vines, and mosses; a pretty arrangement and striking and far fetched, and foreign in its suggestions. The ground, too, has been improved and additions made in the way of plant and floral embellishment until the place looks very attractive. Others of the Bay hotels are also preparing each a line of attractions, chief of which is, of course, its bill of fare. The hungry will be generously fed, comfortably lodged, and cared for during the summer.

Sandusky Weekly Register,
17 March 1897, p. 4.

We are now in the midst of the ice evolutionary period, and its vast and varied processes form an interesting study. Up and down through the island channels, and in and out of coves and bays, miles and miles of ice in broken and detached floes or in solid masses are driving, borne along by shifting winds and beating sunshine wrought a seeming miracle. For a day or two dwellers along the East Channel Shores imagined that all the ice in Lake Erie had suddenly floated away and disappeared. The clearing of a channel core was described as "like a breath." The whole body of ice began suddenly moving, but so silently and imperceptibly that a man working at the end of a dock failed to notice it until he found himself and tools drifting outward into the lake. He called to an assistant employed upon the dock, who, on looking was astonished to see the ice going, and his boss with it. Fortunately a plank long enough to reach the departing ice field, was at hand and after throwing his boots into the water the castaway escaped safely to land--"saved by the skin of his teeth"--as old time revivalists might term it. In a short time scarcely a film of ice was visible along the shore curves, in the outer channel or, in the offing, save the wedgelike masses that had grounded upon Ballast reef.

So summerlike appeared the scene with the unfettered lake lying motionless and blue, with wild ducks and gulls afloat upon its smooth surface, and robins and blackbirds waking the echoes of rock and true bordered above, that observers persuaded themselves that ice and winter had taken their dual departure and talked of sowing cabbage and onions. Conditions were more apparent than real, however, and the shortsightedness of human calculation became obvious, when before the whizzing gale of Friday whole fields and territories of ice illimitable, came surging in from the West and North crowding and jamming channel and passage as far as the eye could reach; wind and current deeply drifting and grounding it and piling it high upon rock and shoal. The violence of the westerly wind caused the water to fall to a very low ebb. The mailcarrier was unable to make the trip across to Catawba and the *American Eagle* which left in the morning for Sandusky did not attempt to face the storm and running ice, but remained in that port.

The twitter of the spring bird has grown faint and the gardener has put away hoe and rake for a day or two, but with the return of sunshine and a change of wind the ice is again seaming and spreading apart. The *Eagle* is expected with its delayed mails. The *Eagle* is said to be doing a good business in the freight and passenger line.

Sandusky Weekly Register,
16 March 1898, p. 4.

Spring birds are already on the wing, and their songs are sweetly suggestive of all manner of spring delights, some of which tillers of the soil and knights of the pruning hook already enjoy while tramping up and down the muddy vineyards. So hard packed was the last snowfall, that it required a long time to melt, which it finally did, dispensing in rushing rills which made streamless Put-in-Bay Island appear for a time like the stream scalloped reaches of the mainland. It left shoals of mud, and the roads were as bad as island roads ever get. Put-in-Bay, however, can boast of nothing in the road line equal to the highways of Mustcash at this season. Touches of genial sunshine and southerly zephyr breaths have perceptibly brightened the sod in some places, and the early wood flowers will soon bud.

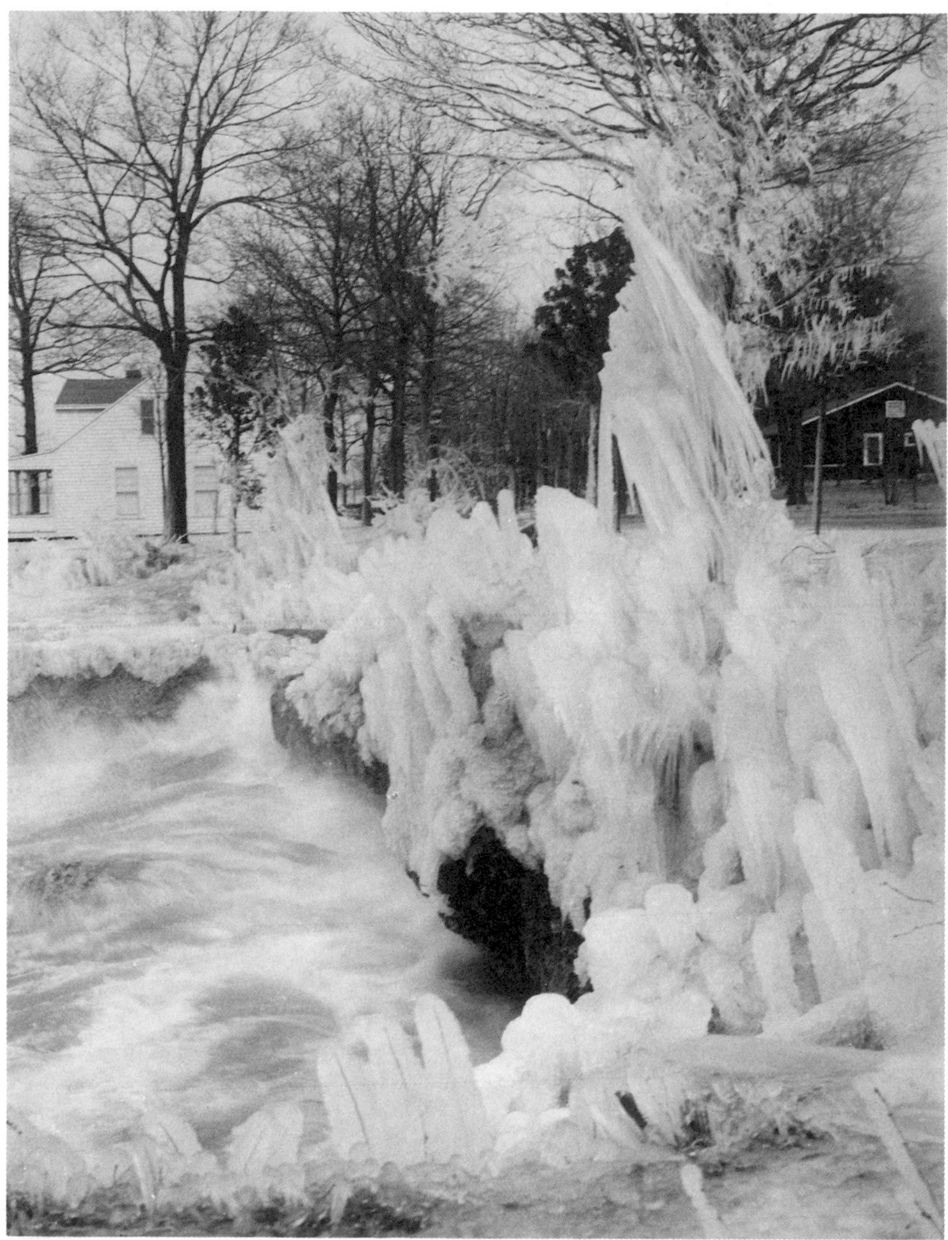

Splash-ice on cliff and shore vegetation, northwest shore of South Bass Island, 16 March 1952.

Sandusky Weekly Register,
30 March 1898, p. 11.

Cisterns and cellars were filled to an overflowing by recent floods of rain, and from husbandmen there was no end of complaint about mud and water standing ankle deep in their vineyard rows. A two gallon jar set out of doors and away from dripping eaves late in the afternoon, caught one third full of water the following night for the windows of heaven were opened and a deluge came down. The jar contained also an angle worm, showing conclusively that said worm must first have ascended--per water spout, suppositiously--before it could descend into the jar; for no angle worm however daft would or could on a dark, rainy night mount the smooth, perpendicular sides of a two gallon jar for the purpose of committing suicide. This seems a practical proof of a sometimes advanced, and frequently laughed at theory, namely, that it sometimes rains angle worms. So it stops before raining "pitchforks" we are, however, content. The bay marsh, Squaw Harbor, has assumed the dignity of a lake, and a very pretty, and picturesque lake at that. Amplified by mighty rainfalls its borders now extend to the foot of Toledo Avenue, and have become a portion of the corporate limits of the town. The gamins are having lots of fun about its banks. The mud hen has begun her shoal water wadings, and the frogs are turning up for their nightly concerts.

"White wings that never grow weary," and wings of all colors, both of birds and boats begin crowding upon our vision. The first solitary sail of the season appeared soon after the ice went down the Lake, but are becoming more numerous as days go by. The busy trafficers can't wait until Uncle Sam sets out his buoys and gets his beacon lights burning, and so they are going it blind, and taking their chances and trusting to luck, and this lovely March weather for propitious voyages; but some luckless day there'll be storm—a regular "snorter," and some of these venturesome craft will be reef wrecked, driven ashore, or sent to the bottom. Our first marine visitor this season was the steamer *Jenkins* which anchored in the Bay last Tuesday night.

Sandusky Weekly Register,
28 September 1898, p. 11.

The rainfalls of the past week have been heavy, and possessors of empty cisterns were made correspondingly happy even if the overflow did inundate their cellars. Some fears of undue moisture cracking open ripened grapes of tender varieties have been expressed. Concords, Porklington, Delawares, and other standard early varieties are now being picked and shipped.

South Bass Island of 1382 acres in Ottawa County, Ohio, is 12 miles from Port Clinton and 31 miles from Toledo. Its permanent year-round population is approximately 375 to 400 individuals. With the addition of summer residents and cottage renters, this number enlarges to 1,500 to 2,000, and with the presence of tourists on certain weekends, the Island's population may swell to over 10,000 people.

References:

Chapter Two, South Bass "Island Jottings"
I. Natural Products and Weather

Anonymous. 1862. "Grapes on Put-in-Bay." *Sandusky Daily Commercial Register*, 3 July. pages not numbered.

Anonymous. 1866. "The Islands. Statistics at Put-in-Bay Township." *Sandusky Commercal Register*, 19 May. pages not numbered.

Anonymous. 1951. "America's most intriguing island [South Bass]." *The Ohio Edisonian* pp. [3-9], July.

Dodge, Robert J. 1975. *Isolated Splendor: Put-in-Bay and South Bass Island*. Exposition Press, Hicksville, New York, x, 166 pp.

Frohman, Charles E. 1971. *Put-in-Bay: Its History*. The Ohio Historical Society, Columbus. viii, 156 pp. Second Printing, 1974.

Gilfillan, Merrill C. 1960. "The Bass Archipelago." *Ohio Conservation Bulletin* 24(11): 3-5, 31.

Hamilton, Ernest S., and Jane L. Forsyth. 1972. "Forest communities of South Bass Island, Ohio." *Ohio Journal of Science* 72: 184-210.

Herdendorf, Charles E. 1985. *Self-guided hike/bike tour of Put-in-Bay, South Bass Island*. Ohio Sea Grant College Program, The Ohio State University, Columbus. OHSG-GS-10, 16 pp. Revised and Reprinted 1993, 46 pp.; 1995, 46 pp.

Hudgins, Bert. 1943. "The South Bass Island community (Put-in-Bay)." *Economic Geography* 19: 16-36.

Jackson, Joan Howison. 1950. Erie Islands mural, a geographic study of the United States islands in Lake Erie. M.A. Thesis, University of Cincinnati, Cincinnati. 110 p., photographs.

Langlois, Thomas H. 1951. "Lake Erie's island vineyards." *Toledo Blade Pictorial*. 1 July, pp. 8-9.

Langlois, Thomas H. 1965a. "The waves of Lake Erie at South Bass Island." *Ohio Journal of Science* 65: 335-342.

Langlois, Thomas H. 1965b. "Ecological processes at a section of shoreline of South Bass Island, Lake Erie." *Ohio Journal of Science* 65: 343-352.

Langlois, Thomas Huxley, and Marina Holmes Langlois. 1948. *South Bass Island and Islanders.* The Ohio State University, The Franz Theodore Stone Laboratory. Contribution No. 10. x, 139 pp.

Martin, Jessie A. 1990. "The Bass Islands," pp. 71-83. *In The Beginnings and Tales of the Erie Islands*. Harlo Press, Detroit, Michigan. [1-8], 9-128 pp. Fifth Printing, 1995.

McCormick, Jack. 1968. "Vegetation in fallow vineyards, South Bass Island, Ohio." *Ohio Journal of Science* 68: 1-11.

McKay, Al. 1971. "Trampling out the vineyards. . ." *Sandusky Register Focus*, 25 September, pp. 1-3.

Moizuk, Ruth Dickerman. [1968]. "Put-in-Bay, Grape Country," p. 37. *In The Put-in-Bay Story Told from the Top-of-the-Rock*. [Published by the author]. 48 pp.

Nichols, G. G. 1888. *Nichol's handy guide book to Put-in-Bay, Middle Bass, and Kelley's Island*. I. F. Mack and Brothers, Sandusky, Ohio. 32 pp.

Ross, Harry H. 1949. "Put-in-Bay or South Bass Island," pp. 20-26. *In Enchanting Isles of Lake Erie*. [Published by the Author]. 80 pp.

Verber, James L. 1955. "The climates of South Bass Island, western Lake Erie." *Ecology* 36: 388-400.

MAIN ENTRANCE TO HOTEL VICTORY, built from 1888 to 1892 at Victory Park.
INTERIOR VIEWS: Main Office and Assembly Hall.

Tillotson's "White Elephant:"

CHAPTER THREE

The Hotel Victory

Hotel Victory, whose construction began in 1888, has been acclaimed as the largest summer resort hotel of its time in America. Erected at Victory Park on the highest land along the southwest shore of South Bass Island, the Hotel overlooked Victory Bay, now known as Stone's Cove. The Victory was a huge, elegant, four-story, frame building painted in soft, harmonious woodbrowns, and crowned with graceful towers. The magnificent structure resembled the Buckingham Palace with flags flapping atop high gables. Broad flights of stone steps led to the wide, high piazzas, which extended across its front. The grounds were landscaped in a Gay Nineties style with rustic bridges spanning ravines, an electric fountain, a boardwalk extending 500 feet to the lake shore, and tree-lined stone trails on which to take leisurely strolls. A copper, bronze, winged Woman Victory statue was erected in 1907 in the center of a parapet enclosed with a stone balustrade located on the extreme west lawn. The Natatorium, or swimming pool, situated in a ravine in front of the Hotel, was first opened in the summer of 1898. It was 100 feet long, 30 feet wide, from three to seven feet deep, covered with a roof to keep out the sun, and lighted at night by electricity. The pool provided a relaxing place where both men and women swam together, a pleasure that was considered shocking in its time. A trolley line with electric cars, connecting between Victory Park and the village of Put-in-Bay, transported guests to the Hotel.

The checkered history of the Hotel Victory finds a place in every book on the history of South Bass Island. The stories reproduced here are selections from this history. Theresa Thorndale's newspaper accounts describe the early stages of its construction. Succeeding stories tell of its grand opening, its plunge into receivership the same year that it opened, its place as a convention center with amusements and entertainment, and finally its complete destruction by fire in August 1919.

Transportation car from downtown Put-in-Bay to the Hotel Victory.

Road from the Caves to Hotel Victory.

Hotel Victory Foundation Emerges

Theresa Thorndale

Sandusky Daily Register,
26 January 1889, p. 1; 3 April 1889, p. 2.

It is rumored that work on Hotel Victory is to be resumed before the opening of navigation. This elephant in embryo has been the subject of so much comment all over the country; that possibly some of our readers who live beyond the center of attraction would appreciate a glimpse of the seemingly illusive and impalpable object, or rather of what there is of it. Though the materializing process is slow, yet the clearly defined outlines of an organic body are manifest, and we have every reason to believe that the blood, bone, and muscle of a live enterprise will yet be developed. The approach to the site of Hotel Victory is by a road which leads from Put-in-Bay harbor to the west dock. From a point near the Island cemetery a view is obtained of the forty-acre tract of land and woodland which comprises the Hotel grounds. This tract--which is the highest elevated portion of the Island--when taken with its surrounding undulations of hills and hollows; its fertile grading barren rock ledges; its broad sweeps of orchard and vineyard; and its magnificent view of lake and adjacent islands, constitute a scene of diversified and unrivalled loveliness. A stately dwelling, built in a style of architecture which forcibly reminds the observer of some foreign villa, as represented in old world paintings, forms a picturesque point in the landscape. Passing down a lane which runs to the left of this foreign looking structure, we enter a field, the surface of which is hilly, broken, and covered with limestone that crops out at every turn in abrupt ledges, sharp points, and jagged edges. Patches of sod have gained a foothold between the rocks, and in the grass season a few cows manage to extract a living from the unpromising soil. Across this field, and in the edge of a forest belt, are the foundation walls of the prospective hotel.

The walls cover an extensive piece of ground, but only one-half of the entire plan; no beginning has yet been made on the other half of the foundation. A person unacquainted with the plans of the building could form but little idea of it from the position of the walls which more resembles some vast fortification than anything else of which we can think. In some places the walls are eleven feet in height, built of limestone quarried on the spot. Broken lines of stonework are seen here and there, and walls are built inside of walls. Heaps of rough, undressed stone are piled on every side in chaotic confusion, suggestive of the work yet to be accomplished. Within the court a well has been drilled and a force pump inserted, from which water is obtained for the mixing of mortar and other purposes, while a frame building erected near at hand serves as a tool house. Just now the place is lonely and deserted as the ruins of some old fort; secluded, yet romantic, as is its situation, and the echo of the woodman's ax and the chirp of birds in the woods nearby, are the only sounds that break its silence. Victory Park is a strip of primitive forest, wild, rough, beautiful, and picturesque. Groups of cedars mingle their greenery with the grey trunks and branches of other forest trees, and over-hang the high precipitous shores that forms the semi-circle of Victory Bay.

Information has been received to the effect that the directors of the Hotel Victory Company and contractor for the same, are to meet at Put-in-Bay about the middle of April to arrange business, and decide the "to be or not to be" of the hotel question.

Sandusky Daily Register,
27 March 1889, p. 2.

Hotel Victory is a plant of doubtful vitality. Though hot-beaded and nurtured long and carefully it shows little indication of life at the present time. This dormant sprig of greatness has been given until the 1st of April to germinate. If no signs of sprouting are then visible, the evidence of its deadness will be considered as established in the minds of many islanders, though some are willing to wait the development of summer showers and sunshine, holding that an enterprise projected on so large a scale requires time for a necessary deep rootage. The whole thing is evidently a "muddle" over which there is much head shaking. Rumor says that a suit is to be entered at an early day by the contractor for work already done on the building, which is yet unpaid. The islanders, many of whom have given toward the enterprise as liberally as their means would permit, are already wishing their money back, as few of them have means to sink in abortive schemes. Some indignantly pronounced the project a swindle, and an indignation, already kindling, will burst forth against the projectors, if a swindle it is proven.

Sandusky Daily Register,
25 July 1889, p. 1.

A sale of cottage lots took place on Wednesday last at the site of Hotel Victory. Only a few sales were closed, but it is expected there will be more soon. The expressions of admiration made by the prospectors concerning the beauty and desirability of the location were many. Work on the Hotel is going steadily forward. A force of masons are engaged on the foundation, and other workmen are variously employed. A vessel laded with a cargo of sand designed for the structure has arrived in the Bay.

Sandusky Daily Register,
1 August 1889, p. 2.

Hotel Victory is proving a substantial reality, instead of a mythical fancy as it has appeared in the eyes of a great many persons. A force of men, numbering between forty and fifty, are now actively engaged upon the structure. One-half of the massive foundation, three hundred feet in length, has been completed, while the remaining half is laid out, and the lower portions of the walls are being put down. A ledge of building stone was recently struck within the Hotel grounds far superior to the rough limestone which has hitherto been used. The quarry is capable of producing a hundred cords of stone, and it is being worked. A number of horses and wagons have been brought from the mainland and are employed at hauling stone, sand, and lumber. A large quantity of the latter material is already piled about the place, which is being drawn from Brown's dock to the site of structure.

Sandusky Daily Register,
7; 14; 28 August 1889, p. 1; p. 2; p. 2.

Work on Hotel Victory is going on uninterruptedly. Two hundred cords of sand have been contracted for, a large part of which has been delivered in vessel cargoes. Seven teams from the mainland as well as a number of island teams are employed about the building site. . . .George E. Gascoyne is constructing frames for seventy windows, which are to be placed in the base of the walls. . . . It is stated by workmen on Hotel Victory that the foundations of the building will be completed this week.

Hotel Victory Formally Opened with Banquet and Ball

Anonymous

Sandusky Daily Register,
13 July 1892, p. 1.

The formal opening of the Hotel Victory was a grand success in every way, and the vast crowd of people that visited Put-in-Bay and enjoyed the inaugural banquet and ball demonstrates conclusively that the popularity enjoyed by Put-in-Bay as a summer resort years ago has been returned with interest by the tireless energy and remarkable ability of J. K. Tillotson. The history of Hotel Victory since its inception several years ago, if written in detail, would make one of the most interesting books for businessmen ever written. It would be a series of chapters of apparently insurmountable obstacles overcome, a series of victories that culminated in the magnificent Hotel Victory.

Although the postponement of the inaugural banquet from June 30 to July 12 was extensively advertised, it did not serve to keep people away. The Hotel has been entertaining guests since June 29, with a constantly increasing list of names on the register. Today everything was in excellent condition and the crowd was taken care of with ease.

The electric cars did not reach Put-in-Bay as soon as they were expected, but they finally got there and the first run was made Sunday evening about 6 o'clock. Of course everybody wanted to ride on the first car, and those that did considered themselves fortunate. Motor car No. 3 made the run with W. K. Archbald of the Westinghouse Company at the motor and J. K. Tillotson on the front platform at his side. When the car ran along the track without a break or slip the passengers grew enthusiastic, but when it ran up the big hill from the cemetery to Victory Park, a great cheer went up from the car that met with a hearty response from guests at the Hotel.

Yesterday a second car was fitted with its motor, and today passengers from the boat landings to the Hotel were transported with safety, comfort, and dispatch. Each of these great cars has a seating capacity of 96 persons and can carry altogether 150 people. The cars are 42 feet long, 8 feet wide, and 12 feet high. Of these, four are motors and four trailers. The combined seating capacity of the cars is 768 passengers, and the combined carrying capacity 1,200. So, it can be taken to Hotel Victory and return without inconvenience to anybody.

Of the Hotel proper so much is to be said of its immensity one scarcely knows where to begin or where to stop. Mr. Thomas Keegan, the builder, says he has figured it out that there are sixteen and one-half acres of flooring, seven and one-half miles of baseboards, and a mile of wainscotting, besides which there are 1,700 doors in the building and about 2,500 windows. Altogether there are 825 rooms, of which 600 are guest chambers. On the building proper there are 458,000 shingles, not including the roof and how many thousand there are on the roofs Mr. Keegan himself cannot say. Of carpets, Manager Henry Weaver says there are over 16,000 yards, mostly Brussels, Ingrain, and Maquette. The main dining room is 160 x 90 feet and about sixty feet from the floor to ceiling. A balcony runs entirely around this great room about fifteen feet from the floor. The ordinary dining room is 110 x 60 feet, the officers's dining room 30 x 40, and the nurses' and children's dining room 80 x 40. The total dining room capacity admits of the seating of about 2,000 people.

Hotel Victory with main entrance (left), a connecting building containing lobby, office, and ball room, and the main dining room (right).

Inside the main dining room of Hotel Victory.

One of the most delightful rooms in the building is the main reception room, 120 x 50 feet, elegantly carpeted and furnished with the handsomest and most comfortable chairs. Smaller reception and party rooms open into the room, and all are elaborately furnished. The office is 90 x 60 feet with beautiful red oak desk furniture and handsome oak staircase. Off from the office is the general reception room beautifully carpeted with Maquette and richly furnished. The writing room, also leading off from the office, is no less attractive. The general parlor is 100 x 60 feet and furnished in keeping with the rest of the house. All three rooms are adequately lighted with incandescent electric light fixtures. Everything is modern, rich, elegant, and attractive. The elevator carriages are models of taste and beauty and are arranged well for the convenience of guests. The counter in the guest bar room is thirty feet long facing the lake. Adjoining it is the billiard room with ten of the best tables made. An object of interest to everyone is the kitchen which, without doubt, is the best arranged and most modern equipped in the country. It is 100 x 60 feet, well ventilated and entered by vestibules from the main and ordinary dining rooms. The great ranges are as interesting as they are massive, and automatic dish washers are among the chief mechanical features of this department.

Today the great structure was gaily decorated with flags, flowers, bunting, and banners. In the main dining room seats for 1,000 guests were tastily arranged in family style, eight at a table, instead of a long banquet table, as is generally the custom. The menu was elaborate and would have been a credit to the finest metropolitan hotel in America. At noon the boats began to unload the excursions, and the dock was a scene of bustle and gaiety, although the number of people was not quite as large as had been anticipated. The electric cars were crowded, and many of the carriages on the Island were kept busy taking guests to the great Hotel. The banquet lasted from noon to 4:30, and the dining room service was the very best. It is a feather in Manager Weaver's cap to have it known that he can handle a great crowd as easily as a small one, and such service is sure to make the house popular. The music was surprisingly good, Hotel Victory orchestra playing throughout the banquet. Tonight the ball room was a brilliant scene of fashion and gaiety. It was characterized by that delightful uniformity that makes people feel comfortable at summer resorts. Dancing was kept up until long after midnight.

Today's opening demonstrates beyond the possibility of a doubt that Hotel Victory is destined to be the great popular, fashionable summer resort of the West, and the Detroit, Cleveland, Toledo, and Sandusky people will be benefited accordingly. Manager Weaver already has numerous applications for private banquets to yachting parties and society people in these cities, and the place promises to be the resort for society gatherings of this nature. Of the history of Hotel Victory there is so much to say that one can scarcely do it justice. Mr. J. K. Tillotson conceived the idea four years ago, and with him to think was to act. He started in to win, and in the face of great opposition carried the project through innumerable ups and downs to an absolutely unqualified success. He knew the people wanted such a resort and were willing to patronize it. On this knowledge he based his efforts. He has bought the land, built the greatest summer hotel in the world, constructed an electric railway, and made business for all the railroads centering in Cleveland, Toledo, Detroit, and Sandusky, and all the steamboats running out of those ports. As for Put-in-Bay, the transformation is remarkable.

Tillotson's Palace Placed in Hands of Receiver

Cleveland Leader

Sandusky Daily Register,
12 September 1892, p. 4.

Judge Ricks of the United States Circuit Court on Saturday appointed George H. Ketcham of Toledo receiver of the Hotel Victory Company, Put-in-Bay, in a suit brought by the Phoenix Furniture Company of Toledo. The bond of the receiver was fixed at $50,000. J. K. Tillotson of Toledo, who has been the prime mover in the Hotel Victory enterprise from the start, brought a cross-bill and secured an injunction against disposing of the securities. The suit was brought in the Toledo division of the United States Court, and the papers are not on file in Cleveland. The Electric Supply Company brought a suit at the same time against the Put-in-Bay Water Works, Light & Railway Company for a receiver. Hon. L. S. Baumgardner of Toledo has been appointed with a bond at $5,000. Those who have been familiar with the state of affairs at Put-in-Bay have known that it was only a matter of a few weeks when the big, new hotel would go into the hands of the receiver. It was a strange coincidence, however, that the receiver was appointed on the anniversary of. . .the Battle of Lake Erie, when Commodore Oliver H. Perry whipped the British fleet under Commodore Robert H. Barclay.

Nearly five years ago Mr. J. K. Tillotson of Toledo, conceived the idea of starting an enterprise that would surpass anything of its kind in America. His idea was to build an immense summer hotel to take the place of the big Put-in-Bay House, which was destroyed by fire about fifteen years ago, and make it the largest hotel of its kind in the world. He succeeded in interesting a few moneyed men in the gigantic plan, but they subsequently withdrew, believing that the project would not be a paying one. After many discouragements Mr. Tillotson succeeded in getting the Hotel project on paper and announced that the Hotel would be open to the public in the summer of 1890. It was named Hotel Victory in honor of Perry's conquest, which occurred a few miles northwest of the Island. There were many discouragements, and but little was done the first year. The opening was postponed until 1891.

Considerable headway was made in forming the Company, and rapid progress was made in building the Hotel. A large number of lots were sold in Victory Park and many persons were induced to subscribe to the stock of the Company. The building was put up with hardly $1,000 visible when it was commenced. Subscribers to the stock paid up their subscriptions, and the money received from this source together with what was realized from the sale of lots enabled Mr. Tillotson to keep the enterprise going. It was utterly impossible to get the Hotel ready for guests in 1891, and the opening was postponed another year. The Hotel was on such an immense scale that a vast amount of money was needed. Many of the firms which furnished material were induced to accept stock in the Hotel Victory Company as payment, and many of the contractors for work were paid in the same way. It was generally believed that the Hotel would be a big paying investment when once opened. Everything was sacrificed to have it ready for the season of 1892. The opening was announced for June 30, but was postponed.

A large number of tickets were sold in Cleveland, Detroit, Sandusky, Toledo, and other lake and inland cities for the opening banquet and ball. With the sum realized from this sale the most pressing creditors were paid, and extra efforts were made to get the Hotel in readiness. It was finally opened to guests early in July. The Hotel was by no means completed, but portions of it were finished in the most luxuriant manner. The reception and drawing rooms were especially rich in their furnishings, and the throngs of visitors who inspected the Hotel during the past season were lavish with praise. Early in the summer the managers gave cognovit notes in payment of a large number of claims. Many of these notes were entered up, and judgements taken against the Hotel Company in Cleveland and many others in Toledo. It is said that over $150,000 has already been put into the project. Mr. George Ketcham, of Toledo, who was appointed receiver, is a young and enterprising millionaire, a public spirited citizen, and a good business man. It is probable that in his hands something will be done to adjust the present difficulties, complete the Hotel, and place it upon a paying basis.

Big Hotel Victory Sold at Auction

Toledo Commercial

Sandusky Weekly Register,
27 February 1895, p. 2.

Under an order of sale duly issued from the office of the clerk of the United States circuit court for the Northern District of Ohio, in the famous case of the Phoenix Furniture Co. against the Put-in-Bay Hotel Co., Marshall Haskell sold the monster Hotel Victory, its grounds, and its equipments at auction in the United States court room at Toledo at 2:30 o'clock on Thursday afternoon. The property is described as lots number nineteen and twenty, range north of the county road, on the main part of South Bass, otherwise known as Put-in-Bay Island, containing twenty-one acres of land, more or less, in the county of Ottawa, being the same property conveyed to the said Put-in-Bay Hotel Co. by Valentine Doller, assignee of Jose de Rivera, and being the same property upon which the said defendant, the Put-in-Bay Hotel Co., has erected a hotel, together with all buildings, structures, improvements, hotel property, out buildings, and appurtenances of every kind constructed or located upon said property, together with all privilege and appurtenances thereunto belonging, which originally cost $260,000. It was sold to Fallis & Company of Toledo for $17,000, or about one-fifteenth of its original cost. The equipment, consisting of all the furniture, carpets, mattresses, pillows, beds, bedding, linen, crockery, glassware, silverware, cutlery, kitchen and laundry outfits, and all other personal property and fixtures located at and being in the said hotel and its appurtenances, which originally cost $79,168.87, was sold to the Phoenix Furniture Company, of Grand Rapids, for $7,000, or nearly one-twelfth of its actual cost.

There was much interest manifested at the sale. The court room was full of men who had come to see how really little the property would bring, and even they were astonished at the low figure. There were only two bidders and the sale was made inside of ten minutes. After reading the official order of sale, United States Marshal Haskell stated that the hotel proper and its equipment would be sold separately, and he offered the furniture for sale first. Bids were a little slow in starting, but at last the representative of the Phoenix Furniture Company offered $3,000. The representative of Fallis & Co. raised the bid to $1,000 and thousand dollar bids were raised until the Phoenix bid reached $7,000 and the Fallis company pulled out. The hotel proper was then put up. This was also started by the Phoenix Furniture Company's man, who bid $5,000. The Fallis man raised it to $10,000, and the bids then went up by the thousand dollar jump until the property was knocked off to Fallis & Co.

The marshal explained that one-third of the expenses of the sale will be paid by the purchaser of the personal property and two-thirds by the purchaser of the realty. The total expense of the case will aggregate $15,000. The aggregate amount of judgements against the property was $303,387.88. The Phoenix Furniture Company held the largest lien. Their's aggregated $90,409.84 with interest at 7 per cent, from July 31, 1889. They held first lien on the furniture and second lien on the property. Fallis & Co. has first lien on the property in the sum of $10,897.32. Other lien holders of large denominations were the Central Thompson Houston Company, $12,131.66; Lock & Schultz, $12,010.96; also $19,086.40; assignees of George St. John, $75,151.05; Second National Bank of Sandusky, $31,080.31; First National Bank of Fremont, German-American Bank of Port Clinton, Third National Bank of Sandusky, one-third interest each in a judgement of $25,794.06.

Grand Dance at the Victory

Theresa Thorndale

Sandusky Daily Register,
28 July 1897, p. 4.

Lovers of the dance were highly favored last Saturday evening by an attraction in the way of a ball given at the Victory. It was reported as a grand affair attended by members of the naval brigade who arrived during the evening.

Many Guests Enjoy Social Doings at Hotel Victory

Anonymous

Sandusky Daily Register,
11 August 1897, p. 5.

This beautiful morning at Put-in-Bay, so bright, so refreshing after the thunderstorm of last night, the swish and roar of the breakers nearby being the only reminder of the wind's late high temper, finds Hotel Victory with a large, though quiet household. The first delegation of Big Four, Wabash, and Clover Leaf tourists, anticipated last week, are gradually giving place to others, and thus from time to time for the next week or two, the inducements offered by excursion rates will bring many extra guests.

At this time, when the resort season is so far advanced, one is impressed (when in the mood for moralizing) with the absence of reserve and superfluous tire, some so-called etiquette in the beautiful spirit of common brotherhood--common love. Then too, when the partings come, one is surprised to find how tightly their new friendships are interwoven in our lives, and we wonder why we say goodbye through such a tell-tale mist, when it is quite natural to think that they may go out of our lives forever today. We have so many good friends, tried and true, at home. It is good, it is best, all are better for having diffused their sympathy, admiration, and affection in just that way.

Social doings at the Hotel for the past few days have not been marked by an extraordinary event, although the same delightful amusements are in vogue to sweeten each passing hour if we will. The hop of last Saturday evening however, while not announced as having any especially attractive features, was unusually brilliant and enjoyable, for there came over from Sandusky a large detachment of the naval reserve (many accompanied by ladies) some from the Toledo reserve, and many visitors from Toledo and elsewhere, who came to join in the festivities. A considerable number of society people from Sandusky were also present, among them: Will Gilcher, Miss Mildred Cline, Mrs. E. H. Marsh, Miss Carrie Lea-Marsh, Miss Jean Abbott, C. D. Peck and wife, Col. and Mrs. W. H. Herbert, Mrs. W. J. Reynard, and P. Matthews.

It was generally remarked that a prettier array of the light, airy costumes of the ladies, so sensibly and charmingly fashionable this summer, had not graced the dining hall this season, the beauty of the scene greatly enhanced by the immaculately white uniforms of the reserves. Sunday evening the regular concert by the orchestra was made still more enjoyable by the assistance of musical talent from among the guests. The generous contributors so enthusiastically received were Miss Bear of Cincinnati, who possesses a sweet soprano voice; Mr. McFall of Detroit, the owner of a rich baritone; and Miss Troy of Detroit, pianist, who acted as accompanist as well as soloist of the evening.

Last evening those of the guests of Hotel Victory, who hoped to skim the placid waters of Lake Erie by moonlight, were doomed to disappointment, for though the trim little *Ogoniz* lay patiently waiting at the wharf, the moon hid her face behind such angry looking clouds that the placard in the Hotel office came down, and the would-be boaters put on their dancing shoes and quickly changed the program to that of an informal dance. In truth, dancing, while always a popular amusement, seems particularly attractive to the young people of late, under the direction of the new master of ceremonies (young, good looking, and an artist in his line), Prof. Louis Schackne of Toledo. To the interested observer who is a lover of the graceful pastime, yet to "pirse" to take part, Professor Schackne's style is a most happy innovation, for instead of the forever and forever "two step," the program is varied by other equally pretty dances.

Yesterday the lobby, corridors, dining room, and outside places of rendezvous were enlivened by the presence of a company of military, the City Guards of Lima, who are at present camping at Johnson's Island, and as a digression from camp life came to dine at the Victory. Their excellent maneuvers on the veranda, their "cheers for the Victory," and their gentlemanly and soldierly conduct throughout their stay won them rounds of applause. As their car "curved the bend" the ladies waved their handkerchiefs and the soldier boys their caps in the jolliest of goodbyes.

Life at Hotel Victory Devoted to Entertainment

E. S. P.

Sandusky Daily Register,
19 August 1897, p. 5.

While yet the Island is flooded with sunshine and the Lake a vast sheet of gently tossing blue, a cool wave has sought out our summer home, quite to the disappointment of the ice-cream and lemonade vendor, and the discomfort of the bather. The white duck man and shirt-waist girl have suffered a transformation.

Conventioners at the Hotel Victory.

Conventioners in Victory Park at the Hotel Victory.

Still it is delightful; and if one is only wise enough when on those sweltering days of packing at home, to lay a foundation for the gauzy garments of summer with one good snug suit, such days as these will be found the best of all. Such an opportunity for that long self promised walk through the woods, or the clamber down the cliffs, or perhaps the ascent of the tower at Hotel Victory where on a clear day one can almost nudge his Port Clinton neighbor, or shake hands with Sandusky, or even watch the boat sway from her moorings at Lakeside to bring over the Methodist friends. In truth, it seems sometimes that the Put-in-Bay Islands are really at their hey day of loveliness when the grape harvest is on, for surely no more beautiful scene is to be met with inside the radius of many miles than these romantically situated green hills of Erie, ere yet the autumn frost has bared the trees, blushing, blooming in their rich purple plenty. There is now considerable very favorable mention of keeping the Victory open until that season say, the middle of September, and in that case, visitors will have experienced the pleasure of seeing the Island in its varying happy moods.

The past week at Hotel Victory has been devoted, for the most part, to the entertainment of another convention, viz: that of the Master Builders Association of Ohio, numbering about two hundred in attendance, including ladies. Moonlight rides on the water, cards, dancing, etc., comprised an attractive social program, and one evening a concert by the "Slave Cabin Jubilee Singers" furnished pleasure for two hours or more. The Company is made up from the Victory's corps of colored waiters and their dusky lady friends from Detroit, and it is especially good for one of its kind.

Today another convention crowd is anticipated, the first delegation arriving this morning via Detroit. It is the annual meeting, for combined business and pleasure, of the Organized Agents of the New York Life Insurance Company, from various parts of the country and under the leadership of Thomas A. Buckner of Chicago, inspector of agencies. The meeting will doubtless occupy the greater part of the week.

One of the most important society events in anticipation at this Hotel is the grand ball to be tendered the Naval Reserves of Cleveland and Toledo and their ladies. In all probability it will be next Saturday evening, which it is expected by the management will for numbers, elegance, and perfect appointments outshine any previous efforts of the season. Another happy affair of the near future is the visit, for two or three days, of a social club of Toledo numbering at least forty couples, further arrangements for which are yet in the hands of the club's entertainment committee.

A recent acquisition to the society of Hotel Victory is the encampment, in the Park, of about thirty members of the Y.M.C.A. of Toledo. All are most agreeable, gentlemanly, and otherwise entertaining young men; and having received a standing invitation to all hotel festivities, ere the first white tent was pitched, are frequent cordially welcomed visitors.

Musical entertainments at Hotel have always been encouraged, and it is well worth mention that never yet has the requisite talent for an interesting and artistic program been found wanting. Last Thursday evening a limited number of the guests were afforded a most rare treat in a musicale arranged by a gentlemen from Cincinnati (who, with his family, are guests for the entire season), Mr. Ratterman. The artists of the occasion were Prof. Romeo Gorno of the Cincinnati College of Music; pianist and violinist, Oscar Ehrgott of Cincinnati, baritone; Mrs. Ehrgott, accompanist;

Ervin Singer of Toledo, tenor, and Miss Nellie Cook, pianist. Sunday evening the program of the regular orchestral concert was varied by some very excellent numbers furnished by Mrs. Finnie of Savannah, Georgia, soprano; Mr. Brady of New York, tenor; Fred Brown of Toledo, baritone, and Fred Brown, pianist.

The Hotel's Floral Garden

Theresa Thorndale

Sketches and Stories of the Lake Erie Islands
1898, pp. 97-98.

The grounds adjoining the Hotel form a landscape garden which nature and art combine to beautify. Profuse but tasteful and exquisite floral decorations appear. Foliage plants and blooms of torrid richness blend with paler hues; while climbing the white walls and stone-pillared steps, masses of maderia, morning glory, nasturtium and woodbine spread a mantle of blossom-starred greenery. Care is taken to preserve natural effects, and in the park, consisting of twenty-one acres, extending to and along the shores of Victory Bay, revels a profusion of flowers, both wild and cultivated.

The greatest charm of the park is its freedom, for the shore upon which it opens is as picturesque as ever conspired to woo the lover of Nature. Masses of beetling rock, of rock cleft and riven as by volcanic action, gird its broken line, while in the caverns indenting their base echoes the sound of waves. As if to screen their roughness, vines and mosses cover and shrubbery and cedar clumps edge and overdroop them.

Fire Sweeps Hotel Victory

Anonymous

Sandusky Register,
15 August 1919, pp. 1-2.

A smoking, charred mass of ruins is all that remains of Hotel Victory, one of the largest hotels of the Great Lakes and for many years one of the most famous summer resort hostelries, as result of fire which tonight swept the magnificent structure and burned it to the ground. The blaze, which started shortly after 7:30 o'clock [Thursday 14 August] and had gained such great headway before its discovery that efforts to check the sweep of the flames were fruitless, was the most disastrous conflagration in the history of the Lake Erie Islands. It removed from Put-in-Bay Island a structure which has been its most famous show place for nearly thirty years.

All efforts to arrive at an estimate as to the loss caused by the great blaze failed because of the absence from the Island of Harry J. Stoops, manager and one of the principal owners of the Victory. In constructing and furnishing the immense Hotel, however, it is said that between $500,000 and $1,000,000 have been spent since its erection, although the property loss today would, of course be much less. Just how much insurance was carried on the structure is also unknown tonight. Some reports have it that no insurance was carried. Others say that only a comparatively small amount had been carried, and that only last week this amount had been reduced by half. In the absence of Manager Stoops, the Hotel was in charge of his nephew, Benjamin R. Mowry of Chicago.

Hotel Victory destroyed by fire on 14-15 August 1919.

Ruins of Hotel Victory following fire of 14-15 August 1919.

Artist's aerial view of the entire Hotel Victory building.

Entire front of Hotel Victory with Victory Park, cliff, and Victory Bay.

There were not more than 20 or 30 guests at the Hotel, and all of them escaped from the fire. The blaze started in the north-west corner of the third floor of the main building. A defective electric light wire, from which trouble had before been experienced, is believed to be the cause. By the time Acting Manager Mowry and other people connected with the Hotel discovered the fire, the flames were already sweeping through the upper floors, and the doom of the Hotel was sealed. A slight west breeze carried the flames through the entire structure. By 8:30 o'clock, the building was a roaring, seething blaze, from which flames leaped 75 feet in the air. The Hotel stands on the highest spot on the Island, and as darkness fell, the view from every part of Put-in-Bay Island was indeed spectacular. Hundreds of islanders and summer visitors flocked to the scene. Scores came from surrounding islands in small boats.

The Put-in-Bay fire department, limited both in regard to fire fighting apparatus and fire fighters, confined its efforts to saving surrounding property as soon as it was seen that the Hotel was doomed. The Schiele residence and wine cellar, just in the rear of the Hotel, was in the greatest danger, and had there been a higher wind velocity, this property and other houses to the east of the Hotel would likely have been destroyed. As it was, the conflagration was confined to the Hotel. A number of guests and persons connected with the Hotel lost their valuables in rooms in the west section of the Hotel. Some furnishings and other valuables were removed from the east section, but for the most part, the contents of the structure were lost in the blaze.

The fire brought to an abrupt close a disastrous season at the Hotel. The Chicago syndicate, headed by Harry J. Stoops had operated the Victory this season without great success, the crowds for the greater part of the season being below requirements for a hotel of the size of the Victory. It was common belief at the Island this week that the Hotel would see an early closing, as one store here had been purchasing supplies from the Victory management.

In size, design and magnificence, Hotel Victory was surpassed by no hotel on the Great Lakes. The main building was of wood in the form of a square with 600 feet frontage, facing Victory Park, and a depth of 300 feet. It was three stories high, with corner cupolas five stories in height. The main portions of the Hotel surrounded an open court 300 feet square. Forming a wing to the main structure and connected with main building by a lobby, office, and ball room, was the magnificent dining room, a structure 155 feet long and 85 feet wide. This room had a height of 52 feet, permitting the location of balconies. This dining room, together with the balconies seated 1,200 people. The Hotel proper had 625 guest rooms, many with baths. The spacious lobby seated 1,000 persons, and it is said that in the corridors of the Hotel there was one mile of floor coverings. The place was steam heated and had three elevators. The furniture, for the most part, was purchased some years ago, but it was of the finest obtainable and of workmanship and material almost impossible to secure today. When Walter E. Flanders took over the Hotel two years ago, he poured thousands of dollars into new furnishings. It has been claimed that he spent upwards of $150,000 in reestablishing the Hotel.

Hotel Victory, long advertised as "the largest hostelry in the Great Lakes region," was a mammoth caravansary designed by architect E. O. Fallis of Toledo. The building was completed in 1892 at a cost of $70,000, by George Feick of George Feick & Sons, contractors of Sandusky, and his brother, the late Adam Feick. It was in process of construction from the fall of 1888 until it opened for business in June 1892. In order to build Hotel Victory the Messrs. Feick found it necessary to establish and maintain their own sawmill and planing mill here; also their own eating houses and dormitories. At one time they had seventy-five carpenters alone in their employ. The steamer *Arrow*, of Sandusky, was used for transporting material and workmen. Frequently the *Arrow* was chartered for special trips, especially on Saturday nights when the men engaged in the work of construction wanted to come home.

The Victory was built for a company organized by J. K. Tillotson from Toledo, in which a number of Sanduskians, among them Capt. Joseph Post, of the Post Fish Company, were interested financially. The venture was a failure from the first; that is, Hotel Victory was always regarded as a "white elephant" to a more or less extent. Those who are in a position to know say that it never made money, and that much wealth was relinquished in unsuccessful efforts to make pay dividends.

Thomas W. McCreary, now deceased, managed the Hotel from 1899 until his death in 1907, when he was succeeded by Col. R. G. Diegle who, for several years had been the Cedar Point Amusement Company's director of publicity. During much of the time that McCreary was manager and throughout the two-year period that Col. Diegle was in charge, the Hotel was owned by the C. W. and J. W. Ryan brothers of Toledo. From 1909 until 1918 the Victory was closed. Late in 1917, however, the hostelry was sold to Walter E. Flanders of Detroit, who operated it in 1918. Early in the present year the property was purchased by the Chicago syndicate headed by Stoops.

Whenever the Victory was open, it was headquarters of Great Lakes yachtmen assembled for the annual regattas of the Inter-Lake Yachting Association. The Hotel had a reputation for aristocracy, and the banquets and balls held there from time to time were always elaborate affairs. Some of the best known men and women of the United States had stopped at Hotel Victory. Among the women were Mrs. Jefferson Davis, widow of the first and only president of the Confederacy, who, for many years, made it a point to spend a good part of each summer here. Presidents and ex-presidents, famous soldiers and statesmen; in fact people from the highest walks of life had at some time or another affixed their signatures to the Hotel register. Among them were former President William H. Taft, the late President William McKinley, the late Senator Joseph B. Foraker, General Nelson A. Miles, General Hiram Scofield, and Robert T. Lincoln, son of President Abraham Lincoln

In point of furniture and furnishings Hotel Victory was, in its early days, said to have been second to no hostelry in the central West. The parlors were elegantly equipped. In every way the place was of a kind that could not but appeal. During the time that it was closed the Hotel was allowed to run down considerable. Before it was reopened however, costly improvements had been made.

Sandusky Star-Journal,
15 August 1919, p. 6.

On the southwest corner cupola was a large American flag. As the fire approached, the halyards burned but the flag was not reached by the flames. Finally the pole itself burned off near the base and toppled over carrying the flag into the sea of fire.

The copper, bronze, winged Woman Victory Statue erected in 1907 in the center of a parapet enclosed with a stone balustrade located on the west lawn in front of Hotel Victory.

Rustic bridge spanning a ravine between the front of Hotel Victory and Victory Bay.

Ruins of the Natatorium, or swimming pool, at Hotel Victory following the fire of 14-15 August 1919.

Staghorn summac invading the ruined foundation site at Hotel Victory, about 20 years later after the fire of 14-15 August 1919.

WELCOME
Main Entrance at Hotel Victory.
Greeting from Put-in-Bay Island,
Lake Erie, Ohio.

Main Entrance to Hotel Victory, South Bass Island.

Front Views of Hotel Victory on South Bass Island.

Rustic Bridge at Victory Park, Put-in-Bay, O.

Victory Park at the Hotel Victory on South Bass Island.

Put-in-Bay, Ohio., Cliffs at Victory Park.

Cliffs and Rocks along shore of Victory Bay at Victory Park.

South Bass Island State Park

The Hotel Victory site was left abandoned after the disastrous fire. Around the old foundation grew a thicket of staghorn sumacs. These woody shrubs are typical of the first stage of plant succession following soil disturbances and fires on South Bass Island. Later a forest of principally sugar maples, with some scattered black cherry trees, replaced the sumac shrubs as the dominant vegetation. This shady tract of approximately 21 acres was purchased from Roy Webster by the State of Ohio in 1946. At a bankruptcy sale in 1938, the State of Ohio also had acquired from the United States Fisheries Company an adjacent tract of about 11 acres located at Stone's Cove. This property had earlier been owned by John Stone and contained a dock, three sheds, and a barn. About 1940, the State of Ohio began rebuilding the Stone Dock and planted tree seedlings of red pine, sugar maple, sweet buckeye, and tulip poplar. A cottage was constructed at the barn site on the hill in 1943.

A description of the Park in the early 1950s appears in a letter written by Ralph D. Richards of Rocky River, Ohio, published in the *Ohio Conservation Bulletin*, 15(4): 27. 1951. He Wrote:

> Permit me to call attention to one of Ohio's most beautiful and interesting state parks. . . on South Bass Island about a mile from Put-in-Bay. Some of the outstanding features of the park are: a pebble beach with quiet, clear water, picnic tables, abundant space for camping, outdoor stoves, free wood, a superintendent who tries to be helpful, a beautiful view of the lake with the mainland in the distance, large lawn for games, and unusual fishing privileges. Boats are well protected by a large, new dock for the fisherman or owner of a cruiser.
>
> . . . It seems to me that more people of the state would enjoy this island park if they knew more about it. Most of the land formerly around Hotel Victory and a part of its beautiful grounds. . . now gives pleasure to the tourist, camper or local resident.

Together the State's two parcels of purchased land formed the 32-acre Stone Cove State Park, now known as South Bass Island State Park administered by the Division of Parks and Recreation in the Ohio Department of Natural Resources. As the magnificent Hotel Victory and Victory Park once did, this Park too overlooks the picturesque Stone's Cove, whose varied shore line meets the Lake at places with pebbled beaches and at other sites with rocky dolomite cliffs. In 1952, guests paid $2.00 per day to rent a cottage, and charges for camping privileges were 50 cents per night for a unit of four persons, the same as elsewhere in the state.

During the 1980s, the Park had 135 campsites and four cabins that accommodate overnight visitors or week-long guests. Facilities available were a public boat launch, boat tie-ups, tap water, a showerhouse, and toilet facilities, but no electricity or sewer hook-ups. Campers with tents, trailers, and motor homes were welcome in the Park. A campsite rented for $5.50 per night, whereas a cabin, a hexagonal structure that combined the best features of a tent with the conveniences of a cabin, was of a higher price per week or per night. In summer, picnicking and fishing are major activities; while in winter, amusements are ice fishing, ice skating, and sledding. On the former John Stone property a few nearly 50-year-old planted trees of red pine, sweet buckeye, and tulip poplar are standouts among the natural vegetation. Until a few years ago, remnants of the foundation of Hotel Victory were still very much evident, but now the ground surface under the sugar maple trees has been graded and leveled to such an extent that the old foundation is barely noticeable. The ruins of the swimming pool, nearby sidewalks, and parts of the stone pillars of the parapet, where the winged Victory statue once stood, are the most visible reminders of the golden era of Hotel Victory. Today, instead of sleeping in rooms in a mammoth resort hotel, overnight guests bring their own sleeping quarters housed in motorized campers or in waterproof tents.

References:

Chapter Three, The Hotel Victory

Anonymous. 1980. “Xanadu on Lake Erie: A delightful outing.” *The People’s Voice* 9: [4 pages, not numbered].

Anonymous. 1940. “Stone’s Cove Park - - Put-in-Bay, Ohio.”p. 24; “[Stone] Cove Park development,” p. 28. *In Ohio Conservation Bulletin* 4(5): 24.May; 4(8): 28. August

Britt, N. Wilson. 1940. “Survey of the vegetation of the Old Victory Hotel site on South Bass Island.” Handwritten manuscript. 7 pp. Copy owned by Ronald L. Stuckey.

Cooper, Barbara Allan. 1985. *Hotel Victory.* [Published by the author, Cuyahoga Falls, Ohio]. 40 pp.

Dodge, Robert J. 1975. “A Room for the Night: Hotel Victory,” pp. 98-102. *In Isolated Splendor: Put-in-Bay and South Bass Island.* Exposition Press, Hicksville, New York. x, 166 pp.

Frohman, Charles E. 1971. "Hotel Victory," pp. 108-112. *In Put-in-Bay: Its History*. The Ohio Historical Society, Columbus. viii, 156 pp. Second Printing, 1994.

Hagerty, Brigid. 1985. "Visit vacationland's state parks." *Lake Front News*, Port Clinton, 23-29 August, p. 7.

Jesse, Mike. 1982. "Hotel Victory: Dream on the rocks." *Sandusky Register*, 29 August, pp. B-1, B-2.

Maguire, Stephen D. 1973. "Trolley line on a small island in Lake Erie." *Railroad* : (July) 50-51.

Molnar, James Steven. 1980. "Grand Hotel: South Bass Island's Hotel Victory was a dream come true for a turn-of-the-century Toledo businessman." *Toledo Magazine, The Blade*, 20 April 1980, pp. 4, 7.

Moizuk, Ruth Dickerman. [1968]. "World Famous Hotel Victory," pp. 27-31. *In The Put-in-Bay Story Told from the Top-of-the-Rock.* [Published by the author]. 48 pp.

Parsons, Natalie. 1979. "*Victory Hotel* burned 60 years ago." *News Herald*, Port Clinton, 28 July, p. 4. Photographs.

Richards, Ralph D. 1951. "Put-in-Bay camper." *Ohio Conservation Bulletin* 15(4): 27. April.

Ryall, Lydia J. 1913. "Hotel Victory," pp. 105-113. *In Sketches and Stories of the Lake Erie Islands*. The American Publishers Co., Norwalk. vi, 546 pp. (Perry Centennial Edition 1813-1913).

Thorndale, Theresa. 1898. "Hotel Victory," pp. 93-99. *In Sketches and Stories of the Lake Erie Islands.* I. F. Mack & Brother, Sandusky. v, 379 pp. (Souvenir Volume).

SOUTH BASS ISLAND LIGHTHOUSE, built in 1897 at Parker's Point.

The South Bass Island Lighthouse

Although rumors circulated in 1894 that a government Lighthouse would be built on Parker's Point at the southwestern tip of South Bass Island, the large red-brick structure did not become a reality until the summer of 1897. The construction of lighthouses in the Island region of Lake Erie were all much earlier than the one built on South Bass Island. The owner of the Island, Alfred P. Edwards, originally wished to sell his island property as a whole rather than by parcels, and so he refused to sell the federal government any tract of land for a lighthouse.Consequently, the originally proposed South Bass Island Lighthouse was erected on nearby Green Island in 1854.

Theresa Thorndale is known to have written two stories in the *Sandusky Register*, which are reproduced here, describing the new Lighthouse on South Bass Island at the time of its construction. Her third story, written under her legal name and reprinted in part, depicts the Lighthouse and its surroundings in winter. The light served for 65 years, before it was replaced in 1962 by an automatic navigational light, as discussed in a fourth story. The new light was installed on top of a steel tower placed at the southwestern corner of the house near the steep west facing cliff along the Lake.

During the five years following the installation of the automatatic light, the Lighthouse was rented by the United States Coast Guard to several families as a summer home. In May 1967, the Coast Guard deemed the property to surplus and released it to the General Services Administration. This agency working through the United States Department of Health, Education, and Welfare (predecessor U. S. Department of Education) offered the Lighthouse and its approximate surrounding 2-acres to qualified educational institutions. The successful application of June 1967 was submitted by The Ohio State University for use by The Franz Theodore Stone Laboratory.

Aerial view of the Lighthouse and automatic light tower in 1979 at their location on Parker's Point (lower right); also view of road and the Lime Kiln Ferry Dock facility (upper center).

The New Government Lighthouse

Theresa Thorndale

Sandusky Daily Register,
27 April 1897, p. 4.

At the tip of a narrow projection which puts out from the south shore, is located the new government Lighthouse, now in process of construction. The spot is reached by a rambling road-way, which winds in its eratic course among rock ledges and through vineyards and peach orchards. The road is very narrow, rutty and rough and terminates at "the jumping off place," where in a lonely but romantic position stands the Lighthouse, overlooking a line of rough rocks, fallen masses of which rise in picturesque confusion above the water and are covered with cedar stumps, wild vines, and mosses. The Lighthouse is mainly of brick. It is an elegant and commodious structure, provided with spacious apartments for the keeper and every modern facility in the way of water supply, heating, sewage, etc. When visited last week by a *Sandusky Register* representative the plumbing was being done and the roof put on and the tower is soon to be annexed. The work is under the direction of the United States Engineering Department and supervised by J. P. Bumpus of Albton, New York, Superintendent of the Tenth Lighthouse District. The appointment of a light keeper will be the duty of the United States Naval Department. The light will range with that of Green Island and Marblehead.

Perched on the shore near the Lighthouse approaches stands a dismantled lime kiln with a stone tower which has proven misleading to the uninitiated who have taken it for the new lighthouse. The difference is appreciated, however, when a view of the latter is obtained.

Ruins of old Lime Kiln at Miller Lime Kiln Dock, South Bass Island.

"Parker's Point" Lighthouse

Theresa Thorndale

Sandusky Daily Register,
28 June 1897, p. 4.

Visitors to Put-in-Bay have found a new attraction in the newly completed Lighthouse on Parker's Point. Individuals with romantic notions about these structures may be intended in a sketch thereof. The preconceived idea of a lighthouse is a tall, massive, round tower of grey stone--storm swept and surf beaten--with a bit of a lean-to for the keeper.

However, the old-styled structure has given place to a reverse model, in which the tower forms the lesser portion, the living apartments in the larger. Very picturesquely situated nevertheless is the new station at Put-in-Bay. Its numerous apartments are ample and airy. They are handsomely finished with gold tinted wall papers and gilded mouldings, lovely carpets, and richly upholstered furniture. The mantels are beautifully inlaid, bronzed and carved, and every thing about the place, above and below, just as nice as can be. The dwelling part is three stories high. The basement is divided into numerous compartments to be used for store rooms, laundry room, and other purposes. The floors are carefully cemented, and the place contains a big furnace with pipes designed to heat the whole building; a cistern and a hydraulic force pump, which supplies the basement, laundry, and rooms on the first floor, yielding from its nozzle rain or lake water as desired. The kitchen is beautifully shellacked, "with ceilings painted to match." A massive new range, with a hot water reservoir, is part of the furniture.

The tower is entered from a high and wide front portico and the lantern reached by three circutious flights of iron stairs. The principal apartments of the lower are the watch and lamp rooms. The former is amply furnished with everything in the way of lighting supplies, and in the latter the keeper courteously unsacks from its canvas covering the lens. It is a beautiful object, catching and holding within its prismatic meshes all the color of the rainbow. It was manufactured in Paris and cost $1,500. Placed over an ordinary light it concentrates and gives its rays an immense power. An iron ballustered platform surrounds the top of the tower outside, from which is obtained a magnificent view. Wild, ragged rocks and half submerged boulders in the foreground, and wide lake stretches, island dotted in the distance.

The light keeper, Harry H. Riley, was formerly mate on the United States supply steamer *Haze*. Having been recently married, the young couple are making their first experiment at housekeeping in government quarters. A neat little case marked United States library and filled with choice literature, works of the best authors, left for Mr. Riley's use, goes to prove that "Uncle Sam" is not unmindful of his employees' intellectual wants; but while he permits the keeper to read away the lonely hours of watching, he expects him to keep everything in and about the station as neat as wax.

An additional lighthouse attache and assistant keeper, who manifests a zealous and watchful care, is "Bill," a cunning fox terrier. "Bill" is a great sailor, having spent several years cruising with his friends and master on board the *Haze*, but takes kindly to life ashore.

The original Lighthouse appropriation was $8,000. The sum was sufficient to complete the Lighthouse.

The Lighthouse in Winter

Lydia J. Ryall

Ohio Magazine
2: 204-205. 1907.

The road leading from the Bay to Parker's Point at the Island's southwest extremity, affords a most delightful drive, even in winter. Pretty summer cottages and the less showy but more substantial dwellings of islanders are seen; the former closely barred and deserted, the latter with smoke curling over snow-white roofs. One's attention is also attracted by a succession of vineyards and peach orchards, which, even at this season, are not wholly destitute of life, though denuded of fruit and foliage. The owners are among them in white canvas coats with high storm collars, buckskin mittens, and rubber boots, pruning away last season's superfluous growths. The highway grows rough with ledges of lime rock, finally narrowing to an unfenced wagon track that has never known the combings of a road scraper. Hedges of red cedar and snow-smothered copses appear, with new and charming scenic effect at every turn of the erratic trail that brings us to our destination.

On the extreme point looms the Lighthouse--not the gloomy, grey structure around which fancy has woven a web of romance-- but an edifice of modern construction. It is the newest, costliest, and most practical for its intended purposes of all the lighthouses on Lake Erie. . . The main building serves the purpose of a dwelling, the tower being the least conspicuous part, save as it adds to the general height. The occupants here live in comfort and even luxury. From the tower is obtained a fine view of the shore on both sides; native cedars fringing with their dark green, the beetling bluffs, and fallen rock masses, and contrasting strangely with the ice hummocks below. Here, also, may be seen a marvelously beautiful object--the lense through which effulgence is shed over Lake Erie in wild nights of storm--for the benefit of mariners. This lense radiates all the colors of the prism. Its purchase price was $1,500. Just now it is kept carefully covered, there being no use for it at this season, all Lake Erie stations having extinguished their lights with the close of navigation.

In matters of house-keeping, "Uncle Sam" is very particular--a regular "hen-hussy," in fact. From tower to basement, everything must be kept bright and shining. To insure absolute primness, he paints the coal bunkers white, and stipulates that they be so kept. The brazen faucets over the cellar washtubs must show a polish equalling that of the lamps in the tower. The present occupants of the Parker Point Lighthouse, Mr. and Mrs. Orlo J. Mason, are courteous to all callers, and in summer many tourists are piloted up the winding tower stairs to the lamp room. Most important among summer visitors, however, and one who always comes unannounced, is the United States Lighthouse Inspector. On the occasion of his visit, everything must be found spic and span, even to the gold braid on the light keeper's uniform, in which he is expected to appear without fail. Winter, however, brings immunity to the light keeper, both from government inspection and curiosity seekers. At this season only the resident islanders pay their visits to the Lighthouse family and find welcome and good cheer.

An example of what wind and wave can do may be seen upon the northwest side of Parker's Point, after a hard wintry gale, when the ice is running. Huge ice drifts shove up and under the rocks; and, grounding in the lake at their base, pile to a height of from ten to fifty feet, forming a chaotic, yet marvelously beautiful spectacle. From Parker's Point, a "road" strikes out across the frozen lake. It is important because it is the route taken by the island mail and its accompanying passengers and fish dealers with their wares. The abrupt shore in the immediate vicinity of the light station however, is accessible only at one place, where it is scaled by a flight of stairs, up which supplies are carried from the government lighthouse tender, the *Haze*. It puts in at stated intervals for this purpose, when the lake is navigable, anchoring off shore.

Light Keeper Has Battle with Elements

Frank S. Snavely

Sandusky Register, Second News Section, 26 September 1926, p. 11.

"Oh, yes," some of us say, "lighthouse keepers certainly have a snap—nothing to do but light up at sundown and then put the beacon out in the morning." Again proving that one half of the world doesn't know how the other half lives. This week almost brought another hardship to Captain William Gordon, "boss" of Put-in-Bay lighthouse and those guiding starts located upon Green Island, Ballast Island, and the buoys in this neighborhood. Captain Gordon, several years ago nearly lost his life when caught in the lake ice, where he was held a prisoner a great many hours, was finally rescued off Port Clinton, more dead than alive.

This week's near-calamity came with the first real test-out of the recently delivered lighthouse boat brought here from Buffalo. The new vessel is a very deep riding launch equipped with a heavy duty Lathrop. Apparently the new boat was as staunch as a life saver, but recent heavy seas absolutely proved its peculiar unseaworthiness. It throws such a spray in a blow that it is impossible to keep the engine running, with the result that it swings around at the mercy of the waves.

Wednesday of this week dawned—just the kind of day to sit around and dream—ideal for a run to Green Island, through Captain Gordon. Accordingly, the trip was made over there—a slight repair made to the light apparatus and then the return started. Several hundred feet off the Green Island dock, a nor'easter started with a sudden squall and then the battle between the boat and elements began. Five minutes passed and Skipper Gordon was half drowned by the spray—another 10 minutes and with a loggy boat half swamped with water, the engine died. That was the beginning of one of the interesting lake battles of the year—a "scrap" to gain a landing and home with about everything in favor of the elements.

Watchers say that there were times when the little craft simply refused to buck the waves any longer, but between engine stops, starts, and all kinds of handicaps, it made its way nearly to the big harbor-entrance buoy, when it could not negotiate the turn. Away he went, with the watchers wondering "what next." Fortunately, he successfully made the point above Stone's dock on the other side of the Island and finally succeeded in tying up back of the old wreck—"*Golden Age*."

It was at Stone's dock that Captain Gordon was given dry clothes and through the kindness of Wilken Webster had the water-filled boat tied out of harm's way. Rather thrilling was the whole experience, but proving the necessity of the government providing better protection for the lighthouse boat.

The Good Life — But a Bit Lonely

Dwight Boyer

Cleveland Plain Dealer, Pictorial Magazine, 26 September 1954, p. 15, 17.

Steadfastly guarding the south passage, a "short cut" between eastern and western Lake Erie ports that eliminates the long trek around Pelee Island, is the South Bass Island lighthouse, a red brick building and tower that flashes a 30,000 candlepower beam far out over the lake. Keeping the light in operation is Paul Prochnow, a civilian employee of the Coast Guard since 1930. On a somewhat remote region of the Island, Paul and Anna Prochnow, keep house in the 57-year-old home and light tower erected when steam and sail still shared the shipping lanes. The only sailing craft the pair see today are the small pleasure craft playing the waters in historic vacation land.

It's a seven-day-a-week job from early March to late December, a job that gets mighty lonesome, as they admit, until you get used to it. But, after 24 years of lighthouse duty, the Prochnows have reached the point where they wouldn't care for anything else. You'd think a lighthouse keeper had little to do other than making sure the light is working, but that's not the case at all. A lighthouse keeper, a successful one that is, must be a jack of all trades. He's a combination carpenter, electrician, painter, plumber, and handy-man-about-the-house.

In the winter the seas splash up as high as the tower, sheathing the entire structure with ice and raising hob with the paint. Spring finds Paul atop a 40-foot ladder, repainting the entire exterior trim. On the exposed southern tip of the Island, the house and tower get the full brunt of the winds sweeping across the lake. Consequently, a continuing routine exists of replacing loosened wires and other gear. All the outbuildings and storage sheds must be kept freshly painted in accordance with Coast Guard regulations. When he doesn't have a paint brush in his hand, Paul is busy hauling supplies from the airport or boat dock, picking up the mail or shoveling the snow from the long drive that leads to the main road.

With its tremendous candlepower, you'd imagine the tower light as having a number of large light bulbs. Instead, you find it to be a single 100-watt bulb, its great power and range made possible by an intricate and highly effective series of reflecting prisms and lenses. In addition to the main light tower, Prochnow also maintains two other navigational aids on top of the Perry Memorial Monument.

During the summer, he and his wife cultivate a large garden, processing much of the produce for their deep freeze locker and reducing the amount of food needed from the mainland and the Island's general store. Mrs. Prochnow also keeps a large flock of chickens for a steady supply of eggs and an occasional chicken dinner. Pauls' biggest summertime chore is caring for the grounds. About the time he finishes cutting the acre or more of grass, it's time to start all over again.

Television has made a big difference in the lives of the couple. Long winter evenings, once passed by listening to the radio or reading, are now filled with visual entertainment. Ideally situated, with little or no interference, they have a wide choice of programs from Cleveland, Toledo, Detroit, and several other Canadian cities.

The pay isn't good, by comparison with the earnings of city dwellers but the house, heating fuel, and utilities are furnished and transportation isn't a problem—they can't go out for the evening anyway. Add to this their freedom from the usual harassing problems of traffic, noisy neighbors, door-to-door salesmen, and you have what Paul and Anna call "the good life." "We'll never be rich," Paul remarked, "but we'll have security, a roof over our heads, and plenty of fresh air. I once made very good money as a commercial fisherman and I quit to take this job. I've never been sorry!"

Automation for Lighthouse; Isle Station for Rent

Anonymous

Sandusky Register,
30 October 1962, p. 14.

The passing of an era will be noted Wednesday, October 31, when South Bass Island Light Station at Put-in-Bay in Lake Erie is changed to an automatic light. On the same day, Paul F. Prochnow, keeper of the light for the past 15 years will retire from Coast Guard service. The characteristics of the light will remain unchanged

Paul and Anna Prochnow in the only known historic photograph showing the interior of the Lighthouse.

for the time being, but it is anticipated that it will be replaced by a single steel tower by early summer. Meanwhile, the officer of the Commander, Ninth Coast Guard District, Cleveland, is soliciting bids from anyone interested in renting the Lighthouse. The land and buildings will remain the property of the Government, although only a small area will be needed for the tower.

Two acres of land on the southwest point of South Bass Island were purchased in 1895 for the station, and the light was completed and placed into operation two years later. The light, which is attached to the two-story brick keepers house, stands 46 feet above ground and 60 feet above the water of the lake. It contains a fourth order revolving lens which displays an alternating red and white flashing light. The white light is 200,000 candlepower, and the red light is 45,000 candlepower. Both can be seen from 15 miles.

Prochnow, who will celebrate his 70th birthday in December, has been a lighthouse attendant since 1930. Prior to his assignment at South Bass Island, in 1947, he served as an assistant keeper at Cedar Point Light Station, near Sandusky, for 17 years.

The contracting officer in the Ninth Coast Guard District, who is soliciting the bids for renting the station, lists the property as consisting of two acres of land, with the following buildings: a two-story brick house containing eight rooms, bath, full basement, and sun porch; a two-story frame garage; and an iron storage building. The light station will be rented by the month, with a lease available for five years.

Lighthouse Life for Family of Nine

Anonymous

Sandusky Newspaper Enterprize,
5 August 1963.

With a bid of $66.50 a month, Ottawa County commissioner and building contractor Harry R. Johnson of Williston has won his family a five year lease on the abandoned lighthouse on South Bass Island. Johnson got the word Friday, took his wife and seven children ranging in age from 11-26 over for a first look at their new home Sunday. Said Mrs. Johnson: "We're delighted. We're teasing Dad about the fact that he's got the old contractor's savvy for choosing the right price." Johnson's bid won over three others ranging from $5 to $45 a month.

The family's plans however, are indefinite. "It's all so sudden," says Mrs. Johnson. "There are all sorts of details to be ironed out." The family first "fell in love" with the Island when Johnson was campaigning for commissioner. He lost his bid

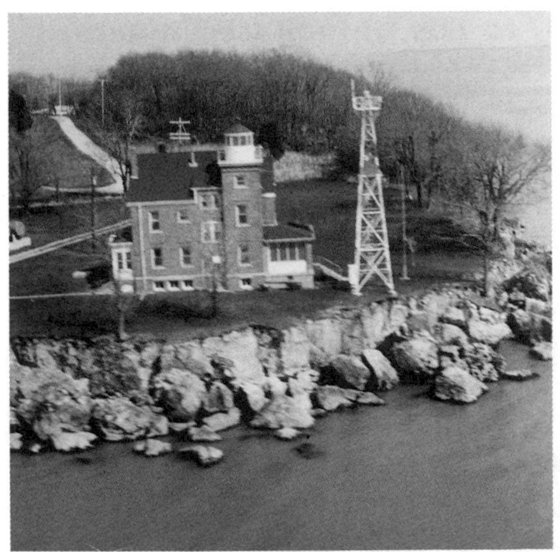

Automatic Light Tower at Lighthouse, 1962.

Nine lighthouse keepers are known to have maintained the light during its 65-year history. The names of these keepers and their approximate years of service have been compiled from several sources: Harry H. Riley, 1897-1899; Enoch Scribner, 1899-1900; Orlo J. Mason, 1900-1908; Charles E. Duggan, 1908-1925; William Gordon, 1925-1940; Frank LaRose, 1940-1941; Robert Jones, 1941-1944; Kenneth Nestor, 1944-1947; and Paul F. Prochnow, 1947-1962. Orlo J. Mason later was a lighthouse keeper at Ashtabula, Ohio; Charles E. Duggan died while serving as a lighthouse attendant; William Gordon, Frank LaRose, and Paul F. Prochnow all retired; and Robert Jones requested a transfer to the Marblehead Lighthouse.

on the Island by a vote of 11-3, but not his enthusiasm. When he heard the lighthouse was for rent, he didn't hesitate to apply.

The site includes two acres of land about a mile-and-a-half from town. Tenants of the lighthouse must remain all year, according to rental terms. Eight bedrooms are in the brick building, which also includes two screened porches, a two-story garage, and a gallery and tower. Johnson says the landscaping has been neglected, but a built-in sprinkling system is on the grounds. There's also oil heat.

Light chamber atop South Bass Island Lighthouse, 1974. Standing on the platform are John and Margie Slagle.

The Lighthouse Transferred in 1967 to The Ohio State University

The application of June 1967 for transfer of the South Bass Island Lighthouse Station property to The Ohio State University, Franz Theodore Stone Laboratory, was accepted, and the Lighthouse with its adjacent acreage was conveyed by *Quitclaim Deed*, dated 27 September 1967, to The Ohio State University. On 10 October 1967, the property was transferred to its Board of Trustees subject to several conditions. The special conditions stated that (1) for 30 years, the Lighthouse is to be continually used for educational and scientific research purposes and (2) an annual report of the Lighthouse utilization is to be submitted to a federal monitor of the U. S. Department of Education, Region V, Chicago, Illinois. The University continued to use this property in

The Lighthouse in winter, about 1976.

accordance with the agreement by enhancing the educational and research mission of Stone Laboratory, and the special conditions of the Deed were met and The University had clear title to the property in 1997.

The grounds are annually used as an outdoor laboratory by the field biological classes of the Stone Laboratory summer instructional program. Soon after aquisition of the property, a bird trap was constructed on the back lawn for research principally on blackbirds under the direction of Dr. Mildred A. Miskimen, who was teaching classes in ornithology during that time at the Laboratory. In 1973, the basement of the Lighthouse was equipped for radiological research by Dr. Walter E. Carey, and as a water quality laboratory under the direction of Dr. Charles E. Herdendorf. Research conducted in these facilities included radiological work and water quality/primary productivity studies associated with the establishment of the Davis-Besse Nuclear Power Station west of Port Clinton. Most of the radiological equipment was relocated to the Peach Point Research Laboratory in 1980. An atmospheric radiation monitoring station is still maintained on the grounds of the Lighthouse in conjunction with the nuclear power station.

During the first five years under operation by The Ohio State University, the living quarters of the Lighthouse were used as a dwelling by summer teaching faculty. Those professors and their families who lived there were Dr. Gareth E. Gilbert, Dr. Ernest S. Hamilton, and Dr. John W. Thieret, all who taught classes in botany at the Laboratory. In the Spring of 1973, the dwelling became the residence of the Laboratory Director, Dr. Charles E. Herdendorf and his wife Patricia for the next three years. After the Director purchased his own cottage on the west shore of South Bass Island in 1978, the Lighthouse again served as a summer dwelling for teaching faculty through 1982. Those who lived there at that time with their families were Dr. Walter E. Carey, Dr. Chester I. Randles, and Dr. John W. Thieret. During the remainder of the year, it was home for Laboratory Managers or investigators engaged in research projects as part of the Center for Lake Erie Area Research (CLEAR). Laboratory Manager John Rupert and his family occupied the Lighthouse in 1979-1980 and Manager Mark E. Monaco was there from 1980-1982. Beginning in September 1982, Larry and Andrea Wilson resided in the Lighthouse year-round until 1988. Mr. Wilson worked for the Miller Boat Line, and Ms. Wilson, the Laboratory Secretary, had been employed since May 1982.

In September 1983, a $50,000 meteorological station was installed on the United States Coast Guard steel tower at the Lighthouse site by the National Oceanic and

Atmospheric Administration (NOAA). The station consists of an anemometer for measuring the direction and speed of the wind; a barometer for recording atmospheric pressure; an air temperature sensor; an electronic unit for collecting, processing and storing weather data; and a directional antenna for transmission of these data via satellite. This sophisticated meteorological station is a cooperative effort of the Ohio Sea Grant Program at the Stone Laboratory and the NOAA Data Buoy Center of Bay St. Louis, Mississippi. Weather information from the Stone Laboratory station is transmitted via satellite to the National Weather Service Center at Wallops Island, Virginia, whence it is then diseminated to other National Weather Service centers. At that time, the Stone Laboratory station was NOAA's most advanced design and the first one operating in this country. Known as the Data Aquisition Control and Telemetry (DACT), it was developed by Magnavox Electronic Systems Company for NOAA. DACT provides valuable weather information by NOAA Radio to recreational boaters and fishermen on Lake Erie.

The Lighthouse property has meteorological sensors capable of detecting environmental radiation and acid rain. These sensors record air pollution as part of the Davis-Besse Nuclear Power Plant monitoring program. A pyranograph has been installed in the top of the old tower which measures sunlight radiation. The new steel tower supporting the automatic light under federal government control had to be moved in 1976 to a position in the lawn southeast of the Lighthouse. If it had not been relocated, the automatic light would have tumbled into the Lake because of the severe erosion of the large rocks that fall into the Lake along the cliffs at the Point. The grounds continue to be a popular place to study shore erosion, cliff-dwelling plants, migrating birds, insects, and other animals.

The Lighthouse in Retrospect

Nearly 40 years has passed since the last keeper climbed the steep, circular steps of the Lighthouse to light and maintain the oil lamp. A few Island residents recall the former days of glory, when the Lighthouse had a caretaker family in residence. L. C. (Cotton) Duggan, in an interview with Robert Boyce during 1987, told of his boyhood years living in the Lighthouse, when his father, Charles E. Duggan, served as caretaker from 1908 until his death in 1925. Cotton, who received this nickname because he had light blonde hair and wore a cap with a cotton top, was four years old when he moved with his parents into the South Bass Island Lighthouse. The family came from West Sister Island, where Charles had been the lighthouse keeper from 1903 to 1908. Cotton

South Bass Lighthouse and location of the Automatic Light Tower, 1987.

Cotton Dugan telling about his boyhood life at the Lighthouse, 1987.

stated that "the light was on from sundown to sunrise during most of the year when the lake wasn't frozen over." Other recollections were of a severe winter when ice piled upon the Island's southern point, blocking the view of the Lake from the kitchen windows. One severe storm sank a tow of barges moving past the Island towards Toledo. A crewman and woman cook from the tow made it to the Island in a lifeboat and appeared about one o'clock in the morning at the Lighthouse. The ice and currents that winter were so severe that they broke the power cable that extends to the Island on shore near the Lighthouse. During wintertime Cotton's mother frequently played the piano, and they watched for the mail to arrive at the Lighthouse Point every day. The mail was carried on an "iron clad" boat with runners which was pulled across the ice. Although Cotton said he was too small in his early years to help with work, such as hauling coal oil and supplies for the Lighthouse, he did, however, mow the lawn, deliver newspapers, and work in orchards and vineyards.

After the death of his father, the Duggan family moved from the Lighthouse, but remained on South Bass Island. Cotton continued working to help support the family by storing ice in the winter and catching fish for wages. For 45 years, Mr. Duggan was a licensed skipper, initially for the Miller Charter Boat Service, and subsequently developed his own charter service after purchasing a 36-foot boat. Now retired, his son "Skip" and grandson "Chip" operate on the Island a miniature golf course, the bus line between the Lime Kiln Miller Ferry Dock and the village of Put-in-Bay, tour trains and trolley, and the purchase in 1988 of the former Parker Ferry Boat Line, serving the village of Put-in-Bay, Middle Bass Island, and Port Clinton. The boat line is now called the Put-in-Bay Boat Line, Inc.

The South Bass Island Lighthouse may be only one of some 750 lighthouses still remaining along the 90,000 miles of United States coastlines, riverbanks, and lakeshores that is owned by a University, according to Dr. Charles E. Herdendorf. Under the University's continued care, the 100-year old Lighthouse "rises above the skyline and greets students and researchers" who come there to study and work. Its prominence at the old Parker's Point on the southwest tip of South Bass Island, attracts the attention of others—families and visitors among the thousands—who cross Lake Erie by ferry boat from Catawba Point to Miller's Lime Kiln Dock. After 100 years of existence, on a day in August 1998, the Stone Laboratory opened the Lighthouse for a public tour. Over 350 visitors made their way through the building to enjoy views from the catwalk in the old tower and the scenic grounds. The Lighthouse is now operated by the University Residence and Dining Halls as an additional housing facility as part of the Stone Laboratory program.

References:

Chapter Four, The South Bass Island Lighthouse

Boyce, Robert. 1987. "Lighthouse still keeps island vigil." *OSU On Campus* 17(3):8. September 24.

Cruickshank, Nancy. 1999. "South Bass Island Lighthouse." Ohio Sea Grant College Program, The Ohio State University, Columbus. Publication OHSU-FS-079. 4 pp.

Heniken, Mike. 1998. "Stone Laboratory opens its doors. Open House activities." *Friends of Stone Laboratory/Twineline* 20(6): 6. November/December.

Herdendorf, Charles E. 1983. "Modern Meteorological Station for South Bass Island." News Release, from file, The Franz Theodore Stone Laboratory. 13 September. Typewritten. 3 pp.

Langlois, Thomas Huxley, and Maria Holmes Langlois. 1948. "The U.S. Light House," pp. 67-68. *In South Bass Island and Islanders*. The Ohio State University, The Franz Theodore Stone Laboratory. Contribution No. 10, x, 139 pp.

Ryall, Lydia J. 1907. "Life in Lake Erie lighthouses." *Ohio Magazine* 2: 204-208.

Ryall, Lydia J. 1913. "Lake Erie Light Keepers, Their Trials and Adventures," pp. 407-420. In *Sketches and Stories of the Lake Erie Islands*. The American Publishers Co., Norwalk. 546 pp. (Perry Centennial Edition 1813-1913).

Thorndale, Theresa. 1898. "[No Lighthouse on South Bass Island]," p. 17. *In Sketches and Stories of the Lake Erie Islands.* I. F. Mack & Brother, The Sandusky Register Press, Sandusky. v, 379 pp. (Souvenir Volume).

Ice House of the Forest City Ice Company, built in the winter of 1893-1894 on Peach Point next to the United States Fish Hatchery.

An Enterprise That Died:

CHAPTER FIVE

The Ice Companies on Peach Point

The harvesting and storing of ice in the winter and selling it in the summer for refrigeration purposes is an enterprise long gone from South Bass Island. In the winter of 1878-1879 Andrew Wehrle & Co. Ice Company began the commercial ice harvesting business on Peach Point. This name is given to the wedge-like projection of land which encloses Put-in-Bay Harbor on the west. The portion of the Bay on the south side of Peach Point is referred to as Fishery Bay. About 1883, it was acquired and operated by the Forest City Ice Company of Cleveland. Expansion of their operation began 10 years later in the winter of 1893-1894, when the Company erected a large building 240 by 180 feet in area and 63 feet in height next to the United States Fish Hatchery building. The total capacity for ice was now increased to 51,000 tons, and runways to transport the ice from Fishery Bay and the Lake to the storage houses were now operated from both sides of Peach Point. The Company's major activity occurred during the winters of 1894 through 1899, as reported by Theresa Thorndale.

The Forest City Ice Company also stored ice in the winter of 1899-00, but the next winter, 1900-01, they operated under the name Columbia Ice Company, and later as the Independent Ice Company. The ice houses were left abandoned, and the land on Peach Point was purchased in 1902 by Louis Schiele and John Hollway. They raised the old ice house buildings and offered for sale 57 parcels of the land for cottages beginning in 1904. The ice harvesting industry died when mechanical refrigeration became available and laws were passed, in the interest of public health, prohibiting the use of natural ice for preserving foods. Descriptions of how the ice was cut and transported to the ice houses for storage are contained in the articles whose citations are given in the list of references, page 81.

The first story reproduced here is by island resident John Brown, Jr. son of the Civil War hero John Brown of Harper's Ferry fame, who describes in detail Andrew Wehrle's Ice Company. Except for the last two stories the remaining stories are paragraphs from Theresa Thorndale's newspaper columns briefly describing the Forest City Ice Company's activity for each winter from 1894 through 1899.

A. Wehrle & Co. Ice Company

John Brown Jr.

Sandusky Daily Register,
3 January 1879, p. 1.

Yesterday, the 29th December 1878, was deserving of notice in the annals of our Island by beginning the work of filling the immense ice houses lately constructed on the beautiful strip of land known as Peach Orchard Point, which lies a short distance west of north from Gibraltar Islandat Put-in-Bay. This Point, bounded by the waters of Lake Erie on the north and northwest; by the waters of Put-in-Bay on the east and south; and extending southwesterly far enough to include about twelve acres of land, is owned by Mr. Joseph De Rivera St. Jurgo of New York. It was lately leased by him for a period of twenty-one years to Andrew Wehrle, Sr., and others of Middle Bass Island, and to Valentine Doller and others of Put-in-Bay Island. This association, under the name of "A. Wehrle & Co. Ice Company," in addition to other contemplated improvements to be made on this cedar and grass-covered Point--the "Put-in-Bay Lovers' Retreat," held in such affectionate remembrance by uncounted belles and beaux--have just finished and put in complete running order five ice houses. They are placed side by side, under distinctly separated roofs, yet the whole forming one continuous roof, as the teeth of a saw; though separated, they are yet connected by the blade.

For those especially interested in such buildings I give quite reliable measurements. The aggregate size on the ground of these buildings is 150 x 150 feet, 22,500 square feet. Each building is 30 x 150 feet in the clear, studding 24 feet high. The houses are set on stone foundations laid in mortar. Sills, 4 x 12 inches for outside walls; studding, 2 x 12 and set three feet from centers. Each building is sheeted inside and out with one-inch common boards. In addition to this, the outside of the aggregated or consolidated building is covered with best quality of tarred sheeting-paper, then stripped with 1 x 3 inch strips, placed two feet apart, then boarded up and down with common barn boards dressed on one side and battened with "O. G." mould battens. Partitions studdings, 2 x 8 inches, set four feet to centers and covered on both sides with common boards; each partition and all outside walls filed with pine saw-dust.

There are two principal runways each 190 feet long, extending from the waters of the Bay to the main building on a grade of two and a quarter inches to the foot; one of these runways to fill two houses, the other three houses. These runways are connected with inside runways which on the descending grade divert the ice from the main runway to the side buildings as required. All runways are made twenty-eight inches inside and of oak. Ice is cut twenty-two inches square. The aggregated capacity of these houses when filled is 540,000 cubic feet, or about 13,000 tons.

In addition to these there is a building 54 x 32 feet, 24 feet high to plate, covering all machinery and tool rooms; engine house 20 x 20 feet, 10 feet plate; also, house to hold sawdust 16 feet into 36 feet, 12 feet to plate, all like the ice house covered with dressed boards and battened. All roofs are covered with the best quality shingles, and have plain cornices, best quality tin valleys and gutters and down spouts, and the entire building is to be covered with two coats of white lead and oil. The ice tools are of the very best quality and procured of Messrs. Barney & Ferris, of Sandusky. Probable cost of building, including filling with saw dust and ready for ice, is $5,500, not including runways, which will cost $2,500 more. The contract for building was made with Mr. George E. Gascoyne, resident architect and builder, September 23rd 1878.

This Company is using the patent elevator of Mr. Louis Zistel of Sandusky, which is now proved at Put-in-Bay to be perfectly adapted to the use of steam as a motive power as well as to horse power. The little portable ten horse power engine for sawing wood, owned by Valentine Doller, was taken over on the ice and attached by belting to Mr. Zistel's elevator. From the very start set the machinery, together with seventy men and the ice, moving with the regularity of clock-work, filled these buildings at the rate of from 75 to 100 tons per hour, with a steam pressure of only forty to fifty-five pounds. Sandusky has reason to be justly proud of her inventor, among whom Mr. Zistel deserves high rank.

Great credit is due to the foresight and business energy of Messrs. Wehrle, Doller & Co., who have secured Peach Orchard Point, using only the northeasterly part for this business, and having left the greater part of the twelve acres for such uses as the far-seeing German intellect can so readily discover. The names of the enterprising men prominently engaged in this undertaking are: General manager, Andrew Wehrle, Sr. of Middle Bass Island; contractor for building, George E. Gascoyne of Put-in-Bay; contractor for elevator, Louis Zistel of Sandusky; superintendent, Valentine Doller of Put-in-Bay; assistant superintendent, George E. Gascoyne. A trip to the islands would be amply rewarded by a view of the workings of the Zistel ice elevator in a model ice house.

Hoping that dwellers in the sunny South may never want for ice nor for the genuine sympathy of those whose blood tingles with the winter's cold of the North (should afflictions again come as in the past year). I remain, yours for all, East, West, North, and South, Put-in-Bay Island, Lake Erie, Ottawa County, Ohio. December 30, 1878.

Tour of Peach Point

Theresa Thorndale

Sandusky Weekly Register,
9 May 1894, p. 9.

Probably the most remarkable of all island localities is that portion of Put-in-Bay called Peach Orchard Point, from an ancient peach orchard there found by early settlers, suppositiously planted by still earlier predecessors who had mysteriously come and gone without leaving upon it the impress of their names or history. Peach Point [includng Oak Point], as it is known for short, is a curving projection of land which encircles with its long arm the waters of Squaw harbor and those of the Bay, amply protecting from the sweep of northwesterly storms and shipping anchored within. This Point is remarkable both for its wealth of wind and picturesque scenery and for the large and important enterprises there centered. It is approached from the bay village by a circuitous wagon road following the shore line, known as Riviera

Boulevard, which, by the way, is a name too metropolitan by far for a road so delightfully sequestered and so unconventionally guilleless of improvements.

Peach Point forms a bewildering maze of scenery, the wildest, most picturesque and beautiful ever crowded into a single territory of like size. From every point of observation, at every turn, whether along the rough rocks, engirding the shores of both sides, or amid inland tangles of cedar clump, shrubbery, vines, and verdure are presented views sufficiently novel and unique to drive an artist wild with delight. It seems, indeed, as if Nature had here become recklessly prodigal and had exhausted her resources in endowing the spot with attractions. The whole Point comprises in fact a magnificent natural park, which did it lay within the corporate limits of the city, would be reckoned of inestimable value. The Point contains but a single dwelling, a cabin, picturesquely situated among forest trees and orchards, rude and unconventional enough and secluded enough withal to suite the taste of the most fastidious hermit.

Despite its seeming defiance of circumscribed rules of art and civilizing influences generally, this untamed bit of nature yet nurses three important enterprizes which along with the rattlesnakes, blowsnakes, peaches, lime, and other products flourish among rock ledges and cedar clumps with rare hardiwood. These enterprizes are namely: The Cincinnati Fishing Club [on Oak Point], the United States Fish Hatchery, and the extensive storage houses of the Forest City Ice Company [on Peach point proper]. The latter, with lands belonging to the Company, occupies the extreme point. The rocks on both sides here terminate in stretches of wide gravel beach, and outlying reaches of low, flat rock over which meeting currents fret and foam, and incoming waves bear shoreward the flotsam and debris of the unsalted seas. The ice houses comprise a huge pile, lonely and deserted, where a night ghosts might congregate with perfect propriety, and robbers hold intrigues without fear of molestation.

The Forest City Ice Company

Theresa Thorndale

Sandusky Weekly Register,
3 January 1894, p. 8.

For months past the Forest City Ice Company, having its headquarters in Cleveland, has contemplated an extension of its already large interests at Put-in-Bay, in the way of new additions to the group of massive buildings on Peach Point as storehouses for Lake Erie ice. The project is now to be carried into effect. Arrangements for the transportation of building material across the lake have been made, and work will begin this week. Five draught horses with necessary outfit and numerous workmen arrived a few days ago via steamer *American Eagle,* and grading for the foundation is now in progress. The contractor for the job, together with a force of carpenters and other workmen, is expected in the week. The ice industry with its increased facilities will undoubtedly become a feature of decided importance to island dwellers, as it will furnish employment to a large number of men.

Of island crops none are more prolific than the ice crop. Its extent and supply unlimited in fact, and no crop more valuable when properly gathered and garnered as the Forest City Company evidently perceive. Already the fields of Erie grow "white unto the harvest," and laborers look hopefully forward to the reaping, glad of an opportunity in these times of financial tribulations to secure remunerative employment of any kind. In coming dog days, when a whole city is groaning with heat

Cutting ice in Put-in-Bay Harbor; Gibraltar Island in the background.

and thirsting for cooling drinks, then the garnered ice will be shipped thither by great barge cargoes and supplied ready to customers at paying prices. The prime crystal quality of island ice puts to shame the murky, sewer-tinted commodity collected in the vicinity of a city as big and black as Cleveland.

Sandusky Weekly Register,
10 January 1894, p. 12.

Some murmurs of dissatisfaction, too, are heard among the ice men. They calculated on ice illimitable. Had they taken "time by the forelook" and been satisfied with what Providence sent, they might already have in store a fair harvest, but not content with good, they waited for better and so got left all around. Some had prospective ice fields marked out ready to begin operations when away it went; and nobody knows whether it will come back again this season or not--excepting for mere fashionable calls. Some think it will, others are sure it will not--a question which will be settled undoubtedly by next April. The Forest City Ice Company have packed up and will probably leave in disgust by Monday's steamer unless by that time there are prospects of a freeze up, so that the largely projected improvements on Peach Point will be largely subservient to the weather.

Sandusky Weekly Register,
28 February 1894, p. 12.

John Croft, of the Forest City Ice Company, who was on the Island six weeks or more, watching the hen on her nest, got disgusted with the prospect and deeming the ice crop a failure for this year, left for more fruitful fields. No sooner had he gone, however, than mercury took a dive to zero and below, and now they say he will come back with men and mules and other outfit to fill the big storage houses on Peach Point.

Sandusky Weekly Register,
7 March 1894, p. 4.

The Forest City Ice Company began last week filling the big houses on Peach Point owned thereby. The ice, when they began, was of clear crystal quality and solid, but a few days at early spring sunshine honey combed and spoiled it, and now the enterprise has been abandoned. The houses are but partially filled.

Sandusky Weekly Register,
2 January 1895, p. 7.

The ice houses now crowd closely upon the United States Fish Hatchery, and in contemplating the great amount of igneous material employed in all these massive buildings, the causal thought occurs: "What if fire should break out," and no fire engine nearer than the Bay, and reached only by a rough, erratic road of rock and rut, by far too romantic for practical purposes.

Sandusky Weekly Register,
23 January 1895, p. 3.

Ice in the Bay is now of a thickness ranging from five to seven inches, but outside it is not strong enough to warrant any very extensive travel with teams. . .Some of the smaller ice storage houses in the vicinity of the Bay have been filled, but the Forest City Company will not begin storing the 51,000 tons, which they expect to harvest, until they can crop an eight inches thickness of the commodity.

Sandusky Weekly Register,
26 February 1896, p. 1.

The laboring forces of the Forest City Ice Company are again in the field. Even before the late heavy freeze the ice was pronounced in good shape for harvesting and work was begun. The thickness and solidity of the product has materially increased within the past few days.

Sandusky Daily Register,
12 January 1897, p. 7.

A hustle is now perceptible all over the Island, anticipatory of benefits expected at the hand of the frost king. The Forest City Ice Company forms perhaps the gladdest lot represented, unless we expect the boy with the new skate sail or the newly commissioned ice yachtsman. The interests of the Forest City Company are so extensive and important that the question of ice or no ice signifies literally to its representatives dividends or no dividends. Then, too, there are many workmen--islanders and others--who largely depend for winter employment upon this great enterprise. Hundreds and thousands of tons will be stowed by the Company if the ice becomes sufficiently thick and solid. Numerous other ice storing concerns owned by island parties likewise stand empty waiting to be filled.

Sandusky Daily Register,
26 January 1897, p. 5.

A thunder shower and a rainbow interluded the weather, and the Forest City Company talked of going to Michiganwhere ice is less uncertain. Then another freeze gave the fast expiring hopes of the ice men a lift and rejuvenated the fishermen.

Sandusky Daily Register,
12 March 1897, p. 5.

The Forest City Ice Company has completed work at its Put-in-Bay Ice houses, and the men and horses which have been employed on the Island since last fall came to the city yesterday morning on the steamer *American Eagle* and have gone to Cleveland.

Sandusky Weekly Register,
12 January 1898, p. 10.

"Taking time by the forelock," the local ice companies began cutting and storing as soon as the crop was sufficiently matured, and an excellent quality of solid, transparent ice from nine to ten inches thick was harvested. Men and teams were busy during the week, and many of the numerous small houses are already filled. The Forest City Ice Company will wait until the ice grows thicker and stronger before cutting. Their work will be immense before the vastly commodious houses are filled.

Sandusky Weekly Register,
16 February 1898, p. 10.

The Forest City Ice Company has come to grief in consequence of the prevailing mild weather, which has knocked flat its icy enterprize. The Company had a considerable force of men employed and had not quite a quantity of the commodity lodged at the bottom of the big Peach Point but the insidious wear of the under currents, the south wind, and a temperature verging upon 60 degrees--as registered at times the present week--spoiled their fun as well as work. They have suspended operations and now await another solidifying process at the hands of old jack.

Sandusky Weekly Register,
16 March 1898, p. 4.

The teams and employees of the Forest City Ice Company took their departure via steamer *American Eagle* Friday morning. About 38,000 tons of ice were stored by the Company. There is still room for several thousand tons more, but it will not be obtained here this season. John Croft, manager of the Forest City Ice Company is still on the Island.

Sandusky Weekly Register,
18 January 1899, p. 10.

The Forest City Ice Company are getting ready to put up ice. A large force of men are at work, and the Company have laid off their field nearly as far out as Rattlesnake Island. Their houses are entirely empty, and a large supply is needed. The Company have only two or three men from ashore. They prefer to hire all island labor. The islanders are thankful for small favors and larger ones in proportion. George Baldwin filled the round house ice storage with success on the 12th and 13th. The ice was eight and nine inches thick and as clear and blue as a crystal. This pure water around these islands certainly furnishes the best ice on the lakes. Louis Miller will have charge of the engineering department at the Forest City Ice Company's this winter. Mr. Miller was engineer on the steamer *Burch* a number of seasons.

Cottages on Peach Point; the John A. Feick House (far left).

Sandusky Weekly Register,
22 February 1899, p. 10.

The Forest City Ice Company are working all the men they can get. Mr. White says it will take him three weeks longer with his present force. The clear blue ice is now 20 inches in thickness. The channel is frozen over every morning, and it takes about 2 hours to open it. The Company have had considerable trouble with their help. The weather has been so cold some could not stand it outside, and the work inside is so heavy they could not do it. Consequently 16 men left on the 13th and some are quitting every day. . . . Eleven additional men came on the 16th for the Forest City Ice Company. The force at that place seems to be changing daily.

Sandusky Weekly Register,
1 March 1899, p. 10.

On the 20th at 3 p.m. the Forest City Ice Company quit work. The soft weather of days previous had softened the ice so it would fall to pieces as soon as it would strike the run. It was 20 inches in thickness, but honeycombed about 16 inches, and would not hold the ice tongs. They will not resume work again this winter unless we have some very cold weather. All of the men have gone ashore. Some walked and some went with the mail. The last teams [of horses] to come across were two owned by J. B. Ward, which arrived at 5 p.m. on the 20th. No one would venture out afterwards. The ice was so mushy, and the horses sank four or five inches into the slush. However, the ice was tough, and all were glad when they set foot on terra firma.

Cottages on Peach Point; the Ross Lewis House (far right).

Peach Point After the Ice Companies

In 1902, two enterprising individuals, Louis Schiele and John Hollway purchased the property on Peach Point from the Forest City Ice Company. They subdivided the land into 57 cottage sites. In 1904, the lot at the tip of the Point was the first one to be sold. It was purchased by the actor Ross Lewis, who built the first cottage in 1904. A number of actors followed by acquiring lots and building cottages on the Point, a place which they found as a haven for rest and relaxation.

Two stories remain in this chapter, and they are concerned with Peach Point after the Ice Companies abandoned their winter enterprize at Put-in-Bay. The first story concerns the raising of two boats left abandoned at their dock by the Forest City Ice Company about 1902. The hulls of these little steamers filled with mud and sank along the south shore of Peach Point where they remained for approximately 20 years. In 1926, they were removed to clear the area for new docks for the residents of Peach Point. The second story recalls the Actors Colony. Eventually Peach Point came to be called the Actors Colony because it was comprised of entertainers who had been in vaudeville. These actors, whose work was generally limited to live theater during the fall, winter, and spring seasons, spent summers at resorts.

Sunken Boats Raised from Shore of Peach Point

Frank S. Snavely

Sandusky Register,
12 October 1926, p. 9.

And out of the crucible of neighborly all-pull-together effort comes a bright new ingot of public convenience. The Bay has a dandy new yacht pier at Peach Point. It came about because there happened to be an ideal leader by the name of John A. Feick, who had the ability to attract a following of good neighbors, willing to put some real money into a venture for everybody's good. The leadership, plus the money has made possible what the Peach Point bunch has long wanted, but what for a long time looked hopeless--a suitable dock for the yachts on the Point side of the Island.

What is now Peach Point at the Bay was formerly the site for buildings of the Forest City Ice Company, a concern which utilized lake ice in by-gone years for commercial purposes. The advent of artificial ice put the lake proposition out of the running, with the result that all of the Point buildings were left to deteriorate, until the property was purchased by summer cottagers and the transformation into nifty little homes took place, leaving two of the old Ice Company's boats to rot at their dock.

As the years went by, these two old hulls, the *Little Jake* and the *Walton*, gradually filled with water until they sunk. Then a big addition of litter and mud made their raising almost prohibitive, from a cost standpoint. So the people living on the Point have all these years been deprived of proper dockage, just because the two wrecks hampered the erection of a suitable pier.

And forever so many moons, public-spirited John A. Feick dreamed of his opportunity to some way remove the wreck obstacle, and build the much needed dock. This week sees the dream realized, because an accident to one of the big steamer docks made it necessary to have a lot of expensive repair apparatus shipped here from Cleveland. Mr. Feick immediately communicated with the owners of the machinery, got an estimate of $35 per hour for raising the wrecks, talked to the neighbors, received their hearty approval to go ahead with the work. In less than a week the last of the old eyesores were bodily dragged out of that part of the Bay. Then the work of building the new dock started, and by next season the Peach Pointers will indulge in its use. They are Ross Lewis, A. J. Lang, Frank Willing, Fred Whitfield, Charles Summers, Emil Schmidt, and of course Mr. Feick, the ringleader.

Restaurant Piano Player

David Vormelker

Cleveland Plain Dealer,
23 August 1949, p. 15.

Sue Snyder, the last of the famed Actors Colony on Peach Point, pounds a piano in the Crescent Restaurant at Put-in-Bay. Always called Sue since entering show business at 18, she is now 71 and says she will continue to play until age makes her take to the rocking chair. "My brother, Ross Lewis, started the Colony and at one time 15 stage couples lived there," Sue said. "When we were all on the Island we used to give many impromptu performances here just for the fun of it. Sometimes I thought the shows we put on here were better than our acts because they were spontaneous.

Actors Colony on Peach Point Not Forgotten

Mrs. Ethan Fox

Sandusky Register, Twin Anniversary Edition, 25 November 1947, p. 15.

"Memories, memories." Many memories of the "golden age" of vaudeville are recalled each time local residents discuss the former "Actor's Colony," which was located on what is now called Peach Point.

Although the spot was called the "Actor's Colony," Fred Allen of radio and screen fame in recent years, would revel in the list of vaudeville "greats" who had summer cottages here at about the turn of the century. Allen on many of his broadcasts mentioned many former vaudeville "names" who appeared on "hills" with him. He would probably recall some of the following listed below.

Mr. and Mrs. Ross Lewis were the first to buy a lot in what was to become the Colony. This home is still in existence, being owned by Henry Leubert, Cleveland. It was formerly owned by the late Emil Schmidt, the wine manufacturer. Another home was built by Mr. and Mrs. John Hemmingway. He was the brother of Mrs. Lewis.

Harry Bannister and his wife Crystal, another noted vaudeville team, added a home to the already well established "Colony." His wife was killed several years later while riding horseback in Texas. Bannister later married Ann Harding of movie fame.

Mr. and Mrs. Fred Whitfield and Mr. and Mrs. Frank Willings and family built homes on the Point and became active members of the group of entertainers. The Whitfields later moved to Port Clinton where he became a theater manager.

The Murdock Brothers, Clyde and "Tex" and their families added two more homes. "Tex," a well-known acrobat, later quit the stage and before his death in Urbana was manager of a hotel there. Jack, a son of "Tex," survives and is well-known in the field of music, directing his own band at present.

Many full length vaudeville shows were put on in the town hall, where a large stage provided ample room for acrobatics, jugling, and other "stunts." Whenever a show was scheduled, those members of the "Colony" who happened to be on the Island at the time, took part. Each member was well-known for his act or team. The island churches, lodges, and civic groups or other "sponsors" derived much benefit from these performances.

The town hall stage curtain, still in use although badly aged, was designed and painted years ago by "Lew" Griffin of the "Lew and Lawrence" Griffin team. These brothers also had homes in the "Colony."

Only one team of the "old timers" remains on the Island, Sue Snyder. Although Sue spends the winter in Columbus with a sister, the rest of the year she lives on the Island and entertains at the Crescent Hotel. Mrs. Snyder. has a summer partner in Mrs. Kay Dalton, Bascom, Ohio, and they are billed as "Sue and Kay."

Sue. and her late husband, Jack, bought the "Wee House" in the Colony in the early 1900's. They later bought "Sunset Cottage" on Victory Point. The latter was sold recently to Mr. and Mrs. Harold Mack, and "Sue" purchased a cottage on Toledo Avenue to be nearer her work.

"Sue." and "Jack," were rated among the outstanding teams of vaudeville performers in the Colony and also rated highly with servicemen in World War I when they "trouped" in Europe. They also played for royalty in England, Belgium, and France. Jack," died a few years ago, and his body was buried in Mapleleaf Cemetery.

Mr. and Mrs. Martin Sands were "names" in the heyday of vaudeville and also had a home in the Colony. The late Thomas B. Alexander, a former island mayor, although not a "member" of the colony, having a residence elsewhere, took part in many of the shows.

Another noted team of the "younger set" and who are the last of the "Actor's Colony" to have a home on Peach Point are Mr. and Mrs. Carl Nixon. The Nixons entertained servicemen and women in the South Pacific and elsewhere during World War II, following in the footsteps of "Sue," and Jack," Snyder. Many local residents during the war received letters starting--"Guess what? We were entertained by the Nixons and was it good to see them." Just like vaudeville, the Actor's Colony is practically gone, but not forgotten.

Peach Point House, gifted in 1938 by Julius F. Stone to the F. T. Stone Laboratory for a housing facility.

Many of the old features of Peach Point are gone. Today, the Point has no peach trees, but is covered with both year-round homes and summer cottages amidst shadetrees, predominantly silver maple, basswood, and hackberry. Norway maples and pines have been planted in the yards. The fish raising business is no longer conducted by the Federal Government, or by the State of Ohio. The Ohio State University maintains the old Federal Fish Hatchery as a facility for the Center for Lake Erie Area Research (CLEAR) and The Franz Theodore Stone Laboratory with administrative offices in the nearby Bayview House. The Charles W. Somers property on the west shore of Peach Point near the State of Ohio Fish Hatchery was purchased in 1938 by Columbus businessman Julius F. Stone. As the donor of Gibraltar Island for the OSU Stone Laboratory, he also gave this property to the Laboratory for use as a housing facility. Named Peach Point House, Loren S. Putnam and his wife Mildred lived there from 1955 to 1973 while he was Laboratory Director.

References:

Chapter Five, The Ice Companies on Peach Point

Dodge, Robert J. 1975. "On, Under, and Over the Ice: The Ice Industry," pp. 119-120. *In Isolated Splendor: Put-in-Bay and South Bass Island*. Exposition Press, Hicksville, New York. x, 166 pp.

Frohman, Charles E. 1971. "Winter: Ice Harvesting," pp. 66-68. *In Put-in-Bay; Its History*. The Ohio Historical Society, Columbus. viii, 156 pp. Second printing, 1974.

Hurt, R. Douglas. 1986. "Cold comfort: Harvesting natural ice." *Timeline* 3(1):38-49.

Kurnat, Alan A. 1988. "The natural ice industry." *Lake Front News*, Port Clinton, 26 August-1 September, p. 3.

Langlois, Thomas H. 1948. "The ice industry at Put-in-Bay." *Inland Seas* 4:41-43; photographs, p. 36.

Langlois, Thomas Huxley, and Marina Holmes Langlois. 1948. "The role of sub-groups within the community: The Theatrical Group," pp. 34-35. "The ice industry," pp. 73-75. *In South Bass Island and Islanders*. The Ohio State University, The Franz Theodore Stone Laboratory, Contribution No. 10. x, 139 pp.

Vormelker, David. 1949. "Still a trouper despite 71 years: One-time Keith Headliner [Sue Snyder] plays restaurant piano." *Cleveland Plain Dealer*, 23 August, p. 15.

United States Fish Hatchery, built in 1889-1990 on Peach Point.
***Shearwater*, the Fish Hatchery's steam launch, operated until 1910.**

Restocking Lake Erie's Fishes:

The United States Fish Hatchery

The United States Fish Hatchery was built on the south shore of Peach Point for the purpose of artificially propagating whitefish. On 2 March 1889, the United States Congress approved a bill that provided $20,000 for constructing and equipping a fish hatchery at a location convenient to the natural populations of whitefish in Lake Erie. Through the efforts of Valentine Doller a parcel of land was acquired from the Forest City Ice Company and donated to the United States Commission of Fish and Fisheries by the citizens of Put-in-Bay for the Hatchery. The general contract for erection of the building was awarded on 12 October 1889 to George E. Gascoyne of South Bass Island, and contract for the necessary steam and water plant was made with Shaw & Kendall & Co. of Toledo on 11 March 1890. The machinery was ready for use in the new building on 16 September 1890.

An Act of Congress approved on 30 September 1890 provided an appropriation of $10,000 for the completion of equipment for the Hatchery, including the purchase of a steam launch for use in the collection of spawn and distributing the fry, the newly hatched fish, to Lake Erie. Plans and specifications for this vessel, the *Shearwater* were prepared by the chief engineer of the Commission, W. B. Bayley and built by the Craig Ship Building Company, Toledo, Ohio. This vessel was used until 1910 when it became obsolete and worn out. A second *Shearwater*, a steel steamboat of the lake tug type, 85 feet long, 16 feet beam, and 8 1/2 feet in depth, was brought into service. It was equipped with machinery that had special requirements for the Hatchery's mission.

On 1 July 1890, J. J. Stranahan of Chagrin Falls, Ohio, was appointed the first Superintendent of the Hatchery. Formerly an Ohio State Senator, he pioneered in evolving methods of fish propagation and published a paper on the subject in the *Bulletin of the United States Fish Commission* (1898). Being active in the American Fisheries Society and because of the interest in his work, he was instrumental in having the thirty-first American Fisheries Society meeting at Hotel Victory during 5-7 August 1902. While here, Stranahan lived in one of the three houses on Squaw Harbor. On 15 April 1900 he was transferred to the Cold Springs Fish Hatchery in Bullocksville, Georgia. Mr. Stranahan was a gentleman of unusual ability, for years being prominent in politics, and later as a highly successful fish hatchery administrator. In the later role, he won the entire confidence of the Ohio fishermen through hearty good will and complete cooperation. While at Put-in-Bay, in 10 years, he doubled the capacity and output of the Hatchery, making it one of the finest in the country. Succeeding superintendents of the United States Fish Hatchery at Put-in-Bay, and their approximate years of service were Seth W. Downing, 1900-1922; David Davies, 1923-1931; and Granville H. Heuchele, 1932-1940.

The "Lost Stories" about the Federal Fish Hatchery concern principally the selection of the site for the building, the awarding of the contract for its construction, a description of the proposed building, and the Hatchery's operation during the early years of its existence. The last three stories tell of the fire that destroyed the store house, the importance of the Hatchery to the nation, and the proposed dwelling for the Hatchery's Superintendent. Theresa Thorndale's descriptive writings constitute over half of the major stories.

Prospective Fish Hatchery

Theresa Thorndale

Sandusky Daily Register,
12 March 1889, p. 1.

Appropriations of over $20,000 have been made by Congress for the United States Fish Hatchery on Lake Erie. Where it will be located is yet undetermined. Put-in-Bay has been suggested as a point naturally available for the purpose, and there is little doubt but that an effort on the part of her men of means would be rewarded by the planting of the enterpize in Island waters, thus furnishing to the inhabitants an additional branch of industry and adding to the trift and importance of the place.

Sandusky Daily Register,
27 March 1889, p. 2.

John L. Gay, a representative of the United States Fish Hatchery; Cyrus D. Osborn, President of Ohio Fish Commission, and Superintendent Henry Douglas, of Sandusky, arrived here by steamer March 20th. The object of the visit being the inspection of shores and waters adjoining for a location of the United States Fish Hatchery, for which appropriations were recently made. On Thursday the commissioners made a tour of the

Island, with its coves and bays, reporting favorably concerning facilities thereof. Should the Hatchery be located at Put-in-Bay, the building will occupy an elevated portion of ground on what is known as Peach Point.

Hatchery Decision Favors Put-In-Bay Site

Marshall McDonald

Sandusky Daily Register,
10 April 1889, p. 2.

The President of the Board of Water Works is in receipt of the following self-explanatory letter:

U. S. Commission of Fish and Fisheries
Washington, D. C., April 1, 1889

C. F. Schoepfle, Esq., President Board of Water Works
Sandusky, Ohio

DEAR SIR: I beg to acknowledge receipt of yours of March 25th, tendering, on behalf of the Board of Trustees of the Water Works of the city of Sandusky, Ohio, a site for the proposed station of the United States Commission on Lake Erie, and further liberal tender of the use of water for said station at a merely nominal rate. I appreciate fully the magnanimous spirit in which your tender is made, and regret exceedingly that important consideration affecting the best efficiency of the station will prevent me from accepting it.

After full consideration of the matter, I have determined to accept the tender of a site on Put-in-Bay, although the working of the station at this point will involve a somewhat larger expenditure per annum for water supply that would be required on the same scale of work at Sandusky. It is very desirable that the station should be, as nearly as practicable, in the center of the fishing grounds from which the supply of eggs for incubation is to be drawn. The largest fisheries are nearly all located within a radius of about six miles of the Island. Port Clinton is distant but ten miles from it, and the extensive fisheries of D. Y. Howell & Co., and others, of Toledo, can be reached daily during the fishing season within fourteen miles by meeting the Toledo steamer. Spawn secured from the fisheries near the Island can be placed in the hatchery jars within an hour after being taken, while plants of fry can be made at any hour, day or night, that it may be necessary to make them.

The most important consideration; however, in determining a preference for Put-in-Bay as compared with Sandusky, is the quality of the water supply, and our ability, by drawing it immediately from the lake, to avoid those changes in temperature during the incubating season which must necessarily arise where the water is to be drawn through the city water works.

I am satisfied that the success and convenience of the general work will be promoted by the selection I have indicated; and, I feel very sure that a careful consideration of all matters in connection with it, will bring the gentlemen of your Board to the same conclusion.

Very truly yours,

Marshall McDonald,
Commissioner

In this connection we desire to add that the location of the Hatchery at Put-in-Bay was determined by federal officers, and that Mr. J. J. Stranahan who introduced the bill in the Legislature, which cedes the ground to the Government, was simply acting at the request of Mr. McDonald, the Commissioner of Fisheries. Mr. Stranahan is an applicant for the position of Superintendent, but it is not likely that he would prefer to live on the Island during the winter to living in the city. We are satisfied that injustice was done him in a recent item in these columns in which it was hinted that he introduced the bill because he desires the Superintendency.

Hatchery to be Built on Peach Point

Theresa Thorndale

Sandusky Daily Register,
18 April 1889, p. 2.

The location of the United States Fish Hatchery at Put-in-Bay has furnished occasion for general rejoicing among those interested in securing accessions to the industries of the Island. John Brown, Jr. has been appointed to survey and set apart one-half acre of land on Peach Point as a building site. This half acre has been presented to the Government for the purpose as above mentioned. Building material will be shipped to the Island at an early date, it is said, and the erection of the structure begun. When completed and set in operation, Put-in-Bay can boast of an enterprise which, in the extent of its facilities and the perfection of its arrangements, will surpass anything of the kind on the entire globe.

Peach Point is a wedgelike area of land which encloses and protects the Bay from the westerly gales. Its shores are wild and picturesque; its surfaces underlaid with limestone which crops out in irregular and grotesque shapes. The shore wall is carved, niched, and caverned. Heavy growths of cedar and other trees, together with wild vines and shrubbery, cover the Point, forming in many places almost impenetrable thickets. In the less dense and more tillable portions of ground, peach trees have found a foothold among the rocks and in blossom time mingle the pinky hue of their branches with the thick, dark foliage of the cedars among which they revel. A partially stagnant though beautiful lakelet [Terwilliger's Pond] is enclosed with a curcuitous line of wooded bluffs, which in the summer season frame in with many hued screens this bit of liquid blue; itself flecked with lily pads and blossoms, and shadowing in its depths the tall weeds and rushes along its margin. This little basin is separated from the lake waters by a narrow neck of land, through which an outlet is perforated; and the stream thus formed is spanned by a bridge, and crossed by a footpath and wagon road, furnishing a most delightful walk or drive through umbrageous thickets, vine wreathed and aromatic with wild fragrance, to the extremity of the Point which ends in masses of flat rock low lying, over which in rough weather the waves dash and the breakers whiten.

The main body of the Point is without an inhabitant. A deserted hut among the trees near the lakelet, and the great ice houses of the Forest City Ice Company are the only buildings, and these by the air of isolation and desertion which surrounds them tend to increase rather than diminish the sense of loneliness which takes possession of the visitor to this spot. At an elevation the highest above the line of bluffs before mentioned, among jutting rocks and briery tangles, where the fiery tongued rattler is supposed to lurk, is the site selected for the Hatchery. The waters which surround Peach Point and lap its shores are clear and limpid, while its protecting arm clasps the calm, unruffled circle of Squaw Harbor [Fishery Bay], a broad cove, distinct in many ways to add advantages to the establishment. The interest which attaches to this enterprise together with the pleasing character of the scenery which environs it, will doubtless prove a future attraction to island visitors.

Operations of the Fish Commission Enlarged

Anonymous

Sandusky Daily Register,
10 June 1889, p. 1.

Mr. John L. Gay, Inspector of Stations of the United States Fish Commission, was in Sandusky Saturday and left for Put-in-Bay on the steamer *City of Sandusky* in company with Supt. Henry Douglas. Their mission was to look after some matters pertaining to the new Government Hatchery to be erected on Put-in-Bay and consult with the fishermen at the Islands relative to the fall supply of spawn. Mr. Gay said that the bids for the new Hatchery had no doubt been received by the Commission at Washington by this time, and they would be duly opened by a board of these officers. The contracts would be speedily let on the receipt of the board's report to Commissioner McDonald. While the specifications call for the completion of the Hatchery within ninety days after the work begins, the appropriation will not be available until July, and it is possible that the new Hatchery will not be ready for use in time for the whitefish spawn in early November. The United States Fish Commission will continue to operate the State Hatchery in Sandusky this fall and winter, the State Fish Commission having accepted a proposition to that effect, whereby not less than 60 per cent of the fry hatched will be deposited in Ohio waters. Supt. Douglas will continue in charge with his efficient corps of helpers.

A *Sandusky Register* reporter in conversation with Inspector Gay gathered some facts pertaining to the work of the United States Fish Commission which serve to show the increased impetus it is receiving under Commissioner McDonald's administration and the enlarged field of the Commissioner's operations. Mr. Gay said that the Hatchery at Put-in-Bay would be in every respect first-class in construction and equipment, that all its apparatus would be of the very best known, and that the Hatchery would be the largest in the world, having an annual hatching capacity, with its 2,500 jars, of quite five hundred million fry.

Fish Hatchery Delayed

Theresa Thorndale

Sandusky Daily Register,
4 July 1889, p. 2.

The contract for the building of the United States Fish Hatchery at this place has not been let, at latest accounts, but will be, it is thought, at an early date.

Sandusky Daily Register,
28 August 1889, p. 2.

No fish hatchery this year, the preliminary legal measures of securing title to land, having taken up the greater part of the season.

Hatchery Contract Awarded to George E. Gascoyne

Anonymous

Sandusky Weekly Register,
23 October 1889, p. 1.

A few days ago the bids for erecting the United States Fish Hatchery at Put-in-Bay were opened at the office of the Fish Commission at Washington. It will be remembered that the building will be 2 storys high in shape of a cross; the dimension lengthwise being 32 x 95 and crosswise 20 x 67. The bids comprise all the work, the concrete, dock, cribbing, and water pipes from the Bay and boiler house.

The bids were as follows:

G. E. Gascoyne, Put-in-Bay	$9,977.24
J. T. Watson, Cleveland	13,500.00
Robt. McQuoid, Cleveland	14,170.00
Doerzbach & Decker, Sandusky	13,500.00
Aug. G. Fettel, Sandusky	13,850.00

The contract was awarded to Mr. George E. Gascoyne on October 12, 1889.

Hatchery Construction Underway

Theresa Thorndale

Sandusky Weekly Register,
5 December 1889, p. 2.

United States Fish Commissioner, John L. Gay, and Superintendent Henry Douglas, have concluded business relative to the collection of spawn at this place and distribution of the same among hatcheries throughout the country. These gentlemen left last Saturday on the *City of Sandusky*. . . The lumber for the building of the United States Fish Hatchery, located on Peach Point, is on the ground; and, the work of excavating and blasting the underlying beds of solid rock and the laying of the foundation is in progress.

———

Sandusky Daily Register,
11 December 1889, p. 1.

Under the supervision of George E. David, of the United States Fish Commission, George E. Gascoyne, contractor, the new Hatchery at this place is rapidly materializing. The foundation is completed, the timber work raised to position, and the building already makes a show, as viewed from the Lake and its adjacent shores.

———

Suppl. Sandusky Weekly Register,
5 February 1890, p. 1.

Work on the United States Fish Hatchery at this place is progressing favorably. The building is under roof, the sides enclosed, and the interior work begun. A dozen machines are employed under the direction of Contractor George E. Gascoyne and General Superintendent George E. David, of the United State Fish Commission. Superintendent David has in his possession some well executed plans and drawings of the structure, representing its varied departments with appliances, which are designed to be first-class in every respect. The building is to be completed in the month of June and will be stocked and set in operation the succeeding fall. Mr. David speaks of the Put-in-Bay location as particularly adapted to fish culture for numerous reasons, among which he assigns the limpid cleaness of the water. The establishment, it is claimed, will be the most extensive of the kind on either continent.

Inside the United States Fish Hatchery on Peach Point.

Tour of U.S. Fish Hatchery

Theresa Thorndale

Sandusky Weekly Register,
9 May 1894, p. 9.

Next neighbor to the ice houses stands the United States Fish Hatchery. The buildings are projected on an extensive scale. Architecturally considered they are elegantly and artistically planned and executed, and form the largest and best equipped establishment of the kind in the world. The structure is located upon the shores of Squaw Harbor [Fishery Bay], commanding a fine view of Gibraltar Island and the Bay with its shipping and adjacent shores. Fronting the buildings is an ample pier at which lie the United States Fish Hatchery, the steamer *Shearwater*, with some smaller boats. The Hatchery occupies a consipicous place and may be recognized afar by the golden fish--a black bass they say--swinging and swimming in either upon the weather vane.

The party, of which your correspondent formed a member, was shown through the main portions of the Hatchery. The hatching of spawn is now in progress and very interesting it is to watch its progress. Midway between the floor and high arched ceiling and ascended by a flight of stairs is a wide platform, upon which are two tanks containing each 6,000 gallons. These are filled from the Lake by means of suction pipes connected therewith. Descending from these tanks runs a system of pipes to what is called the batteries. Here within glass jars are placed the eggs in process of hatching. From the main pipes smaller ones extended, reaching nearly to the bottom of each jar, through them constantly runs a stream of fresh water, causing a boiling, bubbling motion which keeps the eggs in a chronic state of commotion. Each jar thus forms a small but energetic whirlpool that night or day knows no rest. As fast as the water pours in, it is carried off again by a small trough. Having emerged from the egg the miniature specimen of the finny tribe soon wearies of his whirlpool home, and yearning for a larger world with larger advantages, seeks and finds an outlet through the said trough to other aqueducts, and is carried into a large tank of fresh water upon the ground floor, where he is reared and educated for future usefulness. He is so tiny you can hardly see him, but he is afforded room to grow, and when he gets big for the Hatchery he is given the freedom of Lake Erie, or mayhap carted away to some of the rivers and lakes of other localities.

The Hatchery has 4,000 jars, each containing 140,000 whitefish eggs, giving it a capacity of 560,000,000 eggs. This, however, is more than the lake fisheries have yet been able to supply. When running at full capacity 1,250,000 gallons of water are run through the pipes and reservoirs every twenty-four hours. Suction pipes connect with both sides of the Point, so that if one becomes damaged or displaced by storm or ice, water may be supplied from the opposite side. Westward of Peach Point the pipe extends 150 feet into the Lake and is held in place by immense anchor bolts drilled into solid rock. This is found a necessary precaution, owing to heavy ice drifts, which have a terrific power in tearing things to pieces. Weeds, lizards, and debris of all kinds are excluded from the pipe by means of an oblong shaped strainer fastened over the end. The pumping engine does the main work of the establishment. In winter the exhaust steam introduced into radiators heat the interior. The coal bunker is a sort of basement blasted out of the solid rock and holds 250 tons of soft coal. The workshop is a large room devoted to repairs and contains odds and ends of all sorts. Varieties of spawn now in the building are pickerel, pike, and perch. In connection with the work here Supt. J. J. Stranahan has charge also of the pickerel work of the State Hatchery at Sandusky. In his absence in that city Capt. H. J. Fox, Assistant Superintendent, takes charge of the work here, assisted by Messrs. Downing, Curtis, and others. Engineer Barry has charge of the engine room and pumping apparatus.

Sandusky Weekly Register,
2; 23 May 1894, p. 9; p. 4.

The spawn gathering season is now about over. Supt. Stranahan and his force have collected 298,000,000 eggs for the Put-in-Bay and Sandusky hatcheries, the former containing 251,000,000, the latter 47,000,000.

The Ohio State Fish and Game Commission met at Put-in-Bay during the week. The Park Hotel was their headquarters. On Tuesday evening a meeting was called for the review and adjustment of routine business. The Commissioners report the business of fish culture in prosperous condition. The party took a hand at bass fishing, and had altogether an enjoyable time.

New and Old Hatching Jars as Used in the U.S. Fish Hatchery.

Preparations of Pike-Perch Eggs before placed in Hatching Jars.

Large Quantity of Eggs at Hatchery

[Theresa Thorndale]

Sandusky Weekly Register,
2 January 1895, p. 7.

A look through the Put-in-Bay Station of the United States Fish Commission is especially interesting at this time. Never since its erection has it contained so large an aggregation of spawn. During the year now closing 4,300,000,000 eggs were taken. Of these 293,000,000 were pike perch, or what is sometimes known as wall-eyed pike, taken in April and hatched and planted in three or four weeks. One hundred and twenty-six and a half million whitefish eggs and 10,500,000 eggs of the herring, or what is better termed the "ciscoe," are in the Hatchery. The so-called herring of Lake Erie is really a little whitefish and not a herring at all, but a member of the great salmon family to which our brook trout and all other trout belong--a most excellent fish only for its besetting sin--that is in the poet's "Nevermore" of being so plentiful and so cheap that people of ample means cannot think of tasting them. A few lake trout, perch, and grass pike were also taken, and several successful attempts at hybridization were also made.

Some idea of the work may be formed when it is known that of whitefish eggs there were taken this fall 98 1/2 bushels, dry measure, with about 40,000 eggs to the quart. From this statement may be figured the number of tons of adult whitefish averaging say four pounds each which the given amount of spawn will produce, and the mile lengths of cars required for their shipment. By means of its pipe system, its reservoirs and big engines, Lake Erie, or a generous portion of it, is kept steadily pouring through its arteries and glass jars containing spawn in process of hatching and converted into small whirlpools which never cese commotion, until each tiny egg is evoluted into a finny of unmistakable identity. Freak fishes of diverse sorts in bottles are shown the visitor, among which are some one individual head and two bodies. A string of half swallowed fishes, one inside the other, like a lot of tea cups, is a not an unusual sight, all but the last one presumably choked to death in a ravenous attempt to swallow his next door neighbor. With favorable weather the Superintendent expects to collect and hatch half a billion of pike and perch eggs next spring.

Fish Hatchery Force Busy

Theresa Thorndale

Sandusky Weekly Register,
13 April 1898, p. 10.

A novel and interesting scene was afforded visitors at the United States Fish Hatchery during the week, it being the season of rushing work with over one hundred million of fry emerging from their shells and demanding immediate and careful attention. The massive tanks occupying the center of the main floor, into which they found their way from the hatchery jars, fairly teemed with tiny pickerel and whitefish awaiting introduction to the waters of Lake Erie. Tiers of smaller tanks, one above the other, ranged along the side of the building formed so many little lakes in which youthful trout took their first swim.

The Hatchery force were so busy day and night, manipulating the various appliances of the establishment and catering to the wants of its inhabitants directed by Superintendent Stranahan and Assistant Captain J. C. Fox; while, Chief Engineer Wallack and his department shoveled in the coal, kept the pumping engines working, and the water pouring through every vein and artery of the Hatchery's complicated system. Since the improvements recently made, the water introduced from the main feed pipe is used eight times. There are cascades and waterfalls, and rivers and lakes in the hatchery, and the men go to their work with the babble of brooks and gurgle and roar of falling water, making music in their ears from morning till night and more fish to the square foot of aqueous fluid about them than ever dreampt of even by Izaak Walton.

The steamer *Shearwater* has also been in active service, and with her bright colors whipping the breeze, and her swarthy uniformed crew and officers on deck, the steamer presented a pleasing spectacle as she arrived or departed from the wharves. Wherever appeared her red, white, and blue flag, emblazoned with a big fish, there the United State Fish Commission had business, mainly that of planting fish colonies of innumerable extent.

As understood, the products of the winter's hatching are about as follows: Whitefish fry, over eighty millions; herring nearly twenty millions; lake trout, one million. While the more delicate lake trout are still being cared for in the tanks, the whitefish have nearly all been planted. The fry came out better this season than they have done for years. As fast as emptied, the jars are cleared and reset, ready for the reception of fresh spawn, already arriving via the *Shearwater* from various points. The commission expects to take in about four hundred millions of pike perch eggs during the spring fishing season. Among the domesticated pets at the hatchery are three beautiful whitefish taken last December from the "pens." They were covered with fungi and very sore, but were subsequently doctored, entirely cured, and are not quite as tame as the tabbies which make themselves at home in the establishment. An instructive and entertaining feature of the Fish Commission are the views afforded of aquatic life as seen through microscopic lenses. With a magnifying power of 20,000 diameters a vivid and comprehensive insight is obtained of the lower orders of plants and animals invisible to the naked eye. Through these powerful lenses become visible the fish in the unhatched egg; not only is the circulation of the blood clearly seen, but also the red corpuscles of which the blood is composed.

As generally understood, cyclops were a set of giants, having but one eye in the center of the forehead who assisted Vulcan in making thunderbolts for Jupiter. Incredulous persons who had been wont to regard these creatures as having an existence in mythology only are astonished to learn through microscopic revelation that full fledged cyclops exist in the world beneath us not only, but that we drink them every day in unfiltered lake water. These one-eyed monsters are exceedingly numerous, it seems, and furnish abundant food for white and other fishes.

The slimy green scum of our ponds, scientifically known as Algae, seen through this instrument resolves itself into a mass of beautiful ribbons regularly cross-barred in green and gold, such as might form fitting decorations for an Easter bonnet. The crescent shaped Desmid, with a microscopic bumble bee's nest at each extremity, the Rotifer with sidewheel streamer attachment by which he propels himself nimbly through the water in pursuit of his food and his adversaries, the trumpet-shaped Polymorphus and the beautiful and wonderful bell-shaped Vorticella with its plant-like form, its slender spiral stem, and its admonishing power of sudden and complete contraction into a round ball--all these novelties and many more as revealed by the microscope--form a part of our vast lake water populations, whole menageries of which we swallow at every gulp. The most important function of the microscope in connection with fish culture, however, is its use in determining the condition of eggs in process of hatching. Some strong and excellent work in the way of micrographs, showing fish eggs in various stages of development, were recently taken by Superintendent J. J. Stranahan.

Some new improvements are to be made this season on the water front of the Fish Hatchery in the way of floral decoration. A big mound will take the shape of whitefish one in silver leaf and geraniums, and the United States will probably appear in floral red, white, and blue.

Improvements and Changing Uses

During the early years of the Hatchery, several improvements were made to the physical facilities. In 1896 a frame store house 15 x 20 feet, 1 1/2 stories high, was erected on the southwest corner of the station grounds. The old dock was replanked throughout and supplied with new timbers where needed, and a row boat dock, 40 feet by 9 feet, was built at the southeast corner of the building and extending parallel to and 20 feet away from the main dock. A 30-foot channel, 260 feet wide and 7 1/2 feet deep was dredged from the dock outward to deep water. Retaining walls were built on the north and west sides of the main building and on the northeast of the grounds on the lake front. The grounds were graded and seeded and walks were laid. A 60-light gas plant was installed in the Hatchery, and to obviate the possibility of the water supply being cut off, the suction pipe at the end of the dock was placed in deep water in the new channel.

Following destruction by fire of the north store house in June 1899, a replacement was constructed during that summer. It measured 20 by 30 feet, 14 feet high, and was built for $331. The 10-inch suction pipe extending into the Lake on the west side of the Station, which had been carried away by ice in 1899, was replaced by the Hatchery staff for less than $100, although by outside contract it would have cost $750. In 1901 an extension measuring 24 by 28 feet was built onto the main hatchery building. The next summer the warf was rebuilt at the water's edge and covered with 2-inch oak plank, and the channel and harbor were improved by dredging the channel to a depth of 9 1/2 feet and widening it 25 feet.

Through the years the Hatchery propagated principally whitefish, lake herring or cisco, lake trout, pike perch or walleye, yellow pickerel, and black bass. After the State Fish Hatchery was built in 1907, some competition between the two hatcheries came about in their efforts, and so to eliminate this overlap of effort and needless expense, the two hatcheries began working in cooperation. Beginning in 1934, all eggs were handled by the State Hatchery, while the Federal Hatchery provided the boat, The *Shearwater II*, and some of the personnel. In 1938, the Ohio Division of Conservation assumed operation of the Federal Fish Hatchery properties.

Fire at Fish Hatchery; Superintendent Stranahan to Leave

Anonymous

Sandusky Weekly Register,
7 June 1899, p. 10; 21 March 1900, p.6.

The store house at the United States Fish Hatchery burned to the ground at 5 a.m. on the 30th. The alarm was turned in by Edward Haas, keeper of the Put-in-Bay company's dock. The Fire Department soon responded, but the building was a sheet of flames and nothing could be done save to protect the adjoining property. The building was 14 x 20, 14 foot posts with one-half pitch. It was filled with waste, oils, etc. The day before it had been cleaned and everything placed in apple pie order. It stood 50 feet from the main building to the north and the wind being in a westerly direction the Hatchery proper was not damaged. A fire on the Island is something unusual in consequence thereof the entire population were out. Superintendent Stranahan was in Cleveland at the time and was notified by wire.

. . . Superintendent J. J. Stranahan is to take charge of the new hatchery at Bullocksville, Georgia, and will enter upon his duties there April 15. Were he to remain at Put-in-Bay till next July he would have completed ten years as superintendent. Not only many friends at Put-in-Bay, in Sandusky, and along the lakes, but many throughout Ohio will regret that Mr. Stranahan is to leave his old post. A gentleman of unusual ability, for years prominent in politics and a member of the legislature, he has a wide acquaintance. The fishermen, too, will be sorry to lose him.

Fish Hatchery Most Important in Country

Toledo Blade

Sandusky Weekly Register,
19 December 1900, p. 11.

The government of the United States last year expended for the propagation of food fishes the sum of $215,661.56, says the *Toledo Blade*. Of this sum, $9,895.84 were spent through the Station at Put-in-Bay. The collection of fish and eggs alone at this Station cost $5,382.45. Whitefish were handled principally. The expenditures there last year were more than at any other station. Woods Hole, Massachusetts, came nearest with and expenditure of $9,137.90. The next largest was Green Lake, Maine, where $4,678.44 were expended.

Bayview House, built in 1907-1908 as the residence for the superintendent of the U.S. Fish Hatchery; donated by U. S. Government to OSU 1940.

Proposed Dwelling for Hatchery Superintendent

Anonymous

Sandusky Daily Register,
20 March 1903, p. 7.

We learn that the United States Government has made an appropriation for the purchase of a site near the United States Fish Hatchery for the purpose of erecting a dwelling thereon for the Superintendent of the Hatchery. Money is also appropriated for the erection of the dwelling.

Some city capitalist who loves a beautiful spot upon the lake front with the most beautiful scenery should purchase the Peach Point beyond the Fish Hatchery. The abandoned ice houses owned by the Independent Ice Company of Cleveland are located upon this Point. As the Point is not utilized nor beautified and matters are beginning to look dilapidated, the property should be converted into a beautiful site by some city club who look for the loveliest spot on the islands.

Hatchery Property Acquired for the F. T. Stone Laboratory

The anonymous author was indeed correct when he suggested that Peach Point should be utilized for some worthwhile purpose. The next year, 1904, Louis Schiele and John Hollway began dividing the Peach Point property into 57 sites for cottages following their purchase of the land two years earlier. In the years to come Peach Point was to be populated with cozy cottages and summer residents. The dwelling for the Superintendent of the Fish Hatchery was constructed in 1907-1908 by John A. Feick of Sandusky. It was a large frame 9-room house first occupied by Seth W. Downing followed by David Davies until about 1931. The house sat empty for the next six years.

Stone Laboratory Researchers Mary A. and Milton B. Trautman, in the former U. S. Fish Hatchery Building preparing the manuscript for the book, *Fishes of Ohio* (1957).

In 1938, when the Ohio Division of Conservation acquired the operation of the Federal Fish Hatchery Properties, space was made available in the Hatchery building for use by The Franz Theodore Stone Laboratory. With the help of the United States Bureau of Fisheries, all of the Federal Fish Hatchery property was deeded to The Franz Theodore Stone Laboratory of The Ohio State University by congressional act to be used as a fisheries research station. President Franklin D. Roosevelt signed the authorization in the summer of 1940.

The United States Fish Hatchery building itself has been referred to in previous times as the Stranahan Laboratory or the Fisheries Building. Identified during the 1970 and 1980s as the Peach Point Research Laboratory, it was equipped with an analytical chemistry laboratory, a photography laboratory, holding tanks for collected aquatic organisms, a visitor's center, individual working spaces for researchers, offices, and general field research support space. It was the primary facility for faculty and student research funded through the Center for Lake Erie Area Research (CLEAR), and the operation of its Lake Erie water quality monitoring research vessel, the 68-foot R/V *Hydra*. Leased from the United States Environmental Protection Agency, this research vessel carried an analytical chemistry laboratory and accommodations for a crew of eight.

In addition to the Fish Hatchery building, the acquired property in 1940 also contained a shop and a residence. The shop, a board and batten shed on a concrete wall with a basement, was moved in 1925 to its present site between the two hatchery buildings. The building currently is used as a facility for maintenance operations and storage. The residence, known today as the Bayview House, provided a home for the Director of the Stone Laboratory, Thomas H. Langlois and his family, from May 1937 until May 1956. For the next 20 years, the Bayview House was used principally as a living facility for summer students at the Laboratory. Beginning in the summer of 1977, it was converted to the library and year-round administrative offices for all of The Ohio State University's Lake Erie Programs--the Stone Laboratory summer teaching program, the Center for Lake Erie Area Research (CLEAR), and the Ohio Sea Grant program.

References:

Chapter Six, The United States Fish Hatchery

Anonymous. 1940. "Fish Hatchery inherited," p. 12; "Put-in-Bay Hatchery transferred to O. S. U.," p. 10. *In Ohio Conservation Bulletin* 4(4):12. April; 4(7):10. July.

Downing, S. W. 1905. "Collecting, hatching, and distribution of pike-perch: Why the great loss of eggs." *Transactions of the American Fisheries Society* 1905:239-255.

Downing, S. W. 1910. "A plan for promoting the whitefish production of the Great Lakes." *Bulletin of the Bureau of Fisheries for 1908*. 28: 627-633.

Frohman, Charles E. 1971. "Fish Hatcheries," pp. 113-116. *In Put-in-Bay: Its History*. The Ohio Historical Society, Columbus. viii, 156 pp. Second Printing, 1974.

Ryall, Lydia J. 1913. "Fish Hatchery Work at Put-in-Bay," pp. 465-471. *In Sketches and Stories of the Lake Erie Islands*. The American Publishers Co., Norwalk. vi, 546 pp. (Perry Centennial Edition 1813-1913).

Stranahan, J. J. 1893-1901. "Put-in-Bay Station, Ohio."*In Report of the Commissioner for 1889-1900*. United States Commission of Fish and Fisheries. Government Printing Office, Washington, D. C. Individually paged.

Stranahan, J. J. 1898. "The methods, limitations, and results of whitefish culture in Lake Erie." *Bulletin of the United States Fish Commission for 1897*. 17: 315-319.

Thorndāle, Theresa. 1898. "Among the Fisheries," pp. 355-365. *In Sketches and Stories of the Lake Erie Islands*. I. F. Mack & Brother, Sandusky. v, 379 pp. (Souvenir Volume).

Titcomb, John W. 1910. "Fish-cultural practices in the United States. Bureau of Fisheries." *Bulletin of the Bureau of Fisheries for 1908*. 28: 697-757, pls. LXXVII-LXXXIX.

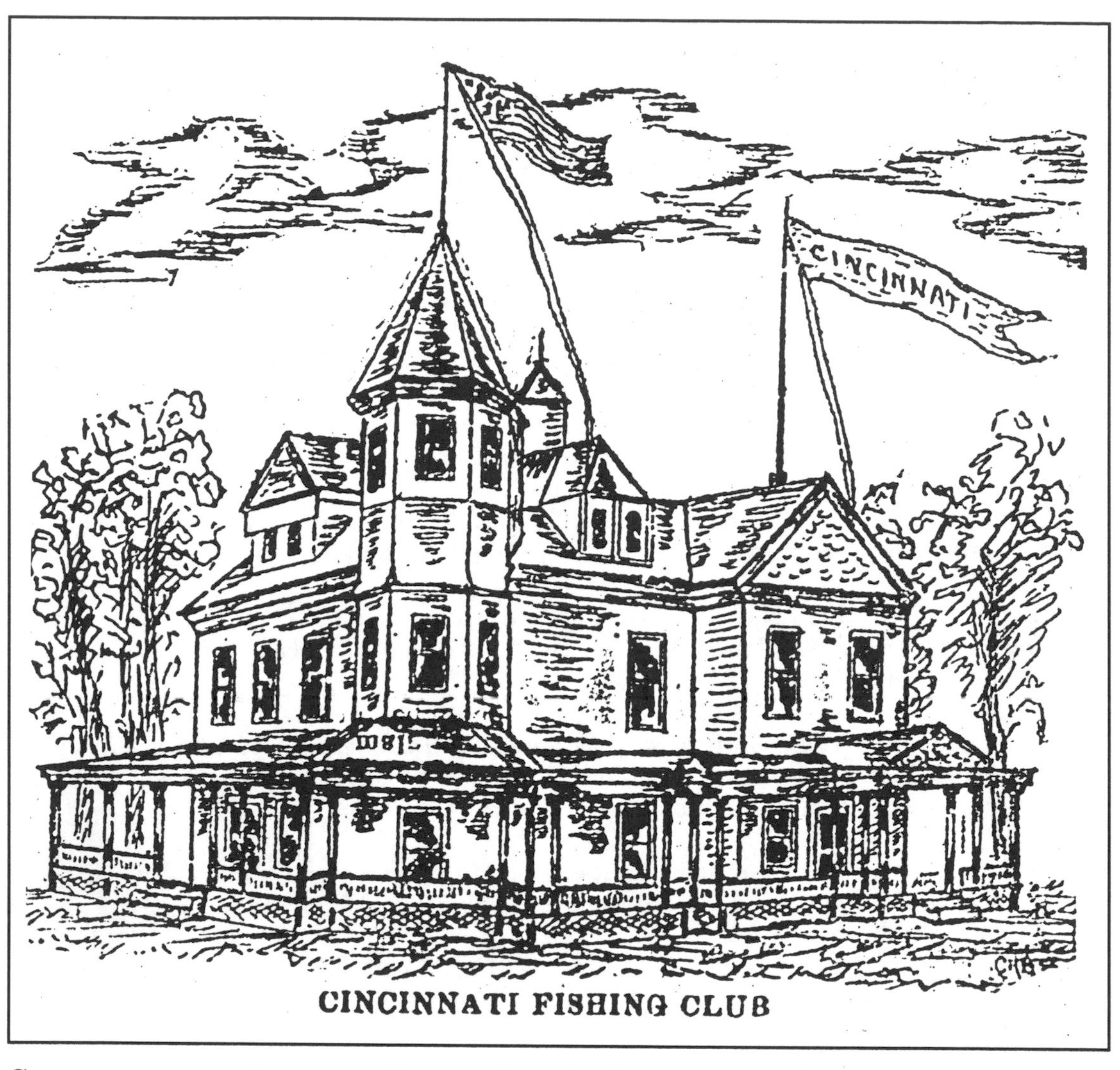

CLUBHOUSE OF THE CINCINNATI FISHING CLUB, **built in 1893 on Oak Point.**

A "Jolly Party" Now Gone:

CHAPTER SEVEN

The Cincinnati Fishing Club on Oak Point

Oak Point is the promontory that extends between Squaw Harbor on the south and Fishery Bay on the north. A gravel bar reaches from the Point southeastward toward Gibraltar Island which lies almost directly east of the Point. The Point and adjacent land on Squaw Harbor and Fishery Bay were purchased from Joseph de Rivera St. Jurgo in 1892 by the Cincinnati Fishing Club, who erected an elaborate 3-story frame clubhouse ready for opening on 4 October 1893. A large boat house was also constructed near the clubhouse at the edge of Fishery Bay. The "Lost Story" reproduced here is by Charles H. Becker, city editor of the *Sandusky Register*, who attended the opening celebration and banquet of the Club. Baker describes in considerable detail the features of the house, and lists those who attended the opening festivities. Theresa Thorndale also provides descriptions of the Club in three short "Jottings."

Because of financial difficulties, the Cincinnati Fishing Club was not able to maintain activity at Put-in-Bay, and in 1898 they sold their majestic Oak Point House and adjacent acreage on Squaw Harbor and Fishery Bay to Captain Elliott J. Dodge. He lived there with his family and operated the property as a hotel, with John J. Day as proprietor in its early years of operation. In 1907 Dodge subdivided and sold portions of the property along the shore of Squaw Harbor for cottages. Ten lots were designated, which he recorded as the Oak Point Subdivision. The remaining property was purchased in 1917 by Arthur G. Smith of Elyria who used the Oak Point House for a summer home. Smith sold about an acre, which included the large house, in 1938 to the Ohio Division of Conservation at a price of $15,000, but retained the boat house, which he later modernized into a pleasant summer home. In 1955, this property was acquired by the Allan brothers, Ford dealers of Port Clinton. Today it is known as Snug Harbor, the summer home of the late Carlton J. "Pinky" Allan (1914-1986) and his wife Ethel, who continued to live there in summers.

New Quarters for Anglers of the Queen City

[Charles H. Becker]

Sandusky Daily Register,
12 October 1893, p. 4.

For many years the islands of Lake Erie have possessed irresistible charms for the disciples of Izaak Walton, and their famous fishing grounds are now known all over the American Continent. Their near proximity to Sandusky, which is well known to be the greatest fresh water fish market in the world, makes Sandusky headquarters for tourists who frequent these popular resorts. Among the group of islands, none are more frequently visited by piscatorial pleasure seekers than historic Put-in-Bay. To Ohioans, and particularly to people, Put-in-Bay has attractions that are unequaled by any other place on earth. That there is no mistake about this is evidenced by the frequent visitations of Queen City dwellers. Col. William B. Smith, who for years has been a connoisseur in the piscatorial art, is the leading spirit among Cincinnati's expert anglers, and it is he who commands almost every fishing expedition out of that city.

Within the past decade numerous efforts have been made by Cincinnatians to purchase property at Put-in-Bay for club house purposes, but without success until recently. In 1878 Col. Smith made negotiations for the purchase of Middle Island, but the deal was never consummated much to the disappointment of all the parties concerned. About a year ago Col. Smith, Mayor John B. Mosby, and Dr. T. W. Graydon succeeded in purchasing about eleven acres of the Joseph de Rivera St. Jurgo estate on Put-in-Bay Island, the sale of which up to that time had been for a long time refused by the owners. The property was later transferred to the Cincinnati Fishing Club, who have beautified the grounds and built the pretty club house that now adorns the spot.

The Cincinnati Fishing Club has been organized about five years and was recently incorporated with the following charter membership: John E. Heatherington, New York; H. M. Little, of New Orleans, president of the New Orleans Sheet Railway Co.; those from Cincinnati being ex-governor Joseph B. Foraker, Mayor John B. Mosby, Charles Fleischman, Frank H. Kirchner, Dr. T. W. Graydon, Col. W. B. Smith, H. M. Ziegler, George K. Griffiths, George T. Sterritt, Captain W. W. Peabody, vice president of the Baltimore & Ohio Southwestern Railroad; H. B. Morehead and A. Howard Hinkle, of the *Cincinnati Commercial Gazette*; Norman G. Keenan, vice president of the Cincinnati Gas Light and Coke Company. The officers of the Club are: Col. W. B. Smith, president; George R. Griffiths, treasurer; George T. Sterritt, secretary.

The location of the new club house is near the northwest part of the Island and is known as Oak Point. It is but a short distance east of the Government Fish Hatchery, which is about the most conspicuous structure in that locality. The front of the building looks toward the morning sun and commands a view of some of the most beautiful island scenery to be found anywhere on the lakes. To the right is Squaw Harbor of Put-in-Bay Harbor, which at all times during the summer season presents a scene of wonderful activity, and to the left lies Gibraltar Island, an emerald setting in the silvery waters, the summer dwelling place of Jay Cooke, the famous Philadelphia financier. The passage between Middle Bass and Ballast Island completes the vista, which to island dwellers must be a joy to look upon.

Mr. George Feick, of Sandusky, was the architect of the new club house, and the builder was Mr. George E. Gascoyne of Put-in-Bay. The construction was begun July 8 and the house was completed, furnished, and occupied on the fourth day of October. The dimensions of the main part are 36 by 50 feet, and in connection there is an L 20 by 24 feet. It is two stories high, with ceilings 10 1/2 and 9 1/2 feet respectively. It is a frame structure with interior oil finish in natural pine. The plumbing and gas fitting was provided by Brohl & Appel of Sandusky, and the gas making machinery was put in by Cincinnati parties. The main reception room is reached by a large front hall in which is also an open stairway leading to the upper floor. Heat for the reception room radiates from a pressed brick fire place that is not only built for comfort but ornament as well. A dining room, kitchen, store room, butler's pantry, dish pantry, refrigerator, and lavatory are also included in the complement of apartments on the first floor. Upstairs are eleven sleeping rooms, each having two beds, and additional room for sleeping is provided in the attic. The upper floor has also a lavatory and closet.

The building lacks nothing in the comforts of modern improvements. It is fitted throughout for hot and cold water which comes from a tank in the attic, and nothing seems to have been overlooked by the builder that would make it a model of perfection for the purpose it has been adopted. Surrounding it on nearly all sides is a ten foot veranda from which members of the Club may "hear what the wild waves are saying" and breathe cooling comfort from the gentle lake zephyrs. The clubhouse property complete cost is in the neighborhood of $25,000. It is a valuable aquisition to Put-in-Bay not alone for its architectural beauty, but in that it greatly enhances the island's popularity as a summer and fishing resort.

The clubhouse was formally opened on Tuesday with appropriate festivities. At 4 o'clock in the afternoon the Club gave a dinner in honor of Commodore George W. Gardner, of Cleveland, who came with a party on the yacht *Wasp*. The collation was served by Max Basse, of Cincinnati, who is the Club's chef. In the evening the club house was brilliantly illuminated and fireworks preceded an informal reception given to the citizens of Put-in-Bay. Col. Smith, presided as master of ceremonies, and in addition to the club members, the following were included among the guests: Hugh McConnell, New York; Commodore George W. Gardner, Capt. A. Peattie, Alfred G. Hathaway and S. M. Williams of the yacht *Wasp*; John Rettig, Cincinnati; Miss Arlin, Toledo; Capt. George A. Brown and Jacob Weis, Sandusky; A. G. Clark, wife and two daughters, Toledo; Judge Lockwood and wife, Mr. and Mrs. Daniel P. Vroman, Mr. and Mrs. Phillip Vroman, Mr. and Mrs. H. L. Ennis, Mrs. C. C. Williamson, George H. Beebe, Miss Blanche Vroman, Miss Myrtle Vroman, Valentine Doller, Frank Miller, George E. Gascoyne, John S. Doller, and Capt. W. H. Ladd, Put-in-Bay. Since the opening of the club house the following names have been recorded on the visitor's register: George H. Tow, George B. Cox, John Frey, August Herrmann, John B. Washburn, D. W. Brown, Willis P. Tharp, Cincinnati; W. J. White, R. R. Holden, Cleveland; A. J. Clark, Toledo.

Members of the Club are now enjoying a season of sport with the black bass. They do not anticipate any extended use of their club house this year, but have planned to be in shape to welcome their guests next season. That much future enjoyment is in store, no one will gainsay who knows anything about Col. Smith's abilities as an entertainer and purveyor.

Oak Point and Peach Point with buildings (left to right), Clubhouse of the Cincinnati Fishing Club, Bayview House, U.S. Fish Hatchery, taken before 1914.

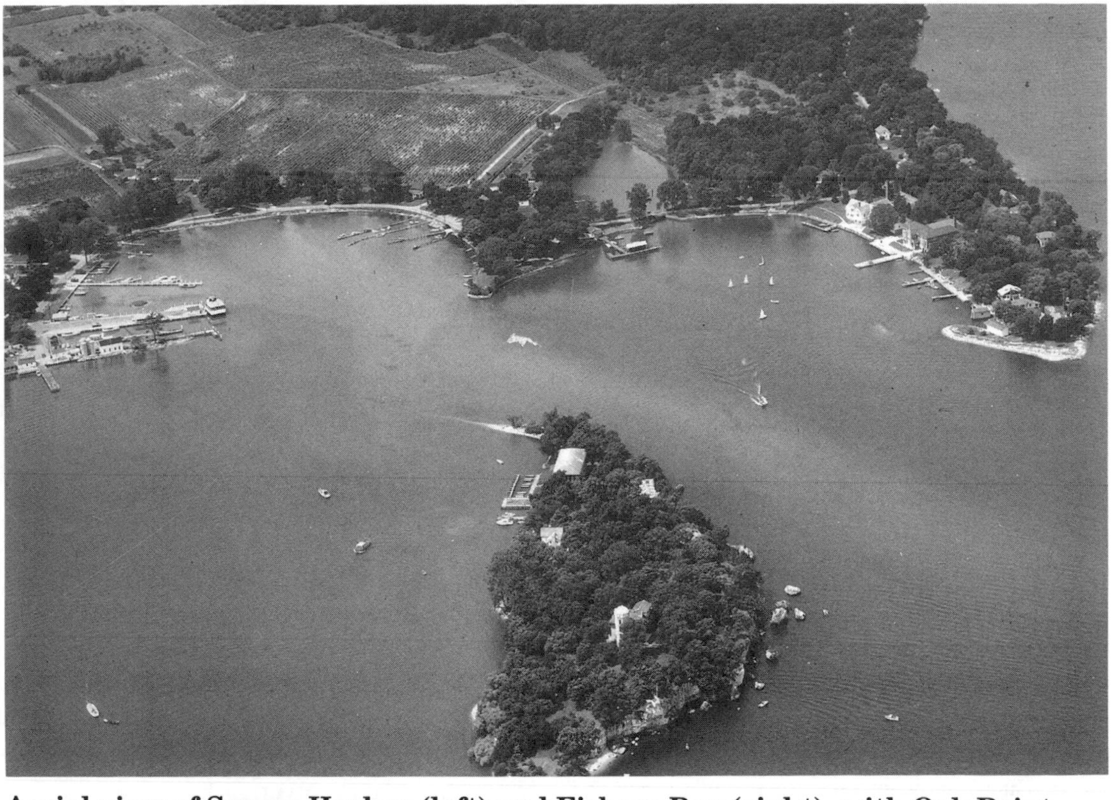

Aerial view of Squaw Harbor (left) and Fishery Bay (right), with Oak Point (left), Peach Point (right), and Gibraltar Island (lower center).

"Jottings" of the Cincinnati Club

Theresa Thorndale

Sandusky Weekly Register,
18 October 1893, p. 4.

The Cincinnati Fishing Club is said to be a jolly party, fond of good cheer and plenty of it. Metaphorically speaking they snap their fingers at adversity and bidding dull care be gone, propose having a good time as they go along. On almost any favorable morning the party may be seen abound for the fishing grounds on board the tug *Ina* with a string of boats in tow and colors flying fore and aft. Charles H. Becker, city editor of the *Sandusky Register*, and Major William Thomas, the *Register's* man on the road, were visitors at the Island last week, putting up at the Beebe House during their stay. The former came to write up the banquet of the Cincinnati Fishing Club.

Sandusky Weekly Register,
2 May 1894, p. 8.

Judge Caldwell, Mayor, and Colonel Mosby, ex-mayor of Cincinnati, will be among the guests at the clubhouse on Oak Point this season; also Mrs. Mosby, Mrs. W. D. Graydon, and other ladies. A water reservoir and windmill is to be erected in the clubhouse grounds, the tower to, or building, attached to contain ample rooms, affording quarters for clubhouse employees --men and boys. A well drilled near the clubhouse is found to contain iron and sulphur in abundance and will be utilized as a health beverage. The chef to be employed by the Club is from the St. Nicholas Hotel of Cincinnati.

Sandusky Weekly Register,
9 May 1894, p. 9.

Just beyond the Fish Hatchery grounds are those of the Cincinnati Club. . . . The new club house and environments are receiving the finishing touches. It is a handsome structure as to external appearance, rising loftily among the oaks, elms, and maples that surround it, and some of the high officials and big money men of Cincinnati will there hold forth during the season. A dock projecting into Squaw Harbor form the club grounds, with a string of prettily painted boats attached, suggests bass fishing. The club members will be on hand, it is said, to begin the week: the tug *Ina* having been chartered to meet them at Sandusky.

Clubhouse Now Hotel

Theresa Thorndale

Sandusky Weekly Register,
15; 22 June 1898, both p. 3.

Every island establishment in the way of hotels, boarding houses, and restaurants from Hotel Victory down are putting on their finishing touches and wheeling into line to be ready for the coming rush. The Cincinnati Clubhouse on Oak Point will be opened for use as a hotel about June 20—Jack Day, proprietor.

Printed invitations have been issued for the opening of the Cincinnati Clubhouse (formerly the Cincinnati Fishing Club) on Oak Point, Put-in-Bay, Monday, June 20th, J. J. Day, proprietor. From the above date to the season's end the Clubhouse will receive and entertain guests.

Oak Point House, a housing facility for the F. T. Stone Laboratory.

Snug Harbor in 1950, with former boat house and Oak Point House.

Oak Point Since 1938

After the Ohio Division of Conservation purchased the Oak Point property in 1938, the house, now referred to as the Oak Point House, was leased to the Franz Theodore Stone Laboratory of The Ohio State University for 15 years, with option of renewal, at one dollar per year. This arrangement was made specifically to encourage the Laboratory's fisheries research program which was largely sponsored by the Ohio Division of Conservation. The Oak Point House was used principally as a facility to house faculty and research students who were obligated to work at the Laboratory on a year-round program which was inaugurated in 1938. The 13-room building was modified into three apartments for married couples, and five sleeping rooms upstairs were available to single students. Meals were served in the kitchen during all months of the year except summer when the Dining Hall operated on Gibraltar Island. Some of the faculty members and researchers who occupied the Oak Point House at some time during the succeeding 15 years were Dr. Bertil G and Lorraine Anderson, Dr. Marion W. and Antoinette Boesel, Dr. N. Wilson and Mary K. Britt, Dr. Bernard S. and Blanche Meyer, Dr. Loren S. and Mildred M. Putnam, Dr. Charles Walker, and Dr. Milton B. Trautman. Some of the married students included Theodore and Mae Andrews, Leonard J. and Lela Bodenlos, Kenneth H. and Alberta Doan, William and Mary Jahoda, Henry and Margaret Merkle, and Owen B. and E. Rosemary "Chauncey" Weeks.

In the mid 1950's when the Stone Laboratory was having financial difficulties, and with the decline in student enrollment and research activity, the beautiful Oak Point House was little used and eventually sat empty. The lease was not renewed, and the building was razed during the winter of 1956-1957. The property was retained by the State of Ohio, and in 1967 a retaining steel wall was erected and small docks constructed along the edge of the Point adjacent to Squaw Harbor. A semi-circular drive and washroom facilities were also added. In 1972 the property became the Oak Point Picnic Area and placed under the jurisdiction of South Bass Island State Park which is administered by the Division of Parks and Recreation of the Ohio Department of Natural Resources. Sitting under the large white oak trees, which have survived the changes at Oak Point, one can still have a breath taking view of Put-in-Bay Harbor, Perry's Victory Monument, and Gibraltar Island. Today, many people can enjoy a picnic lunch on the grounds once occupied by the large elegant clubhouse of the Cincinnati Fishing Club and watch the Put-in-Bay Trolley make its turnaround on the semi-circular driveway.

First Biological Survey of Lake Erie, with Director Jacob E. Reighard (center) discussing research plans with a survey member (left); the lady (right) appears to be newspaper reporter Theresa Thorndale.

United States Fish Hatchery Building with Steamer *Shearwater* at Dock, taken about 1894; headquarters for the First Biological Survey of Lake Erie.

First Biological Survey of Lake Erie

The First Biological Survey of Lake Erie was part of the overall Biological Survey of the Great Lakes conceived in the early 1890's by Jacob E. Reighard, Director of the Zoological Laboratory at the University of Michigan, Ann Arbor. Prof. Reighard called for general basic research that would produce information that could be used to solve biological problems, as they arose in Great Lakes waters. One of the problems in Lake Erie at that time was the decline in the populations of food species of fish. To find solutions to that problem, as well as to new problems that would develop, it was necessary to conduct an exhaustive study of the conditions for fish life and to develop a thorough understanding of their environment and food supply. To obtain a complete knowledge of the life of a species of fish, studies were needed on the entire chain of biological relations existing in the lakes and streams. Accordingly, it was necessary to study not only the fishes themselves, but all the animals and plants in the lakes, for upon these, directly or indirectly, the fishes depend.

In 1898, Prof. Reighard received financial support of approximately $3,000 from the United States Commission of Fish and Fisheries to conduct some of these investigations. The United States Fish Hatchery at Put-in-Bay with its equipment and boats were made available to Prof. Reighard and his associates. Theresa Thorndale gives an account of the first summer's work by naming the principal investigators and stating the problems to be solved. These biological research projects continued at the Hatchery during summers from 1898 through 1901.

Reighard's approach heralded a new and more productive era of limnological research on the Great Lakes. It set high standards for the many subsequent limnological surveys (Smith, 1957). Reighard's investigators were truly a "who's who" in aquatic biology at the turn of the century; their work is discussed further by Stuckey (1988).

Principal Investigators of the First Biological Survey of Lake Erie, a. Jacob E. Reighard (1861-1942), b. Henry B. Ward (1865-1945), c. Herbert S. Jennings (1867-1947), d. Adrian J. Pieters (1866-1940).

Biological Survey Initiated

Theresa Thorndale

Sandusky Weekly Register,
13 July 1898, p. 3.

A scientific enterprise conducted under the auspices of the United States Fish Commission will attract the attention of the scientifically minded. The enterprise in question is a Biological Survey of Lake Erie for the study of its botanical and zoological features along with scientific work of a general character. Members commissioned for this Survey are as follows: Prof. Jacob E. Reighard, Professor of Zoology, The University of Michigan; Dr. Julia W. Snow, The University of Michigan; Dr. Henry B. Ward, Professor of Zoology, University of Nebraska; Dr. Herbert S. Jennings, Instructor in Zoology, Dartmouth College; Mr. Adrian J. Pieters, Department of Agriculture, Washington, D. C. These, together with numbers of assistants and a large mechanical outfit, will be employed.

The party will have its general rendezvous at the Cincinnati Fishing Club; its official headquarters at the United States Fish Commission--the Federal Fish hatchery building which has been fitted up as a laboratory. Here all specimens taken will be duly examined and identified and other experimental work carried forward. Dr. Jennings and wife, the former Mary Louise Burridge of Tecumseh, Michigan, who were married last month, are already here; other members are expected by today's steamers and work will begin at once. The government steamer *Shearwater* will be employed, and every facility undertaking the Survey will be provided by the Put-in-Bay representatives of the United States Fish Commission.

Surveyors Conduct Research on Steamer *Shearwater*.

Biological Survey Progresses Favorably

Theresa Thorndale

Sandusky Weekly Register,
24 August 1898, p. 10.

Under the direction of Prof. Jacob E. Reighard of The University of Michigan, the Biological Survey of Lake Erie is progressing favorably. The work begun this season is preliminary to the execution of one of the most elaborate plans ever projected in North America for the study of fresh water fauna and flora, and

Experimental work is being made a prominent feature of the Survey. Fish Commissioner George M. Bowers has allotted a liberal sum for the same. Some of the problems being studied are:

"The rate of growth of young fishes reared from the egg."

"Food of young fishes, and change of regimen during growth."

"The source of food of aquatic rooted plants."

"The life histories of food fishes reared in aquaria or ponds, and aquatic insects and invertebrates."

"The rate of increase of the plankton as a whole, and of individual constituents."

"The habits, migrations, distribution, and food of fishes and other organisms of the lake."

Associated with Prof. Reighard are representatives from leading colleges and several from the United States Fish Commission. Prof. Reighard is giving attention to plankton problems, and perfection of methods and apparatus. Working with him is Dr. Henry B. Ward of the University of Nebraska, who is conducting his own investigations on parasites infecting fish. Dr. Julia W. Snow of The University of Michigan carries on experimental work with the algae, including identification and distribution of the planktonic members. Other experimental work is being conducted by Dr. Herbert S. Jennings of Dartmouth College on the identification and physiology of protozoans and rotifers, and by Mr. Adrian J. Pieters of the United States Department of Agriculture, who is compiling an

Biological Survey Members standing on the porch of the United States Fish Hatchery, Put-in-Bay. The individual sitting and dressed in a suit appears to be Henry B. Ward.

inventory and preparing life histories of the local species of aquatic vascular plants. Dr. William C. Kendall and Mr. Millard C. Marsh, both of the United States Fish Commission Commission, are investigating the fishes in the waters near Put-in-Bay.

The main portion of the Federal Fish Hatchery of the United States Fish Commission Station at Put-in-Bay, which forms the official headquarters of the Survey, is filled with the apparatus of these scientific workers. Tables covered with instruments, charts, diagrams, and scientific paraphernalia generally are seen; together with bottles, jars, and miniature reservoirs containing specimens of aquatic plants, insects, etc. Fish Commission steamer *Shearwater*, placed at command of the surveyors, makes almost daily excursions about the islands, and to East and West Harbors. Several new and interesting species have been discovered.

Food and Fish Being Investigated at Put-In-Bay

Anonymous

Sandusky Weekly Register,
20 September 1899, p. 11.

The United States Commission of Fish and Fisheries has for two summers past been carrying on investigations of rare importance resulting in scientific data of great value to one of every city along Lake Erie. The work at present is located at Put-in-Bay, where any citizen is made welcome to examine the same and the interesting processes. Prof. Henry B. Ward of the University of Nebraska and secretary of the American Microscopical Society, is heading the work. His learning and

The Large Plankton net.

scientific skill are guarantee that the work will result in both gain to science and profit to the commercial interests of the state. The attempt in this biological investigation of the Lake is to do for lake industries what the state and national agricultural stations have done for the agricultural industries. The design of the government is to make at some place a permanent station, and have also a floating laboratory which can be sent from place to place as need may require. The work of the gentlemen is along both zoological and botanical lines. Fish and the food of fish are the matters under investigation. The stocking of the lakes with proper fish and the means of sure development of the fish after the Lake is stocked are also within their province. Mr. Raymond H. Pond of The University of Michigan replaces Mr. Pieters, and is undertaking an experimental investigation of the nutrition of the vascular aquatic plants grown in aquaria and in the Lake.

The Steamer *Shearwater* with Survey Members testing the efficiency of Reighard and Ward's plankton nets during the summer of 1901.

Hotel Victory Electric Failure Cancels Prof. Reighard's Lecture

Ronald L. Stuckey

Trans. Amer. Fisheries Soc.,
5, 6, 7 August 1902, pp. 17, 18, 22, 38.

Professor Jacob E. Reighard and Henry B. Ward are among those scientists attending the thirty-first annual meeting of the American Fisheries Society being held 5, 6, 7 August 1902 at Hotel Victory. Reighard was scheduled to present his paper as an evening lecture accompanied with stereopticon views aided with an electric lamp in a large assembly room of the Hotel. Regrettably, the lecture was not presented "because of lack of electric current to operate the lamp to be used," and so the evening was spent in the regular business of the Society.

For the same reason, the joint presentation by Reighard and Ward on "A method of measuring the efficiency of quantitative plankton nets," based on research in the harbor at Put-in-Bay also was cancelled. The members, disappointed in not having heard the papers, inquired if it would be possible to publish them in the *Transactions* of the Society. Reighard's answer was, "I do not think so. A good many of the illustrations are colored. I think the most that could be attempted would be an abstract of the articles [papers], perhaps with some illustrations."

[Editor's Note: Based on the minutes of the meeting as published in the *Transactions of the American Fisheries Society* for 1902].

Biological Survey Members sampling with plankton nets on board the *Shearwater*; c,d. Lunch on board the *Shearwater*.

Long-range Contributions and Assessment

The Biological Survey of Lake Erie (1898-1901) was one of the earliest investigations supported by the federal government for basic biological research on the Great Lakes. At least 45 technical publications resulted from these investigations on Lake Erie. The most extensive and detailed contributions were those on aquatic vascular plants by Pieters (1901) and by Pond (1902, 1905), on the planktonic algae by Snow (1903), the protozoa by Jennings (1899a, b, 1900b), and on the rotifers by Jennings (1900a, 1901, 1903).

Some of the aquatic biological facts and principles learned in the Biological Survey of Lake Erie were later incorporated into an important textbook, *Fresh-Water Biology*, compiled by Henry B. Ward and George C. Whipple (1918). This basic book, now a classic and in a second edition edited by Walles T. Edmonson (1959), is widely used by North American students of fresh water biology and limnology. The book is a concise guide to North American fresh-water fauna and flora. It serves not only as a manual for identification, but is also one of the few general sources for the ecology and habits of the organisms. The first edition contained seven chapters written by those who had worked in the United States Fish Hatchery at Put-in-Bay during any one of those four summers that the Survey was in existence. The chapter by Jacob E. Reighard (1918) was on the methods of collecting and photographing aquatic organisms in their natural environments. Julia W. Snow (1918), then associate professor of botany at Smith College, wrote a chapter on the fresh-water algae. Henry B. Ward (1918), then professor of zoology at the University of Illinois, contributed the chapters on parasitic flatworms, round worms, and Gastrotrichida. Raymond H. Pond (1918), late professor of botany at the Texas Agricultural College (now Texas A & M University), prepared the one on aquatic vascular plants. Zoology professor Herbert S. Jennings (1918), then of Johns Hopkins University, submitted the chapter on the rotifers.

The technical information was indeed useful in its day for understanding of the basic biology of Lake Erie and of declining populations of food fish species. These pioneer studies are useful today in assessing changes in abundance and diversity of plant and animal species. For example, the paper on aquatic vascular plants by Pieters (1901) contained a comprehensive inventory of species, in addition to discussions of life histories that are still applicable to the organisms he studied. The 40 species of vascular plants recorded for Put-in-Bay Harbor revealed the great diversity of species at this site, and included some that were rare or that have never been seen here since. Some 70 years later, I rediscovered only 20 of those species. This 50% loss resulted from physical and chemical changes in the water, because of man's increased use of the Bay. During those 70 years, the water became more turbid because of soil runoff from grape vineyards, dredging of channels, and modifications of the shoreline by construction of boat docks and steel retaining walls. Consequently, the result was a loss of certain sensitive submersed species, particularly northern ones, that could not tolerate such changes in their environments. Tolerant species, particularly widespread ones, that can live in turbid, polluted waters have continued to survive (Stuckey 1971, 1978).

After nearly 25 years following Stuckey's 1971 published study on the loss of aquatic plants from Put-in-Bay Harbor, the water of Lake Erie and its bays, particularly Put-in-Bay Harbor, became remarkably clear during the 1990's. Two apparent reasons for this change in the clarity of the Lake's water were (1) mankind's efforts to restore the Lake to its former clear water condition, and (2) the invasion and establishment of the Zebra and qugga mussels. These improved Lake conditions have allowed for the return of nine species of aquatic vascular plants that had disappeared of Pieter's original 40 (Stuckey and Moore, 1995). Noteworthy among these is the appearance of submersed annuals that are dependent on buried seeds for continued survival. The presence of clear water allows for sufficient amounts and kinds of light to penetrate through the water to the substrate allowing for seeds of these annual plants to germinate, grow, and resotre the vegetative plant populations. Those species that were tolerant of and abundant during the time of turbid waters have since declined in abundance.

The Biological Survey of Lake Erie (1898-1901) was the third phase of the Biological Survey of the Great Lakes conceived by Jacob E. Reighard. It followed the surveys conducted at Lake St. Clair in 1893 and at Little Traverse Bay on Lake Michigan in 1894. The Lake Erie Survey was as important as the earlier surveys, in that special attention was given to biological interactions in the lake, in the anticipation that an understanding of these interactions would contribute to an explanation of the decline of food fish species. However, the third survey appears to be less well known than the earlier studies. It was not discussed by historians of Great Lakes limnology, Smith (1957), Egerton (1985, 1987), and mentioned in one sentence by Beeton and Chandler (1963, p. 544).

As the originator of these biological or limnological surveys, Reighard organized teams of uncompensated but extremely cooperative investigators in the various specialities of aquatic biology, and his skill in so doing helped to overcome what might otherwise have been unsurmountable limitations of budget, personnel, and equipment. The chief investigators were in their thirties and the research assistants were in their early twenties. Both groups were intelligent, highly motivated, and committed to publishing the results of their work. Even though they had only small boats and an occasional small steamer for field sampling trips, these survey groups made notable contributions to the knowledge of the Great Lakes biota, and carried out more extensive projects that could have been achieved by a single organization or by a few individuals working independently.

References:

Chapter Eight, First Biological Survey of Lake Erie

Beeton, Alfred M., and David C. Chandler. 1963 "The St. Lawrence Great Lakes," pp. 535-558. *In* David G. Frey, ed. *Limnology in North America*. The University of Wisconsin Press, Madison. xvii, 734 pp. (Reprinted 1966).

Edmondson, Walles T., ed. 1959. *Fresh-Water Biology*. Ed. 2. John Wiley & Sons, New York. xx, 1248 pp.

Egerton, Frank N. 1985. *Overfishing or pollution? Case history of a controversy on the Great Lakes*. Great Lakes Fishery Commission Technical Report No. 41. 28 pp.

Egerton, Frank N. 1987. "Pollution and aquatic life in Lake Erie: Early scientific studies." *Environmental Review* 11:189-205.

Jennings, H. S. 1899a. "Studies on reactions to stimuli in unicellular organisms. II. The mechanism of the motor reactions of *Paramecium*." *American Journal of Physiology* 2: 311-314.

Jennings, H. S. 1899b. "Studies on the reactions to stimuli in unicellular organisms. IV. Laws of chemotaxis in *Paramecium*." *American Journal of Physiology* 2: 355-379.

Jennings, H. S. 1900a. "Rotatoria of the United States, with especial reference to those of the Great Lakes." *Bulletin of the United States Fish Commission for 1899*. 19: 67-104, pls. 14-22.

Jennings, H. S. 1900b. "A report of work on the Protozoa of Lake Erie, with especial reference to the laws of their movements." *Bulletin of the United States Fish Commission for 1899*. 19: 105-114.

Jennings, H. S. 1901. "Synopses of North-American invertebrates. XVII. The Rotatoria." *American Naturalist* 35: 725-777.

Jennings, H. S. 1903. "Rotatoria of the United States. II. A monograph of the Rattulidae." *Bulletin of the United States Fish Commission for 1902*. 22:273-352, pls. 1-XV.

Pieters, A. J. 1901. "The plants of western Lake Erie, with observations on their distribution." *Bulletin of the United States Fish Commission for 1901*. 21: 57-79, pls. 11-20.

Pond, Raymond H. 1902. "The role of the larger aquatic plants in the biology of fresh water." *Transactions of the American Fisheries Society 1902*: 89-96. (Read for Pond by Henry B. Ward at the 31st Annual Meeting of the American Fisheries Society held 5-7 August 1902 at the Hotel Victory, Put-in-Bay, Ohio).

Pond, Raymond H. 1905. "The biological relation of aquatic plants to the substratum." *Report of the United States Commission of Fish and Fisheries 1903*: 483-526.

Reighard, Jacob. 1899. "A plan for the investigation of the biology of the Great Lakes." *Proceedings of the American Fisheries Society* 28: 65-76.

Reighard, Jacob. 1899. "The biology of the Great Lakes." *Science*, new series. 9: 906-907.

Reighard, Jacob, and Henry B. Ward. 1901. "Methods of plankton measurement." *Science* new series 8: 376-377.

Shull, A. Franklin. 1942. "Obituary. Jacob Ellsworth Reighard." *Science* new series 95:344-346.

Smith, H. M. 1898. "Biological Survey of Lake Erie." *Science*, new series. 8: 13-14.

Snow, Julia W. 1903. "The plankton algae of Lake Erie, with special reference to the Chlorophyceae." *Bulletin of the United States Fish Commission for 1902*. 22: 369-394, pls. I-IV.

Stuckey, Ronald L. 1971. "Changes of vascular aquatic flowering plants during 70 years in Put-in-Bay harbor, Lake Erie, Ohio." *Ohio Journal of Science* 71: 321-342.

Stuckey, Ronald L. 1978. "Decline of lake plants." *Natural History* 87(7): 66-69. (Reprinted, 1979, pp. 21-32. *In* John Rousmaniere, ed. *The Enduring Great Lakes*. W. W. Norton & Co., New York. 112 pp.)

Stuckey, Ronald L. 1988. "Jacob E. Reighard and the first biological survey of Lake Erie (1898-1901)." *Michigan Academician* 20: 379-396.

Stuckey, Ronald L. & David L. Moore. 1995. Return and increase in abundance of aquatic flowering plants in Put-in-Bay Harbor, Lake Erie, Ohio. *Ohio Journal of Science* 95: 261-266.

Ward, Henry B., and George C. Whipple. 1918. *Fresh-Water Biology*. John Wiley & Sons, New York. ix, 111 pp.

State of Ohio Fish Hatchery, built in 1907 on Peach Point next to the United States Fish Hatchery.

Hatching Fish For Nearly 90 Years:

CHAPTER NINE

The State Fish Hatchery

The State Fish Hatchery at Put-in-Bay became a reality in 1907, when the Ohio Division of Fish and Game purchased two acres of land adjacent to the northeast side of the United States Fish Hatchery. John A. Feick of Sandusky was contracted to erect a frame fish hatchery building with a lay-out similar to the neighboring establishment. The State facility was planned for hatching eggs of herring, whitefish, and blue pike. Prior to erection of the building, Mr. Feick constructed a two-story frame house to the northeast of the proposed Hatchery site. This dwelling served as the living quarters for the workmen who built the Hatchery. It was probably the second house erected on Peach Point. Later, this house was willed by John A. Feick (sometimes spelled Fyke or Fike) to his grandchildren, and during the 1980s the property continued to remain in the family as a summer home. The two newspaper accounts reproduced here tell of the activity in the Hatchery during its second year of operation and of the fire of mysterious origin that destroyed the building in 1914.

John A. Feick House on Peach Point.

State of Ohio Fish Hatchery at Put-in-Bay, Ohio. Standing left to right: George Senne, George Miller, Captain J. Otto Biemiller, Mitch Hallock, Luke Meyer, Frank Miller.

Fish Hatchery Work at Put-in-Bay

Lydia J. Ryall

Sketches and Stories of the Lake Erie Islands, 1913, pp. 465-467, 476.

One of the most important industries of this country, having for its object the production and conservation of food supplies, centers in the work of the State and United States Fish Hatcheries. Of these, the most extensive on fresh water are stationed along the Great Lakes, the Hatcheries at Put-in-Bay being listed among the largest and best equipped establishments of the kind in America.

The changes more recently made in the buildings and apparatus have materially served both to increase capacity of the establishment and to facilitate its work, which at the beginning was largely experimental—made necessary by the rapid decrease of food fishes, due to lax laws of former years, which gave almost unrestrained freedom to gill netters, poundmen, and trap netters, who combined to make up the innumerable contingent of lake fishermen.

Advantageously situated on a portion of land known as Peach Point, the United States Hatchery had formed for many years a picturesque point in the landscape, when its dignified position was further strengthened by the erection close beside it of a State Hatchery. Though less imposing in appearance, the latter adds materially to the general effect, besides forming an important adjunct to hatchery work in the aggregate.

From the Bay center, Peach Point is approached by a circuitous road following the shores of Squaw Harbor. Grounds of the hatcheries show the usual care required of the employees. The fronting lawns that slope gradually to the sea wall, are kept in perfect condition.

State Fish Hatchery at Put-In-Bay

Anonymous

Sandusky Register,
7 January 1909, p. 8.

The Ohio Hatchery is a good-sized building of the cottage type, shingled sides, red-stained, and close to the water. It was completed about two years ago at a cost $15,000, not one cent of which came from the taxpayer's pockets. It was paid for and is maintained entirely from fisherman's license fees, which amount to $10,000 a year.

This Hatchery receives 332,000,000 whitefish and herring eggs. Next door is the United States Government Hatchery with 363,000,000 whitefish eggs and a million lake trout eggs. Altogether there are 696,000,000 fish eggs in the state and federal incubators, of which from 75 percent to 80 percent will be hatched; so much has man triumphed over nature.

A fish hatchery is the antithesis of a chicken incubator. One is wet and cold and the other dry and warm. The fish eggs are placed in glass jars, the jars placed on shelves, one above the other, and the shelves in rows. They might be likened to the jars of medicines in a drug store. They are so arranged, however, that running water maybe circulated about the eggs constantly. From 350 to 400 gallons of water is pumped every minute, night and day, while the eggs are being hatched.

The Hatchery's capacity is 1,500 jars of which 1,448 are now filled. They are arranged in five batteries of six tiers to a side and on both sides. There are 72,000 herring eggs to the quart and 35,000 whitefish, and the entire number of eggs in the Hatchery consist of 226,320,000 herring eggs and 105,735,000 whitefish. Frank Miller, a native of Put-in-Bay, has been Superintendent of the Hatchery since 1907.

The eggs are collected in November when the fish are spawning. This is done with the co-operation of fishermen, who allow state employees under Deputy Warden Harry C. Crossley, on the patrol boat *Oliver H. Perry*, access to their catch of spawn fish. There were 2,516 fish penned for spawning this year and handled every day. The female fish, as soon as they become ripe, are stripped off the spawn, which is collected in a dry pan, and the milt of the male is added. One male is used to every three females. The fertilized eggs are then placed in tubes for twenty-four hours and are then removed to the glass jars to remain there until April, when the fish are hatched. As in the natural state the spawn is deposited in the lake, where it remains through the winter, so in the hatcheries fresh water a half degree above freezing must be kept flowing over them. The attendants must see that the eggs do not become caked, but remain free in the water. The water flows down from the top row in and out of the jars and so on down into troughs. Each egg contains a food sac, and the first sight of development is when the eyes begin to protrude. Later if the egg, which somewhat resembles tapioca, is held up to the light, the backbone can be seen. As the young fish is evolved in the spring he swims, or is carried out of the jar down into the trough, out of which he is dipped and emptied into a tub. The little fellows are then dumped into the Lake along the reefs of the Island.

In the spring the Hatchery is filled again with pike perch. Of these fish there are 15,000 eggs to the quart, and they hatch in three weeks, or in the case of warm weather, in from twelve to eighteen days from the time of spawning. Saugers, the eggs of which are even smaller, are also hatched in the spring.

The United States Fish Hatchery makes a specialty of whitefish, while the state raises more herring. This arrangement is made so that the two institutions may supplement each other's work. Seth W. Downing is in charge of the Government Station. It is arranged in a manner similar to the state building, except as regards the eggs of the salmon, or large lake trout. These are contained in trays with screen bottoms, like small window screens, half a dozen at a time and sunken in troughs of running water. These eggs do not do Ohio much good, the trout, being large fish, go down the lake to deep water off Erie, Pennsylvania, and Dunkirk, New York.

"That the hatcheries have shown great results has been proven to the satisfaction of even the fishermen themselves," said Paul North, chairman the Ohio Fish and Game Commission. "At first they pooh-hoohed at the idea of a hatchery

The *Oliver H. Perry*, the Patrol Boat for the State Fish Hatchery at Put-in-Bay. Left to right: Mitch Hallock, Captain J. Otto Biemiller, Fred Coom, George Senne.

The *Oliver H. Perry* docked at the State Fish Hatchery, Put-in-Bay.
Left to right: Ed Hass, William Brown, Captain J. Otto Biemiller, George Miller, Tommy Hart (fireman), Ted Phillips, Adolph Fuchs, George Senne, Frank Miller, Henry Miller.

and were even disposed to resent the Commission's activities. Now they are most enthusiastically in favor of the work. Four or five years ago the supply of whitefish and herring in Lake Erie was practically exhausted. A whole fleet of tugs would come back after a day's fishing with only a thousand pounds. Now, due entirely to the hatcheries, there are more whitefish and herring than in the past twenty years. The catch this season was phenomenal, each tug getting a couple of tons of fish a day. Although the price was lowered by the plentiful supply, the proceeds were greater than ever before, and the fishermen had a most prosperous year."

"Of course, it is generally understood that there are more fish in Lake Erie than in all the other of the great lakes combined. At a rough estimate we might say that from 27,000 to 28,000 tons of fish were caught for food in Lake Erie last year. Both the federal and state governments in this work are activated by the knowledge that in propagating fish they are supplying a good food, cheaply."

State Fish Hatchery Building Destroyed by Fire

Anonymous

Sandusky Register,
1 June 1914, p. 1.

The handsome two-story, frame Ohio State Fish Hatchery building was totally destroyed by fire of mysterious origin early his morning. The conflagration entailed a loss estimated by Superintendent Frank Miller at $18,000 to $20,000. The loss is fully covered by insurance. The building was valued at $12,000 and the pumps at $6,000. Superintendent Miller immediately wired General John C. Speaks, chief fish and game warden and that official wired back from Columbus that the Hatchery would be immediately rebuilt.

The fire was discovered about 3 o'clock this morning by the caretaker at the John A. Feick summer residence, but it had a good start before the Island's volunteer firemen and others arrived on the scene. Superintendent Miller says that from what he is able to learn, the blaze started in the carpenter shop on the second story. The structure was a total loss half-an-hour after the discovery

Ruins of State Fish Hatchery at Put-in-Bay Following Fire of 1 June 1914.

was made. All that remains of the building is the foundations and the damaged boilers. None of the hatchery equipment or furnishings were saved.

The building was erected in 1907. It stood just north of the United States Hatchery building. But for the fact that the wind was from the south, the Federal Hatchery would likely have been destroyed also. It took hard work to save the summer home of John A. Feick, of Sandusky. This was the nearest residence to the Hatchery.

"There had been no fire in the building for over a week," Superintendent Miller says, and there was no oil, waste or other materials on the second floor where the blaze started. A strong suspicion of incendiarism is held by some of the island people, but hatchery officials doubt that theory.

All of the spring hatchery work had been completed, and there were no fish eggs or fry destroyed in the blaze. Had the blaze occurred several weeks earlier the eggs, from which millions of fry now in the Lake were hatched, would have been destroyed.

At the Ohio State Fish Hatchery, more than a thousand million fry are produced annually. The principal species propagated artificially at the State Hatchery are whitefish, herring, and blue pike. It is estimated that if only 4 percent of the fry hatched at the State Hatchery grew to maturity, it would add annually more than 50,000,000 pounds of fish to the supply of Lake Erie.

The revenue derived from fees for licenses on trap nets in Lake Erie amounts to more than $20,000 annually, and this sum was used in maintaining the Put-in-Bay Hatchery.

Fish Hatcheries: Past and Future

Thomas H. Langlois

The Ohio State Fish Hatchery . . .
Typewritten Manuscript.[About 1948]. 6 pp.

A biological experiment, started nearly 80 years ago, is the hatching of artificially fertilized eggs of several species of lake fishes which began in 1868 at Castalia, Ohio, and at Northville, Michigan. Every year since then, fish eggs have been obtained from Lake Erie by commercial fishermen for state and federal agencies to incubate and hatch into fry which are placed back in the Lake. No apparent necessity for such operations existed when the experiment was started, but declining abundance of fishes was recognized as a possibility, and some hope prevailed that propagation might make more fish available in the Lake.

Comparisons have been made of the catch records with the records of hatchery output of fry, and these studies have shown that the hatchery output is high whenever the fish have been abundant enough to yield lots of spawn, but that the catch is not high during the third and fourth years after large fry plantings. The conclusion is inevitable that the abundance of fish in Lake Erie is due to circumstances other than the production of fry in hatcheries.

Although the evidence against the value of hatcheries is strong enough to justify recommendations that hatcheries be discontinued, the hatcheries are still operating. They probably will be continued until an enlightened public opinion insists that the wasteful expenditure be stopped.

Aerial view of Peach Point showing United States Fish Hatchery (left) and State of Ohio Fish Hatchery (right).

State of Ohio Fish Hatchery, built in 1914-1915 on Peach Point.

A New Hatchery and Its Uses

Following destruction of the wood-frame building, an attractive, two-story red brick structure was erected on the same site during 1914-1915. The contract was with John C. Feick Construction of Sandusky who erected it at a cost of $90,000. In 1928, the Hatchery contained nine batteries, each one holding 288 glass jars, with a total capacity of 2,592 glass jars. The total capacity for each species was whitefish, 362,880,000; herring, 635,040,000; pike perch or walleye, 1,270,080,000; and sauger, 2,322,432,000. To prevent a total loss of all eggs in the Hatchery because of a breakdown in the machinery, the equipment was in duplicate. This equipment consisted of two 18,000 gallon storage tanks, two big forty horse power boilers and pumps, 16 large wooden tanks, and other minor equipment.

Through the years the Hatchery has specialized in propagating whitefish, herring, walleye, and yellow pickerel. Since 1969 coho salmon and chinook salmon have been raised to stock rivers and streams in northern Ohio. Between 600,000 and 700,000 coho salmon have been produced in one year at the Hatchery. During the summer of 1985, 150,000 steelhead trout were raised in the Hatchery.

The Hatchery has been useful for other related purposes. From 1918 until 1925, the facility served as the laboratory and classrooms for the summer field biology program of the Lake Laboratory of The Ohio State University, which had been relocated from Cedar Point. The building has comfortable sleeping quarters, a kitchenette, and a meeting room. It has been a popular place for state officials to take lodging while on visits to northern Ohio and Put-in-Bay. During the 1980s improvements were made by installing a new generator, new plastic pipe plumbing, improved electrical service, and a public display area. Between 17,000 and 20,000 people tour the Hatchery each year.

The Hatchery is under the jurisdiction of the Division of Wildlife in the Ohio Department of Natural Resources. At the time of this writing, the employees were Steven and Sue Riddle. The former served as Superintendent for 11 years. Previous superintendents and their approximate years of service were Frank E. Miller, 1907- ; George F. Miller, -1933; ?;Bert Millen, 1941-1947; Ernest H. Miller, 1943-1963; Russell E. Smith, 1963-1973; Donald Hair, 1972-1978; Gary Isbel, 1978-1979; Steven Riddle, 1976-1987.

At times, through the years, the Hatchery has been plagued with financial difficulties. The State's vessel, the *Oliver H. Perry*, under the captainship of J. Otto Biemiller, was retired in 1933 because of an economy measure. The next year the

Superintendent Ernest Miller attends jars with fish eggs.

Interior of the State of Ohio Fish Hatchery at Put-in-Bay.

State Hatchery combined efforts with the Federal Hatchery, and one of the consequences was that the Federal boat, the *Shearwater II*, was placed under the captainship of Mr. Biemiller, and funded from both federal and state sources. He operated the boat until his retirement in 1938. The operation for 1950 was maintained at about 75% capacity, with the supply of spawn limited to that provided on a voluntary arrangement with commercial fishermen, instead of paying them for the fertile spawn. Because of a shortage of revenue, a decision to close the operation of the Hatchery in May 1985 was made by the Chief of the Division of Wildlife, Max Duckworth. A reversal of this decision was announced about a week later and was reaffirmed by Governor Richard F. Celeste, when he made a public appearance at the Hatchery on 26 August 1985. Clayton H. Lakes was appointed as the Division's new chief following the resignation of Mr. Duckworth earlier in August.

The Put-in-Bay Hatchery is the smallest facility operated by the Division of Wildlife. The concrete raceways and fiberglass tanks are contained within a single building. Although no longer is use, the old coal-fired boiler is still present. Fuel oil tanks now occupy the once-laden coal bins. Water is no longer pumped directly from the lake. Three wells drilled into the island supply the necessary 1,200 gallons per minute.

Hatchery to Become Education Center

Anonymous

Put-in-Bay Gazette,
April 1991, pp. 1-2.

The Ohio Department of Natural Resources has announced plans for the conversion of the State Fish Hatchery to a fishing educational center. The last fish in the hatchery, steelhead known also as rainbow trout, will be released into mainland streams next month according to hatchery superintendent Dave Insley. The conversion of the Hatchery comes from the facts that fish production on the Island is inefficient because of poor water sources and that more money is available for the funding of educational facilities, rather than for the usual function of hatcheries. Other reasons for the change are limited production capability and logistical problems in transporting food and supplies over to the island. The South Bass hatching operation does not compare favorably to the fish production exhibited at other state hatcheries. For purposes of demonstration fish will still be kept at the hatchery to enhance the educational displays.

In 1985 an attempt existed to close the Hatchery, but efforts by the then state senate president Paul Gilmor (R-Port Clinton) helped to keep it open. Insley claims islanders are happy about the State making the Hatchery into a visitor's center. He said, "They (the islanders) make their money off the tourists. The more there is for tourists to do, the longer they'll stay and spend money here." Funding is now available to the extent of $200,000 for replacement of the roof, gutters and windows, as well as rehabing the exterior masonry on the building. Another $24,936 will go toward design and architectuals services.

Renovations in the 77-year old Hatchery should increase the area for displays, and build a class room and auditorium inside the 15,000 sq. ft. building. One official stated, "We're looking at changing it from something people can view in a few minutes into something that people can spend a couple of hours looking at." Plans call for two naturalists to be hired to give tours of the center. It is anticipated that visitation will increase from 30,000 visitors per year to 100,000 after the center is completed.

On a trial basis in 1997, the Hatchery first operated as a fish education center with displays for public education. The official opening for this purpose came in 1998. Melissa Hathaway, whose office is in Sandusky, is the current Supervisor.

References:

Chapter 9, The State Fish Hatchery

Anonymous. 1938. "Captain Biemiller retires." *Ohio Conservation Bulletin* 2(3): 10.

Anonymous. 1949. "Limited operation of Put-in-Bay hatchery approved." *Ohio Conservation Bulletin* 13(12): 11.

Anonymous. 1985. "Island fish hatchery closing." *Sandusky Register*, 9 May, p. C-2.

Associated Press. 1985. "Wildlife shakeup revealed: Decision to close South Bass hatchery upset Celeste. *News Herald*, Port Clinton, A-1, A-2.

Cranson, Jeff. 1985. "Powerful *friends* reopen fish hatchery." *Sandusky Register*, 27 August, p. A-13.

Dodge, Robert J. 1975. "Growth and Progress: Fish Hatcheries," pp. 37-38. *In Isolated Splendor: Put-in-Bay and South Bass Island.* Exposition Press, Hicksville, New York. x, 166 pp.

Frohman, Charles E. 1971. "Fish Hatcheries," pp. 113-116. *In Put-in-Bay: Its History.* The Ohio Historical Society, Columbus. vii, 156 pp.

Kah, Bill. 1953. "Men in the field [Ernie Miller]." *Ohio Conservation Bulletin* 17(9): 21.

Kah, Bill. 1957. "Production line walleyes." *Ohio Conservation Bulletin* 21(8): 14-15.

Kah, Bill. 1963. "Resource employes retire [Ernest Miller]." Ohio Conservation Bulletin 27(9): 22-23.

Kriss, Claudine. 1985. "Some question closing of local fish hatchery." *News Herald*, Port Clinton, 9 May, pp. 1, 5.

Kriss, Claudine. 1985. "Help given to save hatchery: Manager says Gilmour's plan may be too little, too late." *News Herald*, Port Clinton, 6 June, pp. 1, 5.

Kurnat, Alan A. 1985. "Put-in-Bay's Fish Hatcheries." *Lake Front News*, Port Clinton, August 9-15, p. 15.

Langlois, Thomas H. 1942. "Review of fish culture history." *Ohio Conservation Bulletin* 6(10): 12-13.

Langlois, Thomas H. {About 1948]. "The Ohio State Fish Hatchery on South Bass Island in Lake Erie." Typewritten Manuscript, RLS copy, 6 pp. [See page 127 for introductory portion of this manuscript].

Langlois, Thomas H. 1954. "Artificial propagation [of fish]," pp. 386-395. *In The Western End of Lake Erie and its Ecology*. J. W. Edwards Publisher, Inc., Ann Arbor. xx, 479 pp.

[Piatt, Charles E., Jr.]. 1974. "Rearing salmon for the Great Lakes: Intricate hatchery procedures are behind the Ohio plan which puts Pacific salmon in Lake Erie." *News in Engineering*, The Ohio State University 46(6): 12. November.

Ryall, Lydia J. 1913. "FishHatchery Work at Put-in-Bay," pp. 465-471. I*n Sketches and Stories of the Lake Erie Islands*. The American Publishers Co., Norwalk. vi, 546 pp. (Perry Centennial Edition 1813-1913).

Tertuliani, John. 1988. "Put-in-Bay Hatchery," pp. 20-21. *In* "Ohio fish hatcheries: Science helping nature." *Ohio Wildlife* 1(2): 16-21. May.

Wascko, Harold. 1957. "Walleye stocking in Ohio." *Ohio Conservation Bulletin* 21(3): 14-15.

Wickliff, Edward L., and George F. Miller. 1928. *Artificial propagation of fish in Ohio*. State of Ohio, Department of Agriculture, Division of Fish and Game. The F. J. Herr Printing Co., Columbus. 13 pp.

GIBRALTAR ISLAND, "Emerald Gem of Lake Erie," a view of the northeast end with Perry's Lookout in the center. PERRY'S LOOKOUT ATOP THE HIGH DOLOMITE CLIFFS, American flag, Needle's Eye, and swimming area at northeast end of the Island. FALLEN ROCKS along north side of the Island.

Gibraltar Island:
I. The Years Preceding Jay Cooke

Gibraltar Island the, "Emerald Gem of Lake Erie," is a high promontory rising above Lake Erie's waters consisting of a solid six-acre mass of dolomite rock lying at the entrance to Put-in-Bay Harbor. The Island has several natural features that have been identified with names because of their varied shapes, sizes, and surfaces of the exposed rocks, or they have been named because of significant past events that have occurred there. These natural features are the Glacial Grooves, Perry's Lookout, the Needle's Eye, the Sphinx Head, and the Fallen Rocks along the northwest shore. In addition, the Island, itself apparently received its name from its resemblance to another Gibraltar Island, the famous British fortress at the western end of the Mediterranean Sea. Here too, in Lake Erie, during the War of 1812, Gibraltar Island served as a fortress against the British fleet.

Originally, Gibraltar Island was included in that portion of northern Ohio which was owned by the State of Connecticut. Its title was transferred to Judge Pierpont Edwards of Connecticut, in 1807, and then to his brother Colonel Alfred P. Edwards, in 1836. The latter supported an active program for establishing a Monument on the Island to commemorate Commodore Oliver Hazard Perry's naval victory over the British fleet in the Battle of Lake Erie, 10 September 1813. Edwards agreed to cede land on Gibraltar Island for the Monument together with stone, lime, and hydraulic cement to be used in its construction. In 1845 the Island was occupied as the camping ground for a large number of surveyors and engineers employed by the federal government in making charts and maps of the Lake.

Four topics are covered in this chapter. The first account concerns the natural features and relics on the Island. In the second story, Dr. Charles E. Herdendorf, Director of Stone Laboratory from 1973 through 1988, tells about his excursion on the British

Gibraltar Island and the naming of the Lake Erie Gibraltar Island. Burials constitute the third topic. The lengthly anonymously written account in the *Sandusky Register* of the laying of the cornerstone for Perry's Monument on Gibraltar Island constitutes the fourth story.

Natural Features and Relics

Some of the natural rock features on Gibraltar Island are the Glacial Grooves, Perry's Lookout, the Needle's Eye, the Sphinx Head, and the Fallen Rocks. The Glacial Grooves are deep-cut striations extending northeast-southwest along the north shore at the west end of the Island. These Grooves, formed about 10,000 years ago, are tell-tale remnants of the Wisconsinan Glaciation in North America. The rocks were abraided by a massive force of granite and other rock materials buried under a mile of ice and moved by the advance and retreat of the Glacier. Local legend has it that Perry's guns were hauled onto the Island at the site of the Grooves.

The highest point, an overlook at the east end of the Island, provides a panoramic view of the Lake. Formerly capped with a flagstaff, this point, known as Perry's Lookout, is named because of local legend which claims that Commodore Perry cited the approach of the British fleet from here. To the contrary, however, the actual approach was discovered by a lookout at the mast head of his ship, the *Lawrence*. Below this 40-foot overlook and to the north is a narrow opening in the rock at water level, known as the Needle's Eye. To the south is the swimming area and the Sphinx Head. Along the east and north side of the Island, huge Fallen Rocks emerge from the water like mammouth gray ghosts in the shadows of the night. These Fallen Rocks tell a story of the ceaseless weathering and erosion of the steep rocky cliffs by water, ice, and wind, that have been scouring the Island for thousands of years.

Two other relics at Gibraltar Island bear testimony to former days and events. A small canon, supposedly one of Perry's guns and mounted on a two-wheeled carriage, was used to fire a signal to welcome the Cooke party upon its arrival. After the carriage fell apart, the gun was removed to Perry's Lookout, where it was mounted on a rock ledge and where it still remains. On the south side, but not far from the Castle, hangs a large bell, brought from South Mountain, where according to legend it was used to call the slaves. Originally it came from England, and after it was installed on Gibraltar Island, it was used to summon the Cooke family to morning prayers and meals. Prior to 1987, the bell was rung at 6:30 a.m. each morning, except Sunday, to wake students to begin their day of classes at Stone Laboratory. The bell is only rung now in case of fire on Gibraltar Island.

Gibraltar Island, a view of the northeast end with cliff face of Perry's Lookout, Needle's Eye, and swimming area.

Glacial Grooves at southwest end of the Island.

A Legend for the Naming of Gibraltar Island

Charles E. Herdendorf

Put-in-Bay Gazette,
December 1984, pp. 4, 7.

Gibraltar— the rocky British fortress at the entrance to the Mediterranean Sea— has long been regarded as the namesake of Gibraltar Island in Put-in-Bay Harbor. Indeed, if scale is discounted, the shape, kind of rock and sentry-like position of these two rocky outcrops are quite similar. This similarity is particularly evident when viewed from a boat returning to harbor. But how did the Lake Erie Island come to be called Gibraltar? The following is one hypothesis.

In August 1984, I flew to Switzerland to attend a conference about lakes and present a research paper on Lake Erie. After the conference I decided to visit the Mediterranean Rock of Gibraltar in honor of its namesake in Lake Erie. Getting to this Gibraltar Island was not easy, and after traveling by train, bus, taxi, and then confronting on foot the Spanish guards, it was impossible to get to the Island because only Spanish citizens and Gibraltar residents could cross the border from Spain. Somewhat discouraged, but inspired by the outline of the Island's sheer cliffs in the misty moonlight, I was determined to enter the Island via air flight from the country of Morocco on the north coast of Africa. This effort was successful, and for the next three days I roamed the Rock from one end to the other, from top to bottom, and even inside its caves and 32 miles of tunnels. My guide, a taxi driver named Jack, took me to several of the historic sites and told of many battles and their heroes. At Trafalgar Cemetery, I became aware of an event that provided another similarity between the two Gibraltar Islands.

During the Great Napoleonic Wars, one of the fiercest battles in naval history was fought near the Straits of Gibraltar in October 1805— the Battle of Trafalgar. The famous Lord Nelson commanded the British Fleet and defeated the combined French and Spanish navies. Lord Nelson, in his full dress uniform, was a conspicuous figure as he stood on the bow of the flagship *H.M.S. Victory*. He led the British fleet into a bloody battle as the enemy sailed out of the harbor at Cadiz.

Serving with Lord Nelson as a young Lieutenant aboard the 74-gun, *H.M.S. Swiftsure* was Robert Heriott Barclay. Only seven days before the battle, the Admiralty confirmed Lord Nelson's appointment of Barclay to this commission after eight years as a midshipman. Barclay, wounded at the Battle of Trafalgar, was to lose his left arm in another engagement with the French two years later.

Lord Nelson was more severely wounded. His life hung by a thread as he was cared for in a stretcher fashioned from a rum barrel. The battle waged for a long time. The *Victory* fresh from England with a clean hull was faster than the algae laden French ships and sailed down the line shooting out upper riggings, turning as she approached each ship to fire cannons into the stern where timbers were weakest.

After the battle, the victorious British fleet returned to Gibraltar with its captives and the gravely injured Lord Nelson. Some say he was carried in the rum barrel, more dead than alive, to an inn which still stands near the west shore of the Rock. Young Barclay remained with his admiral until the end came at that lonely outpost in the Mediterranean. Having lost that day the man he revered most, Barclay remained undaunted in his service to the crown. In a touching letter to his father, the Rev. Peter Barclay, he relays the glory of the victory and the sorrow of his losses.

Eight years later, Barclay now a captain, finds himself commander of another British fleet in yet another lonely outpost— Fort Malden, at what is now Amherstburg, Ontario, near the headwaters of Lake Erie. In September of 1813, the Battle of Lake Erie took place. A lookout posted on the high cliff of an island in Put-in-Bay Harbor warns the commander of the American fleet, Oliver Hazard Perry, of the presence of the British ships to the Northwest. Commodore Perry sails out of the harbor, past the high cliffs, to engage the enemy.

Again the battle was furious. Although the Americans were victorious, Perry must give up his flagship the *Lawrence* and row to the *Niagara*. Captain Barclay is wounded twice, his right arm shattered. Over 40 men of the British squadron are killed during the fight; except for the officers, their bodies are thrown overboard as they fall. The American fleet and the captured British fleet anchor at Put-in-Bay Harbor, the wounded are cared for and the dead are buried. Perry sends his now famous message to General William Henry Harrison, "We have met the enemy and they are ours." The lakes are cleared of British naval defense and General Harrison is now free to invade Canada and attack Fort Malden. He plans these military actions with Commodore Perry at Put-in-Bay.

The discouraged Barclay, a true officer and gentleman in the British tradition, writes home to his lovely fiancee, Agnes Cossar, in England, that his wounds have left him "less of a man." He releases her from their engagement. She writes to him at Put-in-Bay, saying that "as long as there is enough of him to contain his soul she will marry him." Heartened by this news, he begins to recover.

While Barclay remains at Put-in-Bay, he is treated graciously by Perry. They eventually become friends and have long talks about naval strategy and past battles. In relaying the tactics of other encounters, Barclay offered that as he

Robert H. Barclay (1785-1837)

approached Put-in-Bay harbor after the battle, the rocky cliff north of the small island protecting the harbor reminded him of another fray— Trafalgar. He reminisced how the Rock of Gibraltar loomed in the distance on that victorious but sorrowful day. Intrigued by this notion, Perry called the rocky island in Put-in-Bay Harbor "Gibraltar" in honor of his respected foe.

Soon the War of 1812 would conclude. At the recommendation of Perry, Barclay was unconditionally paroled and returned to England and to Agnes. Likewise, I boarded the midday plane bound for London when my visit to historic Gibraltar was ended. By early evening I had caught a train from Gatwick Airport to Portsmouth, England and was on the Brittany Ferry bound for St. Malo, France, and new adventures. Darkness fell as the ship steamed quietly out of Portsmouth Harbor, and there above the quay was the silhouette of Nelson's flagship *Victory*, still maintained by the British Admiralty after 200 years of service.

Burials

At the northeast end of the Island is a small pebble beach and on the grassy slope above it overlying the bedrock were markers for two men. Originally, the graves were marked with wooden headboards, "James Ross--Died August 11, 1848" and "John Elliott--Died Sept. 18th, 1848." The former's headboard was replaced by a flat stone marker, but it became broken and disappeared in the late 1970's. A new marker with a date of Aug. 11, 1848 was placed at the site during the 1990's.Dr. Thomas H. Langlois, former Stone Laboratory Director, wrote in his research notes on the South Bass islanders that James Ross was one of Commodore Perry's men who remained on South Bass Island. After the man's death on 11 July 1817, he was buried on Gibraltar Island. However, this individual is not that James Ross, but another Ross of unknown origin. In a handwritten memo concerning James Ross, Langlois noted that he had misread the date, and that it correctly was 11 August 1847, as pointed out to him in 1948 by Theodore H. Phillips, former caretaker of Gibraltar Island.

Caretaker Phillips further stated, as recorded by Langlois, that when the Stone Laboratory classroom building was being constructed, the excavator found bones of a man located near where the second west end basement window was to be placed in the new laboratory building.

No sign of a coffin existed, but the soil around the bones was black from decomposition of flesh and clothes and perhaps a burial sack. The bones were sent away and reported to have been those of a six-foot two-inch white man in his thirties, with every tooth in his head. Phillips suggested that it was probably Ross, and he may have died of the cholera raging then in Sandusky. His bones were kept in the Castle library at the time Phillips reported to Langlois, but their whereabouts today is not known. Perhaps some truth exists in statements by former Stone Laboratory students that they have heard or seen ghosts in Cooke's Castle.

Another burial is recorded on Gibraltar Island by Daniel Vroman, son of Philip Vroman, one of the earliest residents on South Bass Island. The younger Vroman wrote an undated sketch of Put-in-Bay on a piece of wallpaper, which has been transcribed and published in 1948 by Langlois and Langlois, "The first funeral I ever attended was from the frame or rear part of the V[alentine] Doller residence. This was before V. Doller came to the island. The house had been built for the people who operated the saw mill and the family in charge lost a little babe. The interment was on Gibraltar just up from the Cook[e] dock between two maple trees. The whole cortege went over in one row boat. I could pick out the spot until lately I think one of the trees may have been removed."

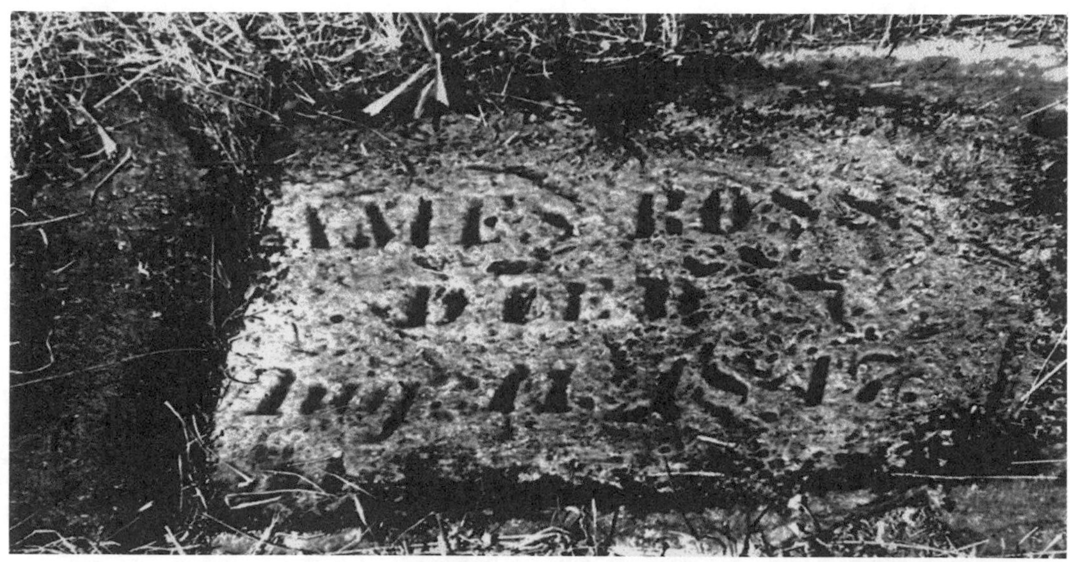

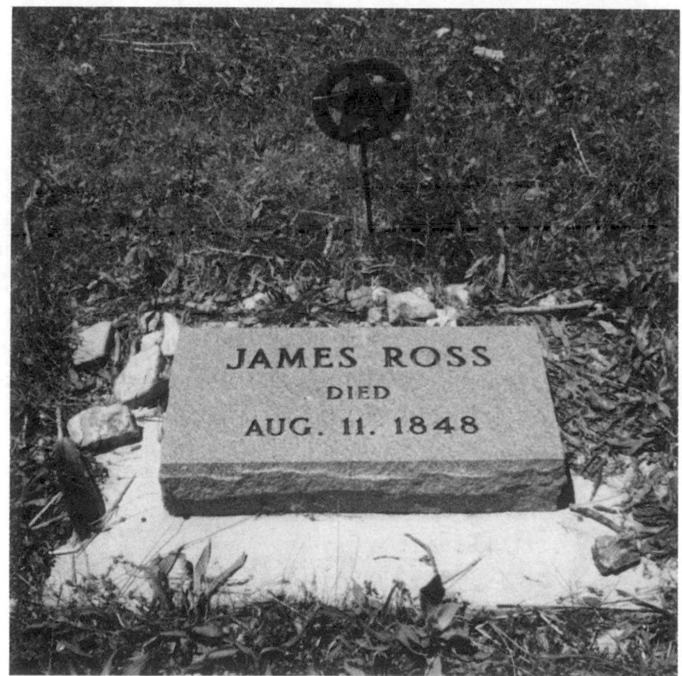

Gravestones at the east end of Gibraltar Island for James Ross. The upper photograph shows his earlier stone marker with the apparent date of Aug. 11, 1847. The lower photograph shows a new marker for James Ross with the date of Aug. 11, 1848.

Laying of the Cornerstone of the Perry Monument

The first proposal for the erection of a suitable monument on Gibraltar Island came in June 1852, when "The Battle of Lake Erie Monument Association" was formed to raise funds for the project. By the time of the second meeting, held in 1858 on the *Arrow*, as it traveled from Sandusky to Put-in-Bay, Gibraltar Island had been purchased in 1854 by Joseph De Rivera St. Jurgo, a New York merchant of Spanish origin. He offered to grant free half of, or whatever was a sufficient part of, the Island for the erection of the Monument. The climax of the Association's effort came on 10 September 1859 when the Monument's cornerstone was laid on Gibraltar Island during a gala celebration at Put-in-Bay.

Anonymous

Sandusky Daily Commercial Register,
12 September 1859, p. 2.

The tenth of September 1859 dawned inauspiciously. The night previous the rain began to fall in dashing showers, and at breakfast time the clouds were lowering, and there was every indication of a rainy day. But the people, in the enthusiasm of their patriotic feelings required something more than a rain storm like this to dampen their ardor, and at an early hour were moving in great masses to the steamers lying at the docks in Sandusky. The *Island Queen* was at once loaded down, and started for the Islands. She carried the Yagers with their Brass Band and the Sandusky Artillery Company. *Arctic* and *Granite State*, lying at the foot of Columbus Avenue, were also quickly filled to the extent of their capacity, and were also soon moving out. The *Bay City* lay at the dock of the Sandusky, Dayton & Cincinnati Railroad. At an early hour she was boarded by hundreds of the citizens of Sandusky, and upon the arrival of the cars on the S.D.& C. Railroad there was a great rush made for her, and she was in a few minutes obliged to shove from the dock to keep from being swamped. She put out leaving from seven to eight hundred disappointed persons behind.

The *Pearl*, which had early in the morning taken a load of excursionists from Port Clinton to the Island, came over to Sandusky and took back a full load; but notwithstanding this there must have been over five hundred persons left in this city, who were anxious to join in the great demonstration at Put-in-Bay. The Free Masons, as a body, who were to lay the Corner Stone with their peculiar ceremonies, were among those left behind; but the *Bonnie Boat* came to their relief, and they were landed at the Island in time to perform their part of the day's programme. So great was the desire of the disappointed persons to reach Put-in-Bay, that it became necessary to station a guard at the gang way of the *Bonnie*, to keep her from being overloaded.

The *Arctic*, *Granite State*, and *Bay City* arrived at Put-in-Bay at about the same time. The propeller *Gov. Cushman* from Cleveland, the *Ocean* from Detroit, loaded down to the guards, the *Sea Bird* from Toledo, and the *Island Queen* from Sandusky, had already arrived. Following in rapid succession arrived the *North Star* and *May Queen* from Cleveland, and the *Western Metropolis* from Buffalo and Cleveland, the *Forester* and the propeller *New York*, from Toledo, and the *Pearl* and *Bonnie Boat* from Sandusky, making in all, with the United States Steamer *Michigan*, anchored in the Bay, fifteen steamers. Besides these, there were two United States Revenue Cutters, the *Jacob Thompson*, Capt. Marun, and the *Jeremiah S. Black*, Capt. Ottinger, two steam tugs, and innumerable sail crafts, forming a semi-circle about the passenger steamers. The scene was the most imposing ever witnessed on the chain of Lakes, and cannot be described. The roar of the cannon, the strains of music from a half score of brass bands, the shouts from thousands of persons whose enthusiasm knew no bounds, the waving of handkerchiefs by the ladies, the wilderness of streaming flags, the steamers and large sail craft lying at rest, the multitude of small sails with their white wings spread to the breeze flitting hither and yon on the sparkling waters of the Bay, and the swaying mass of human life, combined to produce an effect indescribable. He who could witness all this unmoved, is indeed a lamentable stoic. In him whose bosom did not glow with honest national pride and patriotism, our country has an enemy. We as a people are safe so long as we hand with such enthusiasm upon the noble deeds of those whose bravery and blood have purchased and perpetuated to us the national liberty and independence we now so fully enjoy.

At 2 o'clock the Perry's Monument Association was called to order by Capt. Larman, of the U. S. steamer *Michigan*, who officiated as temporary President in the abscence of Hon. Lewis Cass, President of the Association, and Hon. Rosa Wilkins, one of the Vice Presidents who was designated to act as President in case of the regular President's absence. The Throne of Grace was then eloquently and fervently addressed by Rev. S. A. Bronson, of Sandusky, in a prayer appropriate to the occasion. After the music from one of the Brass Bands present, William S. Pierce, of Sandusky, Treasurer of the Association, was introduced, who made the following remarks:

LADIES AND GENTLEMEN: I am requested by the Board of Management to occupy your time, for a few moments, in a statement of their doings since the last Anniversary. As soon as it is practicable, after the permanent organization of the Association under such favorable auspices at this place a year ago, a meeting of the Board was convened at the city of Sandusky. It was made the duty of the Board, consisting of fifty members in different parts of the country, by the Constitution, to appoint an Executive Committee. Among the other acts of that meeting, the Board appointed A. H. Moss, F. P. Barney, and J. A. Camp, Esqrs. of Sandusky, Hon. Samuel Starkweather of Cleveland, M. R. Watte, Esq. of Toledo, Hon. J. A. Campbell of Detroit, Capt. Stephen Champlin of Buffalo, and Capt. W. W. Dobbin of Erie, as their Executive Committee.

One of the first and most important duties which devolved upon them, to which they gave much time, attention, and study, was the procurement and adoption of a suitable plan for the Monument. H. P. Merrick, an architect of Sandusky, furnished to the Committee different designs for the Monument, which were exceedingly creditable to his taste, his attainment, and skill. They were in the form of an obelisk and were highly appreciated by the Committee, and indeed thought worthy of adoption. About this time, however, there was a person in Ohio, the fame of whose genius had taken such hold of the public mind, that your Committee, advised by discreet friends of the measure, believed it would not be doing justice either to the talent in our midst, or to the enterprise, not to give him a commission. I need hardly mention his name, who will share in the fame of our venerable President, the Secretary of State of the United States, of our most worthy Vice President, the Chief Magistrate of the State of Ohio, to having given to their noble brows and commanding features almost the immortality which their exalted virtues and patriotic services have given to their names.

The Board of Management issued a commission to T. D. Jones, Artist, as he professionally and humbly writes his name. How well he fulfilled that commission, let the spontaneous and unanimous voice of thousands answer, in their expressions of approbation and admiration of his design. It has been declared by many, who with cultivated taste, have had the opportunity of foreign observation, to vie with the proudest monuments of the Old World in beauty and appropriateness of design. The Board of Management congratulates the Association on the eminent success of Mr. Jones, in the conception and perfection of his plan, and they feel proud that the progress of the arts in our country is so illustrated by his genius in the West. Joseph De Rivera St. Jurgo, an accomplished Spanish gentleman of the city of New York and the proprietor of these Islands, has contributed as a free gift one half of Gibraltar, with a declaration that the Association can have the whole, if necessary, for the site of the Monument. The Board of Management would thus publicly express their acknowledgements and obligations to him and the thanks of the Association for his generous deed.

Your Committee have devoted much time to the location of the exact site of the Monument, the laying of the foundation, the preparation of the cornerstone, the arrangements for this celebration, the so respondence with friends of the enterprise throughout the country, and to the other duties of their appointment, which I can not take time to relate. With regard to the solicitation and collection of subscriptions, which have been volunteered, your Treasurer has felt very great sensitiveness, which has been sympathized with by the Committee, in making any call on the public before the object of the Association had progressed so far as to command the deserved confidence of the century. They preferred, therefore, that the expenses, by no means inconsiderable, should be otherwise defrayed, and have not until quite recently made collections--not until the site was procured, the plan of the Monument adopted, and arrangements made for laying the cornerstone. What they are now doing meets with great encouragement.

Cast your eye on yonder beautiful island, where we are about to lay the cornerstone of the Monument. Observe the symmetrical formation of Gibraltar--how its rich verdure extends to its rock girt base. Behold its elevation, high above the waters of the Lake--higher than is necessary to protect the waters within the Bay from the turbulence of the waves without when maddened by angry winds. See! what a lookout there is and that all around it can be seen as far as the eye can reach. Mark well its firm foundation. It is made of everlasting rock; and resist the thought, if you can, that it is the design of God's residence--that it shall be a mission of this age, when the people have become refined and wealthy, grateful to God for the rich heritage of blessings which we can enjoy as fruit of the sufferings and sacrifices of our fathers--reverencing the memory of our fathers for their pure virtues and heroic deeds. On this foundation of rock a Monument shall arise, towering aloft towards Heaven, to be seen by every mariner, and every traveler, and every seeker after pleasure or of health, up and down the Lake and amid these Islands, worthy of the Battle of Lake Erie--worthy of Perry's Victory--worthy of a nation's abounding gratitude. The Board of Management most cordially and earnestly invite you all, that you co-operate with them, and unitedly and individually do your part in this patriotic duty.

After a short intermission, filled up with music, Hon. Rufus R. Spalding, of Cleveland, orator of the day, was introduced to the audience. He said, in substance, that the most prominent feature in a people's characteristics was the veneration of the great events in their history. These events are embalmed in traditionary lore. They will be known and talked of when the actors in them are forgotten. The Pyramids of Egypt have evidently been erected as a national expression of a peoples' admiration of some noted event or era in their national existence. Who gives a thought to him who was the master builder of these vast structures. It is only to know what event the building of these master piles were intended to commemorate that causes speculation. Marathon and Salamis would be familiar to men when the classic names now identified with them have been buried from sight. Bunker Hill would form the key note to American patriotism when the name of Prescott was forgotten.

The orator then glanced at the causes which led to the late War with Great Britain. England had become the conceded mistress of the sea, and was arrogant and overbearing in her relations with those powers she deemed weaker than herself. Her war vessels in a number of instances overhauled American merchantmen, and even small armed Government vessels mustered their crews and from them were pressed into His Majesty's service persons who the British officers claimed were British subjects. Of this number, many proved to be native American citizens. This series of outrages was a prominent cause of the War.

The American plan of war was to invade Upper Canada and wrest that province from the British if possible. This plan was thwarted by the inglorious surrender of Gen. William Hull, and the defeat of Gen. Wilkinson. The Northwestern border became the scene of numerous outrages perpetrated upon American citizens by the British soldiery and their savage allies, the Indians. It was deemed expedient to fit out a lake fleet to co-operate with Gen. William H. Harrison's land forces. The charge of this work was given to Capt. Oliver Hazard Perry. The orator then detailed the disadvantages Perry labored under in prosecuting his charge, and gave a succinct history of the manner in which these difficulties were overcome, the sailing of the fleet for the upper end of the Lake after its completion, and the famous naval engagement near Put-in-Bay, September 10th, 1813, and the conduct of the gallant Perry on that occasion.

The survivors of the engagement, who were present and on the Island--Dr. W. T. Tailiaferro of Cincinnati, who was a Kentucky volunteer on the *Somers*; William Blair of Lexington, Richland County, a volunteer on the *Niagara*; and Mr. Tucker, of Adams County, Ohio, a volunteer on the *Caledonia*--were then introduced, and Mr. Spalding addressed them. He said they were venerated by those who had congregated to celebrate the great event in which they had been actors. Those whose blood had been spilled in fighting under the brave Perry were regarded as martyrs to the cause of American rights.

The orator closed by reference to the Monument whose cornerstone was to be laid this day on Gibraltar IslandIt should be constructed so that it might be a fair type of the heighth, the strength, and permanency of our patriotism. We cannot do justice to Mr. Spaulding's oration in this brief resume. We would have given it entire had such been the desire of the orator. A patriotic song was then sung by Ossian E. Dodge and a number of other vocalists of Cleveland. A benediction was then pronounced by Rev. J. B. Walker of Sandusky, after which there was a display of the military present --the Cleveland Grays, Detroit Light Guards, the Sandusky Yagery, an artillery company from Cleveland and one from Toledo, and the Sandusky Artillery Company--all under the direction of Maj. Gen. J. A. Jones Norwalk, of the 17th Division Ohio Volunteer Militia, accompanied by his own staff, and Brig. Gen. H. N. Bill of Sandusky, and staff.

The Masonic Fraternity, under the direction of J. N. Burr and D. G. Master of Ohio, then proceeded in full regalia, with all their appropriate emblems, to Gibraltar, where the cornerstone of the Perry Monument was duly laid with the imposing ceremonies peculiar to that order. The following articles were placed in an air-tight copper box within the cornerstone: by the Monument Association: Declaration of Independence, Constitution of the United States, Constitution of the State of Ohio, Constitution of the Battle of Lake Erie Monument Association, Names of the President, Vice President of the United States, members of the Cabinet and the principal officers of the Army and Navy, Senators and members of Congress of the United States, Governor and other officers of the State of Ohio, Officers of this Association, History of the Battle of Lake Erie, Programme of this days proceedings, Coins of the United States, Papers of the day.

The Masons placed in the cornerstone: Holy Bible, Book of the Masonic Constitution, Constitutions and By-Laws of the Grand Lodge of Ohio, By-Laws of Science Lodge No. 50 of the Free and Accepted Masons, Sandusky City, Papers of the day.

Thus ended the proceedings of the day--a day not soon to be forgotten by the people of the lake shore cities. The concourse of people was tremendous. Not less than fifteen thousand could have been present. Some estimates place the number at 20,000. Everything went off well, and no one seemed dissatisfied with the demonstration.

Considering all circumstances, there was a remarkable immensity from [blurred word]. The only accident worthy of note occurred to the stewart of the *Granite State*. As he was passing up the plank from the dock to the *Gov. Cushman*, he slipped upon a mellon rind and fell into the water between the dock and the boat, striking his head against a projecting timber of the dock. He was stunned, and sank twice before relief was extended to him. He was fished out and placed under the hands of a physician present, who soon brought him from the chill under which he was laboring when he was rescued from the water, and had him in a quiet sleep. The contusion on the side of the head was barely a flesh wound, and not at all dangerous. One or two others, in their anxiety to reach the boats, fell into the water, but were taken out without difficulty, having received no injury beyond a good "ducking."

There was but one fight, we believe, and that was between two drunken men. One was carried from the field dripping with the blood drawn from his nose by a random blow from his antagonist, we believe.

The side-showmen were there, of course. A pair of horned elks had been caged for the occasion, and of course drew those who had come to see the "show" through. The fat woman was also there, and the keeper, in his calico hunting shirt, made the noise, and the amount of its peculiar to his class of humanity.

The bulk of the excursionists from this point had a tedious time getting home. The *Bay City* as soon as she got a comfortable load on board, shoved off, and went home. The *Arctic* was so crowded that she would not venture out with her load, and waited until the *Bay City* and the *Pearl* could come to her relief. The *Bay City* got in with her second load about midnight. The *Pearl* and *Arctic* were still later.

References:

Chapter Ten, Gibraltar Island
I. The Years Preceding Jay Cooke

Frohman, Charles E. 1971. "Gibraltar Island." pp. 37-43. *In Put-in-Bay: Its History*. The Ohio Historical Society, Columbusvii, 156 pp.

Langlois, Thomas H. Research notes on South Bass islanders. Archives, Hayes Presidential Center, Fremont, Ohio.

Vroman, Daniel. Undated. "An original record of early life on South [Bass] Island," pp. 129-130. *In* Thomas Huxley Langlois and Marina Holmes Langlois. 1948. *South Bass Island and Islanders.* The Ohio State University, The Franz Theodore Stone Laboratory, Contribution No. 10. x, 139 pp.; see also, pp. 177-179. *In* Thomas H. Langlois. 1947. "Sidelights on the Erie Isles." *Inland Seas* 3: 173-179.

The Jay Cooke Mansion, also referred to as the Jay Cooke Castle, built in 1865 by Jay Cooke on Gibraltar Island. Monument to the Battle of Lake Erie erected in 1865 by Jay Cooke "to mark the corner stone of a proposed monument commemorating Commodore Perry's Victory at the Battle of Lake Erie Sept 10 1813." Jay Cooke (1821-1905), patriotic financier of the Civil War.

Gibraltar Island:

II. The Years During and Since Jay Cooke

Gibraltar Island was sold again on 27 January 1864, this time to Jay Cooke who obtained it from Joseph De Rivera St. Jurgo for $3000, although some accounts give the purchase price as $3001. The property, however, was still subject to the erection of the Monument commemorating Perry's Victory. Cooke, a powerful banker, investment broker, railroad baron, and "patriotic financier of the Civil War," originally from Sandusky and later of Philadelphia, marked the cornerstone the following year with a granite monument containing a bronze-like vase on top and bronze tablet reading:

> ERECTED
> BY
> JAY COOKE
> PATRIOTIC FINANCIER
> OF THE
> CIVIL WAR
> TO MARK THE
> CORNER STONE OF A
> PROPOSED MONUMENT
> COMMEMORATING
> COMMODORE PERRY'S
> VICTORY AT THE
> BATTLE OF LAKE ERIE
> SEPT 10 1813
>
> "We have met the enemy
> and they are ours"

By 1868, the "Perry's Monument Association" proposed to build the Monument on Put-in-Bay Island instead of Gibraltar. However, the actual construction of a monument was a long time coming into reality, but it finally was erected in 1912 as a 352-feet high Doric column on South Bass Island at Put-in-Bay.

Jay Cooke's Castle

The year following his purchase of Gibraltar Island, Jay Cooke built an elaborate 15-room Victorian stone mansion, to which for the next 40 years he, his family, and distinguished guests were to make regular pilgrimages. Cooke's Castle stood among a grove of hackberry, blue ash, and Kentucky Coffee trees on the high eminence at the eastern end of the Island. The four-story, octagonal stone tower on the east side of the building served as an observation platform from which he and his guests could see fine views of the Lake and the archipelago. Several frame additions were added onto the west side of the Castle to the extent that it "now rambles in careless dismay." An ardent admirer of Commodore Perry, Cooke adorned the walls of his Castle with pictures of the Battle of Lake Erie and its renowned hero. The furnishings in the mansion were in keeping with his outstanding position in the financial world. Through the hospitable doors of the Castle passed four generations of his family and countless guests, among them soldiers, statesmen, clergymen, and business leaders, many of whose names were household words at the time.

The Cooke family first visited their summer Island from 15 June to 29 June 1865. Visits were regular during the bass fishing season each year in May-June and September-October from 1865 until 1873, and resumed on 15 May 1880 and continued during summers through 1904. The "lost stories" reproduced in this chapter are about Jay Cooke's life on Gibraltar and what happened to his beloved Island after his descendents no longer had use for it. With respect to the latter part of this statement, Gibraltar Island in 1925 came into the possession of The Ohio State University to become a field biological laboratory. The Island was a gift from University Trustee member Julius F. Stone, who made the purchase from the Cooke family heirs, Charles and Laura (Cooke) Barney.

Castled Gibraltar and Its Lord

Theresa Thorndale

Sketches and Stories of the Lake Erie Islands, 1898, pp. 271-273.

With natural forest and exhuberant vegetation both wild and cultivated clothing its rocks and covering its whole extent, like an emerald gem in a setting of blue, appears Gibraltar Island. It is a mass of rugged rock poised above the surface of Lake Erie within hailing distance of Put-in-Bay. In its quiet, yet picturesque and striking scenery, Gibraltar takes unquestionably the first place among the islands of the lake--a fact clearly evident to its present proprietor, Jay Cooke, when about thirty-five years ago it came into his possession, and with the multi-millions at his command, he set about fitting it up as the ideal summer abode which it has since become. . . .His stately villa, crowning castle-like the Island's highest elevation, overlooks the treetops, forming a picturesque point in the landscape.

All that wealth and cultured taste can suggest combine with natural attractions, and the effect is charming. The surface is broken by rock ledges. Romantic paths wind in and out among trees and shrubbery. Floral arbors, niches and caverns, natural and artificial, with rustic huts, bridges and rockeries, appear. There are boats and boat houses, and ample wharves and ornamental structures of various kinds scattered about the grounds.

The shore scenery is marvelously beautiful. . . .Probably no portion of the visitor's experience at Put-in-Bay is so dream like and enchanting as a rowboat ride around Gibraltar when the harvest moon--newly risen--traces its wide pathway across the waters, silvering its waves, intensifying the shadows among arched and caverned rocks, and bringing into bold prominence every jutting crag. Wierdly white among huge fallen rocks lie the moonbeams. They thread the Needle's Eye, penetrate the watery cavern at its base, and silver the heights of Perry's Lookout, capped by a flagstaff and a nearby old cannon from Perry's Battle. The moonbeams flood the white beaches of cloven shore niches, and soften the rugged outlines of the rock masses seamed and rent by wave and ice action in prehistoric times. The rock masses forming islands in miniature are covered each with tufted bluebells [harebells] and grasses, vines and mosses which, fostered into crevices, flourish luxuriantly without a particle of earth. With a faint breeze astir, may be heard within the chambered passages far under the rocks the reverberations of breaking swells. The tree-clad slope of Gibraltar appears sharply outlined against the clear sky, and the lights in and around its sheltered villa twinkle through the foliage.

Memories of Jay Cooke and Glimpses of His Island

Lydia J. Ryall

Sketches and Stories of the Lake Erie Islands, 1913, pp. 314, 317-319.

Having circumnavigated the Island, the visitor approaches the landing and moors his boat by the side of numerous others which are lying at the ample docks in front of an artistically constructed boathouse. From this point a gradually ascending walk leads upward along the Island's slope to its summit, where, amid the exquisite blendings of natural beauty with artistic embellishment, stands the old villa, its massive tower and walls of gray stone showing picturesquely through drooping branches. A monument of chaste design, commemorating Perry's Victory, occupies a conspicuous spot near the villa. A rustic summer house, bathing houses and pavillions, a cave down among the rocks, together with winding pathways and romantic nooks at every turn, conspire to render the place an ideal resort.

Within the wide entrance hall of the mansion hang two valuable old paintings, both representations of the battle of Lake Erie. A large room in the base of the octagonal tower is used as a library, many cases filled with books appearing. . . .The parlors are furnished handsomely and in faultless taste. Among the pictures adorning the walls is a novel and interesting photographic production representing four generations of the Cooke family, all bearing the same name, designated as follows: Jay Cooke, Sr., Jay Cooke, Jr., Jay Cooke the third, Jay Cooke the fourth, the latter an infant with long skirts, resting contentedly in the arms of its great-grandfather. . . . The family of Jay Cooke numbered four children, two sons and two daughters: Jay Cooke, Jr., Rev. Henry R. Cooke, Mrs. Charles Barney, and Mrs. Butler, all of whom have families of their own, and with them spend a portion of each summer at Gibraltar.

Of black bass fishing Mr. Cooke was especially fond, and his unrivalled success in the pursuit of this game fish won him renown among the island denizens. For his fishing cruises Mr. Cooke usually chartered a tug, together with row boats, oarsmen, and ample provision, and that he and members of his party, including the boatmen, had a good time, goes without saying. Most of the fish taken were given to the oarsmen, or divided into lots and distributed among the island people.

Famous Old Castle of Jay Cooke

Anonymous

Sandusky Register, Centennial Edition, Third Section, 31 December 1922, p. 5.

A few miles from the southern shore of Lake Erie, on the highest portion of the pile of rocks, raising out of the waters of Put-in-Bay, known as Gibraltar Island, stands today, still intact, though untennated, the large, turreted gray house of Sandusky limestone, built in 1865 by Jay Cooke, the distinguished financier of the Civil War. Known as his "Castle," it was for so many years the summer house of his family, and the scene of many gay and carefree gatherings of the most distinguished visitors of the time.

Jay Cooke died on February 16, 1905, and his last visit to the Island dates back to the previous summer, but the house is kept just as he left it, with all its furnishings intact. It is thought that the government will eventually purchase as a museum this relic of an august past, so closely related to the history of the nation as a whole, and thus preserve the treasures of the mansion as a memorial to Jay Cooke.

Of the importance of the personality of Jay Cooke in the troubled days of the Civil War, and the magnitude of his achievement for the nation in successfully financing the campaign of the Union, the present generation is perhaps not so vividly aware as was the past. Both Grant and Lincoln reiterate the assertion in their correspondence that the victory could never have been won without his assistance. The former wrote to the banker in the crisis of the conflict: "You are doing more than all the generals of the Union Army, for without your aid we could not fight."

The story of his life is generally known. Born in Cooke's Corners, now North Monroeville, near Sandusky, in 1821, as the son of Eleutheros Cooke, who was later representative in Congress, he received his education in Sandusky and had there, too, his first business experience. At an early age, he went east, and found in the banking house of Clark & Co., in 1838, the calling to which he was particularly adapted. In the course of a few years he had gained advancement to a partnership, made an independent fortune and finally in 1858, retired, having accumulated the experience whichpaved the way for his work in the Civil War.

The drives for Liberty and Victory loans in the years 1917 and 1918 utilized a system of universal publicity, through the press, branch agencies, placcards, circulars, and personal salesmanship, with which the public has long been familiar. It it is not generally known, however, that the originator of this intricate organization was Jay Cooke, who in the early sixties revolutionized the methods of floating government bonds and spent more than a million dollars in advertising, to effect the sale of papers to the amount of $2,000,000,000. Mr. Cooke was also instrumental in establishing the national banking system by the legislation of 1863.

It was almost in the shadow of these great happenings, that the Castle on Gibraltar Island was planned and built in 1865, to afford a measure of rest and recreation by the busy man of affairs on a spot near to the place of his birth, and endeared to him by early memories.

The *Detroit Saturday Night* printed on November 4, 1922, a personal impression of a visit to the Jay Cooke mansion by Harlan E. Babcock, with some historical reminiscences. "The work," Mr. Babcock says describing the completion of the house, "was finished early in 1865 when the 'Castle' received its first party of visitors and a memorable house-warming it is said to have been, with Jay Cooke and his wife as host and hostess. The guests were distinguished Washingtonians and relatives and friends from Sandusky."

"Each year in May, Jay Cooke went with his family to remain three weeks at his Gibraltar home, which became nationally famous. He returned there late in September or early in October for an outing of similar length, and during these periods the house was filled to overflowing with relatives, business partners, and friends and their families, particularly if they were fishermen, able to share his own enthusiasm for the Waltonian report. At such times came Chief Justice Solomon P. Chase; Hon. F. E. Spinner, Treasurer of the United States; Ohio Senator and Mrs. John Sherman; Gov. and Mrs. Rutherford B. Hayes, the latter a relative of the Cooke family; Rev. T. DeWitt Talmadge, widely known Pastor of Brooklyn Tabernacle; Senator Pomeroy; Civil War Gen. and Mrs. William T. Sherman; Gen. J. K. Moorehead of Pittsburgh; and many others of note.

"Here upon the waters by day and around the cheery open fires at night, while the lake roared and wind soughed in the boughs of the trees, there was much happiness. The rooms, with wide windows and massive doors, all bordered with heavy mouldings, had an air of large simplicity. The library, the first-story tower room, was stored with standard works, and the bed rooms above it, surveying the lake, were the choicest of slumber places."

Porches on the side toward Put-in-Bay Harbor (upper).

Porches on the Side Toward Lake Erie (lower).

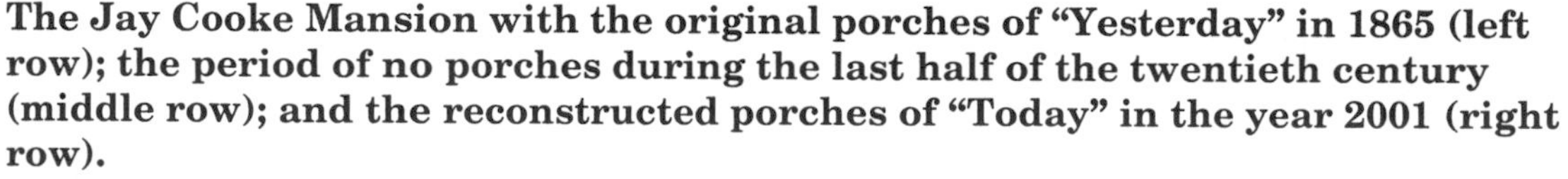

The Jay Cooke Mansion with the original porches of "Yesterday" in 1865 (left row); the period of no porches during the last half of the twentieth century (middle row); and the reconstructed porches of "Today" in the year 2001 (right row).

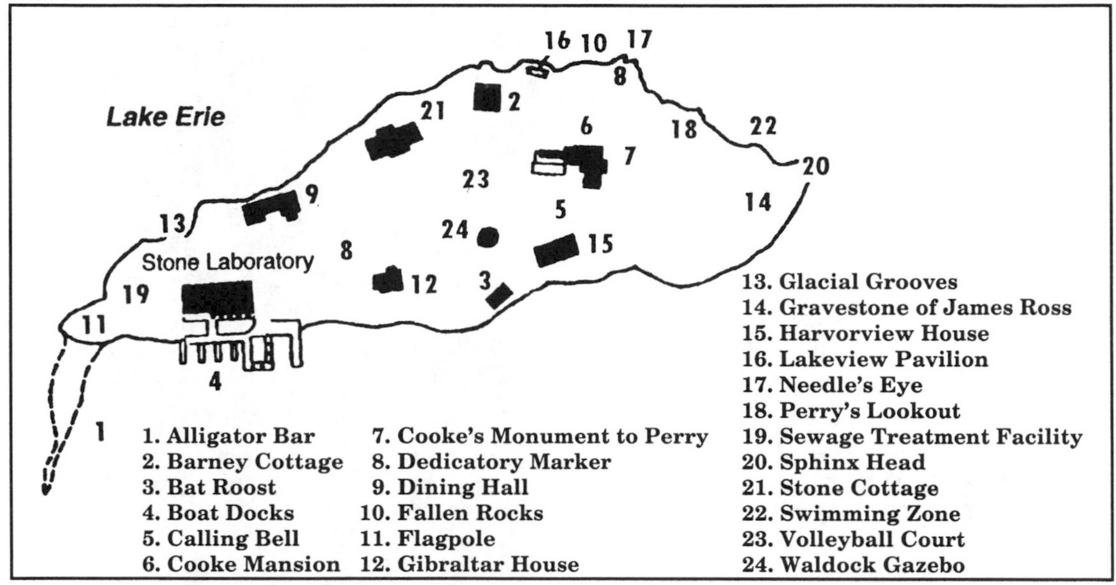

Map of Gibraltar Island with locations and names of buildings and natural features in the year 2001.

A Permanent Home for the O.S.U. Lake Laboratory

When Dr. Raymond C. Osburn became chairman of the Department of Zoology and Entomology at The Ohio State University in 1917, he arranged to have the function of University's Lake Laboratory relocated to South Bass Island. The Laboratory, the site of summer field studies for students in the biological sciences, was moved from the University's own building on leased land at Cedar Point to the State Fish Hatchery at Put-in-Bay. Beginning in 1918 classes were held during the summer months in the upper story of the Hatchery Building, when these rooms were not in use for hatchery operations. According to Director Osburn, the classroom space was quite inadequate, and the living quarters for the students that was available in nearby housing was miserable. From the time that Prof. Osburn became Director of the Lake Laboratory in 1919, he longingly eyed the unoccupied nearby Gibraltar Island as a possible future and permanent Laboratory home. He also had the concurrence of this idea from his core teaching faculty at the Laboratory. In a reminiscence statement written in 1946, Osburn described how he was able to acquire Gibraltar Island for the University's Lake Laboratory.

50-Years of Lab History

Raymond C. Osburn

Archives, The Ohio State University.
Handwritten Manuscript, 1946

Fifty years ago, at this time in 1896, I was one of the first two students at the Lake Laboratory, which had just been established in Sandusky by Professor David S. Kellicott. . . .When I returned to The Ohio State University in 1917 to take the duties of the chairmanship of the Department of Zoology and Entomology, I found that the Laboratory, which had been transferred to Cedar Point in 1903, could no longer be used, so I began at once to look for a better situation. Several of my biological colleagues at the University advised me to give it up as "it could never amount to anything." However, my many years of experience at summer laboratories, . . ., had well inoculated me with the idea of the value of biological laboratories. I could not give up the idea of a laboratory for fresh water biological research and teaching.

I knew of the earlier work of Jacob Reighard of Michigan and Henry B. Ward of Illinois in the Lake Erie region (Chapter 8), and they assured me that it was the richest region they knew for biological work, so when I became director in 1919, I arranged to have the Laboratory transferred from Cedar Point to the State Fish Hatchery on South Bass Island. During the summer months, the upper story of the Hatchery was not in use, but we held classes there although it really was inadequate, and our living quarters were miserable. The attendance, nevertheless, increased to such an extent that in a few years, we were literally "bursting out at the seams."

Raymond C. Osburn (1872-1955), Laboratory Director (1919-1936).

"What to do was a serious problem. I finally learned that the Island of Gibraltar might be bought from the heirs of Jay Cooke, but how to finance the purchase was a grave difficulty. After much cerebrating I finally presented the matter to Mr. Julius Stone of Columbus for advice in interesting some good angel in presenting it as a memorial. I remember well my conversation with Mr. Stone and his reaction. After asking me many keen questions he said "I have always felt that the future of humanity depends upon biological investigation and have always wanted to do something worth while for biological research. You go ahead and see what kind of dicker you can get out of the owners of Gibraltar Island. . . ."

The purchase was consummated in June 1925, too late for us to make use of the place that summer. The old wooden buildings on the Island, now removed, were used for laboratory work in the summer of 1926. The basement of the present brick laboratory building was erected by the use of emergency funds, for use in 1927 and 1928, and the structure completed in time to be dedicated in June 1929. That year and the next one were the peak years of attendance, with 50 and 55 graduate students. Then the lean years of the depression hit the young teachers and graduate students and the attendance dropped.

It had always been a part of our plan to have a permanent director and research personnel to carry on investigations throughout the year, and in 1932 the details of the project were prepared for the action of the Board of Trustees of the University. The day before the Trustees were to meet President Rightmire called me into his office to say that the finances of the University were in such shape that it did not seem advisable to proceed at that time, and asked me if I would consent to serve on the summer plan until things looked better.

My years were interesting ones, including the transfer of the Laboratory to Put-in-Bay, its growth from almost nothing at the end of World War I, the development of the facility and especially the contact with so many fine students from every state in the Union. I hesitate to say how many doctor's and especially master's degrees have been completed on the work begun, or completed here. Approximately 200 research papers have been published in connection with the work done at this Laboratory by 1946.

Though much hard work has been completed, occasional disappointments have occurred. I am happy to have had a part in the development of this institution. Only a few students were here the past four years during World War II, and the present group is small, but attendance should increase again. This is the pleasantest place I have ever worked in the summer, and the richness of the fauna and flora will continue to provide research problems indefinitely. Fifty years is a considerable period in the life of a man, but for an institution it is of little consequence, and I feel confident that the next 50 years will become more productive in research and study than have been the past fifty years.

Gibraltar Island Given To O.S.U. By Columbus Man

James E. Pollard

Sandusky Daily Register,
21 June 1925, p. 1; *OSU Monthly* 16(9):7-0. 1925. June.

Gift to The Ohio State University of historic Gibraltar Island in Lake Erie as the site for a biological laboratory was announced at Columbus Saturday. The donor is Julius F. Stone, Columbus manufacturer, and a member of the University Board of Trustees.

The Island, consisting of approximately six acres, has been in possession of the family of Jay Cooke, the famous Civil War financier and native of Sandusky, for more than 60 years. It contains the famous stone castle-like Jay Cooke mansion of more than 20 rooms, a six-room bungalow, and several smaller structures. The names of the Island and mansion will be retained by the University.

Gibraltar Island, at the entrance to Put-in-Bay, was used as a lookout station by Oliver

Hazard Perry during the War of 1812. Tradition has it that it was from the cliff at the eastern end of the Island that the approach of the British fleet was discovered, and Perry promptly sailed out to give it battle. . . .The Cooke mansion was built in 1864-65, as the Civil War was coming to a close. Part of the lumber and millwork used in construction temporarily fell into the hands of the Confederacy during that War. Some of the construction material is supposed to have been aboard the *Island Queen* when the vessel, plying from Sandusky to the islands on 19 September 1864, was captured by John Y. Beall, the Confederate raider and his associates. The *Island Queen* was then set adrift and became grounded in 10 feet of water upon Chickanola Reef off Ballast Island. The capture was one of several events that occurred as part of the plot to free the Confederate prisoners on Johnson's Island in Sandusky Bay.

Aquisition of Gibraltar Island, in the opinion of Prof. Raymond C. Osburn, Director of the Laboratory since 1918, will afford the University an opportunity for the work "unequalled in the middle west." It will permit more than twice as many students to attend as could be accommodated in the old quarters on the second floor of the State Fish Hatchery. The conditions for work at Gibraltar Island, Director Osburn believes, are unsurpassed. "Lake Erie," he says, "is the richest of all the Great Lakes for laboratory purposes. At slight cost the buildings now on the Island can be adapted to the needs of the Laboratory and its staff." It is probable that fifty students, besides the instructional staff, can be accommodated at the new site. Only advanced undergraduates and graduate courses are offered, and research work is especially stressed at the Lake Laboratory.

The Island is well wooded, has its own water supply and lighting facilities, is easily accessible from every direction, and because of the deep water surrounding it, is assured of freedom from pollution. All of the buildings on the Island are furnished.

Julius F. Stone (1855-1947), Laboratory Donor.

While no statement was made as to the purchase price, it is known that the gift is the second largest ever made to the University. It is one of a number Mr. Stone has made to the institution over a long period of years.

Mr. Stone's only condition is that Gibraltar Island shall remain the property of the University and its use be devoted to teaching and research as a permanent site for the Lake Laboratory. In his formal offer to the Board of Trustees, Mr. Stone said he had a desire to see the University contribute largely to the conservation of the natural resources of the Great Lakes.

References:

Chapter Eleven, Gibraltar Island
II. The Years During and Since Jay Cooke

DeCregorio, William A. 1979. "He Paid Abe Lincoln's Bills: Ohio Tycoon Jay Cooke Drove the Union Bandwagon." *The Columbus Dispatch Magazine*, 10 June, pp. 51-53.

Frohman, Charles E. 1971. "Gibraltar Island," pp. 37-43. *In Put-in-Bay: Its History*. The Ohio Historical Society, Columbus. viii, 156 pp.

Hallock II, S. N. 1982. "Ohio's Gibraltar." *The Columbus Dispatch Magazine*, 5 September, pp. 10-11.

Langlois, Thomas H. 1951. "Jay Cooke and his mansion on Gibraltar Island." *Toledo Blade Pictorial*. 4 March, pp. 16-17.

Larson, Henrietta M. 1936. *Jay Cooke: Private Banker*. Harvard University Press, Cambridge. xvii, 512 pp.

Moizuk, Ruth Dickerman. [1968]. "Put-in-Bay, Gibraltar and Jay Cooke," pp. 33-35. *In The Put-in-Bay Story Told from the Top-of-the-Rock*. Published by the author. 48 pp.

Oberholtzer, Ellis Paxson. 1907. *Jay Cooke: Financier of the Civil War*. George W. Jacobs & Co., Philadelphia. Volume 1, xi, 658 pp; Volume 2, vi, 590 pp.

Pollard, James E. 1935. *The Journal of Jay Cooke or The Gibraltar Records 1865-1905*. The Ohio State University Press, Columbus. xi, 359 pp.

Ryall, Lydia J. 1913. "Memories of Jay Cooke and Glimpses of His Island Stronghold," pp. 305-320. *In Sketches and Stories of the Lake Erie Islands*. The American Publishers Co., Norwalk. vi, 546 pp. (Perry Centennial Edition, 1813-1913).

Sayers, Isabelle S. 1976. "Cooke's Pride." *The Columbus Dispatch Magazine*, 14 March, p. 47.

Thorndale, Theresa. 1898. "Castled Gibraltar and Its Lord," pp. 271-278. *In Sketches and Stories of the Lake Erie Islands*. I. F. Mack & Brother, Sandusky. v, 379 pp. (Souvenir Volume).

Death of James Fullerton, "Uncle Jimmy," from Injuries Received in the *Eagle* Explosion

Anonymous

Sandusky Daily Register,
25 May 1882, p. 4.

Marker in Crown Hill Cemetery for "Uncle Jimmie" (1813-1882).

James Fullerton, of Ballast Island, the old man who was so terribly scalded in the steamer *American Eagle* explosion, died at the Bing House in Sandusky yesterday morning [24 May 1882] about 10 o'clock, making the fifth death that has resulted from that accident. Fullerton was a native of Ireland. He had resided on Ballast Island for a number of years. When a party of Cleveland gentlemen purchased that Island seven years ago "Uncle Jimmy," as he was familiarly called, was its only resident. The Cleveland parties erected a club house and laid out grounds on the Island, and "Uncle Jimmy" was given general supervision of the establishment and its surroundings. He was of kind and obliging disposition, was always faithful to his trust, and soon became a general favorite with the club and their numerous guests at the Island.

On last Thursday morning "Uncle Jimmy" came to this city from Ballast Island to make some purchases and intended returning on the steamer *Jay Cooke* with Mrs. George Gardner and Mrs. James Barnett, of Cleveland, who had come here to go over on that boat to the club house, but he was unfortunately induced by a friend to take passage on the *Eagle*. When the boiler of that boat exploded he was in the cabin and was most frightfully scalded. Mr. George W. Gardner and General James Barnett, of Cleveland, members of the Ballast Island Club, were notified yesterday of his death and came here last evening to arrange for the interment of the remains. A brief funeral service will be held here this morning and the body will be taken to Put-in-Bay for burial in Crown Hill Cemetery. The deceased [Born 1813] was in his seventy-ninth year and has no near relatives in this country.

CHAPTER TWELVE

Theresa Thorndale: Adventures and Romance

Theresa Thorndale's book, *Sketches and Stories of the Erie Islands* (1898) has been viewed by some of today's serious historians as a book for historic inaccuracy. For example, the late Robert J. Dodge, historian and author of *Isolated Splendor: Put-in-Bay and South Bass Island* (1975), wrote in the *Put-in-Bay Gazette* (May 1986, p. 12) that he considered Miss Thorndale "to be unreliable as an historian." Rather than totally dismiss her work, the serious historian, who intensely studies her book and who is already acquainted with much of the island's history, should be able to separate fact from fiction, and to set apart her novel stories from accurate news of that time period. With reference to the immediate South Bass Island area, her book chapters on Put-in-Bay history, Perry's Victory, Capture of the Steamers *Island Queen* and *Philo Parsons*, Hotel Victory, Pen Sketches of the Brown brothers, Gibraltar Island, Geological Features and Caves, and the Federal Fish Hatchery are based on facts of their time, many of which were personally obtained by her through interviews and/or trips to the sites. Now coupled with her newspaper stories, many of which are reproduced in the preceeding chapters of this book, what more factual historical material can be expected of these times at this place. It becomes the duty then of the historian to separate the facts from the fiction, and draw one's own conclusions. In this book, factual information has largely been sought in Miss Thorndale's articles, corrected if necessary, and then reprinted. The following two stories written by Theresa Thorndale are reproduced here from her book. They are believed to be autobiographical, but with her name changed. Both stories are of adventures in which Miss Thorndale participated or certainly could have participated.

Under A Steamer's Headlights: Two Silly Girls and Their Adventures

Theresa Thorndale

Sketches and Stories of the Lake Erie Islands, 1898, pp. 111-118.

To begin, I may state incidentally that I was born and bred in a section of country lying well inland, and until a few weeks previous to the occurrence which I am about to related, had never seen a boat, save the tiny models in toy shops nor a body of water bigger than "Taggart's mill pond." I experienced then a rapture inexpressible when first I sighted Lake Erie, wide rolling in all the reflected blue and golden glory of summer skies. And when in amongst the sleeping islands, emerald dotting her broad bosom, I was borne and sighted the shifting sails, grey and white, of cruising vessels, and the pretty painted pleasure craft gently rocking on the bay, the scene impressed me like a dream. I questioned my reason as to whether the pictures were real, and wondered whether the "Isles of Greece," where "burning Sappho loved and sung," were lovelier than these. The bulk of my knowledge concerning great waters had been gleaned from poetry and fiction and I was proportionately susceptible to romantic impressions. The depth and mystery of the blue expanse where it met and blended with the horizon was to me awe-inspiring, and when the skies darkened and the waters turned green and black with storm, and turbulent waves thundered among caverned rocks, I was fascinated by the sublimity of a scene so new and novel.

I loved, feared and venerated the *Neptune* of the inland seas and felt anxious to be on a friendly footing with this particular deity, hoping thereby to gain the freedom of his wide domain. Sailing and rowing afforded attractions irresistible which I was eager to enjoy, but was afraid of the water. A thought of its depth and the thinness of the boat's sides between it and me caused a choking sensation in my throat. With a trusty oarsman I felt no especial timidity, though still there remained an aching void which could only be filled by a personal and practical knowledge of boats and oars. To obtain complete satisfaction I must learn to row. Once formed, the idea grew and strengthened, and one afternoon I found myself on a little wharf that projected into the waters of a quiet cove. The spot was romantic. The surface dimples were flashing gold and crimson from the westering sun and the faintest of zephyrs stirred the shore trees. Moored to the cribbing was a skiff, blue and white painted, in which lay a pair of oars.

"Now it's your time," something whispered. I obediently loosened the chain which held it and slipped down the cribbing into the boat. The water, as seen by the pebbled bottom, was but two or three feet in depth.

"Should I fall in or the boat capsize I can't very well drown, because there isn't water enough." The thought gave me courage.

Cautiously adjusting row-locks and oars, I was soon in the midst of my experiment. I kept the boat for a time in water shallow enough to wade, in case of wreckage. Having studied the movement of oarsmen I now endeavored to imitate, but sometimes my right oar struck bottom in a most provoking manner, while the left barely skimmed the surface, and vice versa. Still the boat moved and I was exultant, for I could row. Little or nothing knew I, it is true, about feathering, backing and curvetting, and having lived on a farm, might have turned a two horse wagon in far less time and space than I should have required to turn a boat; still I got along amazingly — so I thought — diffidence began evaporating and boldness grew apace. I resolved to pull into deep water, a daring venture, but the boat showed no signs of treachery or insubordination. Confidence in myself, and it became stronger, my strokes bolder, if not more dextrous, and I ventured still farther until the boat was lifted by the gentle roll of undulating swells from the westward. How delightful! The motion was like swinging, with space illimitable above and below. Read and his exquisite Neapolitan song came to mind, and a stanza went jingling though my brain. I sang, "Rocking on the Billows," "Song of the Sea," and "Life on the Ocean Wave," and thought of Grace Darling and in my soul emulated her daring spirit. Thus I found myself luxuriating in a heaven of my own creation, when a young woman, an acquaintance, appeared on the shore. I invited her to join me, and nothing loth, she accepted. With some difficulty I got the boat headed landward, and later, we together quaffed nectar to the fresh water *Neptune*.

Arra evinced a slight distrust of my abilities, when she learned that I was handling the oars for the first time. However, I was the better of the two, since she had never pulled an oar, and never had indulged aspirations along the oar pulling line. There was no danger, obviously, of Arra usurping my place, so I laughed at her fears, sang "Bounding Billows," and she became more courageous.

I was growing heroic to a painful degree, and having like Alexander conquered the world, yearned for more worlds to conquer, when an idea flashed upon me dazzling with its brilliancy. I had long wanted to visit an adjacent island lying in the distance; "why not now?"

My companion thought it a risky undertaking and objected, but I overruled her objections and we started.

"We can easily get there and back again before dark," I observed, and so thought, but had miscalculated both the distance and my ability as an oars woman. Had our course been direct, we might have progressed favorably, but I knew nothing about fixing a point on shore by which to keep the boat in line, so Arra kept constantly bothering me with —

"You're too far to the right, " or "You're too far to the left" — until I ardently longed to box her ears, but contented myself with the demand: "Who is rowing this boat?"

We thus described a course which might have suggested the "worm" fence seen in rural districts.

Outside we encountered a passing steamer. I was somewhat alarmed, having heard of small boats being run down by larger craft; but we got by without difficulty, and my fear of steamers was at once dissipated.

The sun went down under a cloud which rose to meet it, and we missed the sunset scene which we had previously anticipated. Other clouds came up and overspread the sky. Twilight shades were gathering, and still we had not reached our destination.

"It seems as though we should never get there," observed Arra.

"We're bound to get there," I replied, buckling in energetically. It was beginning to get dark when we reached the island,

"Let's not land," pleaded Arra nervously. "Nobody lives there but an old hermit, and I'm afraid."

Now, on this bit of terra firma was an old tree with a big eagle's nest. The nest was the nearest

Ballast Island, with two girls, a rowboat, rocky cliffs, and a gravel beach.

The Steamer, *Jay Cooke*.

approach to an eagle I had ever known, and I could ill brook the disappointment of not seeing it. Once more, then, I overruled Arra's objections, and we quietly beached the boat.

"We'll arm ourselves with sticks, and if the hermit comes out of his hut yonder we'll go for him."

I seized a fragment of ship timber that had washed ashore. Arra picked up a broken lath, also tossed up by the waves, and we quietly stole along a gravelly stretch, and were soon beneath the eagle tree. The big nest on its top, outlined against the sky, was built of twigs and small limbs of trees. After a moment's contemplation thereof, we hastened back to our boat.

"Dear me, how dark it is getting, but never mind, we're homeward bound."

I adjusted the oars and we were off. There was no moon, and only an occasional star appeared through the cloud rifts. The zephyr had freshened to a breeze, a strong current was setting through the channel, and we made even slower progress than when coming.

"I'd like to know what ails this old boat, I can't keep it straight!" It did behave very badly with the current against it. My hands, too, were blistered, and I was getting very tired, but I steered as well as I could by a light gleaming from a cottage window in the cove from which we had started. To while the tedium, we began telling stories. I was in the midst of a narration, when Arra interrupted me.

"Say, we had better hurry and get out of the way, the *Jay Cooke* is coming."

"I don't care anything about the *Jay Cooke*," I replied and resumed my story.

A few minutes passed, and Arra again poked me up with the remark:

"I think you'd better keep the boat straight and row faster; the steamer is not far off, and coming right this way."

"Do let her come; we're here first."

I would not deign a look, and so persistently returned to my story. I did not finish it, however, for Arra again broke in:

"If you don't row faster we'll be run down, just as sure as the world! It's so dark they can't see us, and she's coming straight toward us."

The churning of the steamer's big wheels did sound ominously near, and for the first time I turned and looked. She was indeed but a short distance away, and I saw that we were directly in her course, her port and starboard lights glaring full upon us. I felt a sudden alarm, but confident of being able to clear her, began pulling with all my might. At that place, however, the channel curved visibly to avoid hidden rocks, and veering to starboard, the steamer appeared to follow us. My alarm grew, while strength began failing. My hands trembled, and despite every exertion the progress of the boat was scarcely perceptible. The steamer was now but a few yards distant, and coming at full speed. The thunder of her great wheels sounded frightful, and her red and green eyes blazed down upon us like those of a monster.

I spoke not a word, but my thoughts were all awhirl.

"She is following us; we must turn and row the opposite way!" flashed through my mind.

"No, there's but a moment left; before I can turn the boat she will have passed over us!" flashed back.

I made another effort to send the boat forward, but my hands were nerveless.

"'Tis useless; we are lost! Another instant and we shall be under her wheels! In the darkness her crew will never know, and we shall be left to our fate."

These were some of the thoughts that spun through my brain while the red and green eyes of the monster loomed above us, holding mind by the spell of their fascination. Already life and consciousness seemed slipping away. She was upon us. We were directly under her bow and awaiting the final shock when — was it luck or Providence? — she suddenly veered. Whether by accident or whether the pilot sighted the struggling boat I will probably never know, but an instant turn of the helm "hard a-port" saved us by a hair's breadth. The steamer passed us close; our boat trembled and was nearly swamped by the great waves from her wheels. It was some moments before we fulled recovered our senses. The steamer was then far past, and taking the oars, which had fallen from my hands, I headed the aimlessly drifting boat toward our destination.

"I hope after this experience you'll know better than to toy with steamers."

Arra spoke wrathfully and reproachfully, but thoroughly humiliated I answered never a word. I heard, nevertheless, and heeded her wise counsel, and will continue to heed it to the end of my days.

Romance of the Ice Plains

Theresa Thorndale

Sketches and Stories of the Lake Erie Islands, 1898, pp. 146-154.

A young country girl of poetic temperament and romantic ideas was Nettie Blake. Anything real or imaginary, combining in its make-up a semblance of novelty or variety, appealed to her sensibility. With these natural tendencies, she was fond, intensely fond, of sight-seeing and adventure; but her poor little life had been narrowed down to the limits of a very common-place neighborhood, burrowed like a partidge nest in the midst of an extensive farming district.

A little brown house on her father's little farm was the only home that Nettie had ever known, and although very comfortable, and she loved in a general way its surroundings, the girl longed for a change — the more ardently longed when the family newspaper made its weekly visitations to inform her concerning the great world and its doings; of its stir and enterprise, its strange sights, its wide prospects, and its panoramic scenes of beauty and magnificence. In novels, too, she had read — while her mother softly chided — about the great world's heroes and heroines; of its storied beauty and bravery, bold adventure and tragic situation, chivalrous deeds and daring — until two worlds instead of one grew upon her consciousness: the one apparent to outer sense, the other to an inner perception; the one real, the other ideal.

The people of the neighborhood were old-fashioned, slow, plodding rustics, prosaic in ideas, uncultured in manners. They read little, and thought and cared less concerning matters beyond the affairs of everyday life, from duties and neighborhood gossip.

Two or three little villages were within reach of Nettie's home, but they were dull, poky places. Even the largest and liveliest seemed half asleep. Only twice could she remember having seen the place fully awake — once when "Barnum's Greatest Show on Earth" chanced to strike it like the tail of a great comet, driving the inhabitants nearly frantic with excitement; then again when the governor of the state, an ex-member of the legislature and the town mayor addressed a political gathering on the square, and a brass band played "Hail Columbia" and "Marching Through Georgia." On these important occasions, as she remembered, all the farmers for miles around had flocked to town with wives, children and sweethearts, and all the roads approaching were lined with "buck-boards," piano box buggies and big grain wagons drawn by heavy farm horses, and the country had virtually taken possession of the town. People congregated upon the streets, crowding densely the narrow pavements, and forming a wondrous conglomeration, with rustic humanity largely in preponderance. Country youths appeared in every style of apparel, from blue drilling overalls and cowhide boots to more pretentious suits, showy neckwear and abundant jewelry. Lanky, wide-mouthed specimens of the *genus homo* were there, with frowsy locks and hayseed clinging to their coat collars. They rolled from cheek to cheek prodigious quids and expectorated freely — now and then sending up a vociferous "hip, hip, hurrah."

"Look at the goslings!"

Nettie was in the crowd and her attention was attracted by this uncomplimentary observation. The "goslings" indicated proved to be a neighbor's sons, and she mentally compared them with her ideal heroes, was disgusted at the contrast and went home more dissatisfied than ever. How she detested these common place "clodhoppers." True, they were good, honest fellows, but she ached to see a real hero — one who could achieve something gallant besides steering a cultivator, hoeing corn and cracking a whip behind a team of plow horses. For relief, Nettie turned to mother Nature, but this usually beneficent dame had provided but sparingly for hungry-eyed Nettie Blake, as the scenery about her home was tame and uninteresting. Still there were a few redeeming traits in the landscape. "Walnut Ridge" lay a mile to eastward, which, with the morning sun touching its forests, and tinging its vapors, formed to her a sort of inspiration. It overlooked vast stretches of country upon the other side, and she often climbed its summit to catch, as it were, glimpses of the Beulah of her dreams. Beyond it swept the waters of "Eagle Creek," a very quiet stream at its ordinary level, but somewhat boisterous when on the rampage. Nettie took as kindly to water as does the wild duck, and "Eagle Creek" was to her a source of solace in the summer season. With her girl companions she fished and bathed in its waters, and loitered along its banks of pebble and shale, watching the swift current and wishing that upon it she might drift, with the sticks and leaves, out to the great ocean and the great world which is encompassed. Poor little Nettie!

In winter when the stream was frozen and the trees on "Walnut Ridge" were bare and colorless, her dissatisfaction grew apace. A meager supply of literature afforded some relief, and she liked to talk of what she read, but Mistress Blake was too busy with household cares to listen, and old man Blake would only wrinkle his forehead, and say as how "gals ought to let such rubbish alone an' 'tend to their work."

To her most intimate friend and associate, Mandy Johns, who was several years older than she, Nettie ventured to introduce a book of travels, but Mandy was piercing a quilt of the "wild goose chase" pattern, and lost all connection of what her companion was saying.

Amanda has been piercing quilts for the last ten years. Quilt-piercing was her especial fad, her one accomplishment, and she pursued it with astonishing pertinacity — never so marked as since Ben Peters had begun paying her attention. She was evidently indulging hopes matrimonial — which if not realized would be no fault of hers — and all that she could find of any earthly interest to talk about was her quilts and Ben Peters.

A vision of Ben's red hair, coarse hands, long legs and number thirteen boots rose before Nettie, and in disgust she turned to "old Gregory" the cat. He was the only created being that showed her any appreciation. This patriarchal feline always listened to her with at least respectful attention.

It was under these trying circumstances that Nettie longed for "the wings of a dove that she might fly away to some secluded isle where Mandy's quilts and Ben Peters' big feet might never intrude," and, as if in response to her wish, there came a letter from some distant relatives containing an invitation to visit them. They lived on an island of the lake archipelago, and now that the backbone of winter was nearly broken and the steamer beginning to run, Nettie must come and make them a visit —so the letter read. After some demur on the part of her parents, the girl secured permission to go. She had never been over fifteen miles from home and her heart was all aflutter with expectation, though the undertaking seemed formidable. "Two hundred miles to Lake Erie and a trip by steamer. Just think of it!" Now she should see something of the big world, its big waters and big enterprises, and perhaps meet some of its big heroes.

Nettie required no very elaborate preparations for her visit, and so after a fifteen miles' drive to the nearest railway station, and a few hours' ride on the through express, she found herself boarding a small iron-clad steamer at Sandusky. She gazed in wonder at this, the first object of the kind her eyes had ever beheld, and had she been informed that the craft was a first-class ocean liner, never a suspicion of the difference would have suggested itself, so impressed was she with its size and dignity. Imagine her astonishment, however, to find the lake a vast outreaching plain of ice with no apparent boundary. All the ice that had ever formed on "Eagle Creek" was not a circumstance compared with this gigantic sweep. She had no idea that Lake Erie was so big — comfortably big — and yet it formed but a small part of the big world. Then as the staunch craft under a full head of steam drove into the great floes, and the cabin windows rattled, and the strong timbers quivered from bot to stern, and the chandeliers overhead swung to and fro, Nettie became frightened. "What if the steamer should stick fast or go down in this awful crush?"

Poor little Nettie! So this was seeing the world. Already a dreadful homesick feeling was creeping over her. Had the girl's parents know the condition of the lake they would not have permitted her to come — of this she felt assured — and now she should probably never see home again, nor parents, nor Eagle Creek, nor "old Gregory." Even Mandy's quilts and Ben Peters' ungainly presence would have been a solace to Nettie in this awful crisis — poor little girl. She would have cried had she not been too frightened to shed tears; and how she lived through those long hours of suspense she hardly knew, while heavy clouds of smoke and rushing steam poured from the chimneys, blackened the sky, and the powerful engines groaned with their enforced labor, and the steamer's armored prow butted heavily into masses of drift many feet in thickness. Sometimes the steamer struck with such force, and came to a stop with such a shock as to throw the passengers from their seats. Then with reversed engines she would back for some distance, and again drive headlong into the obstruction, while the great floes seamed and buldged and the water churned into foam by her wheel spouted up the sides. At such times Nettie would thrust her fingers into her ears to shut out the horrible, crushing, grinding noises. They touched at one of the islands where it was found necessary to repair some slight damage sustained by the steamer in her scrimmage with the ice. This done, they continued on her way.

Nettie was approaching her destination, but when still a half mile from shore, the steamer blew her whistle and came to a sudden stop. The captain entered the cabin. Said he:

"We shall not be able to make port, owing to the heavy ice drifts, and will be obliged to put off passengers and freight where we are."

A new and greater terror seized Nettie. How dreadful to be put off on the treacherous ice so far from shore!

What was to become of her? With palpitating heart she followed the cabin passengers down a flight of stairs to the lower deck. On reaching the gangway she saw groups of islanders coming out over the ice to meet the steamer, forming what seemed to her a strange procession, some walking, others upon skates with large triangular sails in their hands, by the aid of which they moved very rapidly. There were objects too that looked like great V shaped sleds, having masts all aflap with white canvas and aflutter with bright flags and streamers, the upper portion resembling the boats she had seen in pictures; there were coming towards them with astonishing swiftness. There were sleighs, too, and cutters with horses attached and men and boys with large hand sleds. This spectacle was reassuring and, assisted by one of the deck hands, Nettie passed down the wide plank to the frozen channel surface.

"Are you Nettie Blake?" queried a young lady."

"I am, and you are —"

"Alice Benton, your cousin."

"Oh, I am so glad, I've had such an awful time!" exclaimed Nettie crying for joy.

"This last cold snap had made the ice pretty tough again; we meant to have written you to wait until the ice broke up a little, but you got through all right, so it don't make any difference." We thought that you might come today, so we drove out to meet you — here is the cutter."

On the front seat holding the reins was seated a young man whom Alice introduced as her adopted brother Fred. He had dark hair, fine dark eyes, and intelligent countenance and pleasing manners, but so queerly dressed. His attire was of pale yellow canvas, with wide flapping trousers, loose, bagging blouse, and a hat termed a "sou'wester." All sailors and fishermen wore them — Alice informed her —and as Fred had figured as mate on an upper lake transportation vessel, his dress only signified his calling.

The "bold sailor boy" of the girl's romantic dreams had become a living reality, and the ugly, yellow oil suit was proportionately transfigured.

What a refreshing change from plowmen in blue drilling, wood choppers with brawny fists and farm boys generally.

Nettie drew a sigh of relief when once again her feet touched terra firma, but the thought of being so far from home and upon a remote island caused a queer sensation, and yet how romantic it all seemed. She saw many objects which were new and novel to an inland dweller, but being very tired was glad of the rest afforded at the pleasant fireside and hospitable board of her relatives.

ENTRANCE TO CRYSTAL CAVE. U. S. MAIL arriving at Put-in-Bay Post Office. SCHOOL HOUSE at Put-in-Bay, South Bass Island.

CHAPTER THIRTEEN

South Bass "Island Jottings"
II. Caves, Mail Service, and Graduation

These introductory remarks from page 13 continue to discuss the revived activity responsible for more tourists coming to South Bass Island during the late 1970's. One of these reasons was that increased efforts to clean up Lake Erie were moving in a successful direction, and as vacationers realized more income for social spending, the popularity of boating, sailing, and fishing, especially for bass and walleye, began to bring more people to the Island. During summers of the 1980's, tourists of record numbers made visits to the Island. New shops opened, buildings were repaired and painted, new cottages were constructed, and the erection of new hotels were discussed and built. In the summer of 1987, the Perry Holiday first opened its door for business. Transportation to the Island is by two Ferry Boat Lines, the Miller Boat Line, a 20-minute trip from Catawba Point to the Lime Kiln Dock on the south shore, and the Put-in-Bay Boat Line, formerly a 1 1/2 hour trip from downtown Port Clinton to downtown Put-in-Bay can today be taken on the *Jet Express*, a trip of 22 minutes. Island Airlines flies from Port Clinton to the Island's airport in the southwest part of the Island. Transportation of many forms can be had on the Island—automobile, bus, bicycle, golf cart, cab, trolley, and moped, but no rental cars. Motorcycles are discouraged. A tour train departs from a depot in downtown Put-in-Bay for a narrated tour of the Island.

In the village and even elsewhere on the Island are restaurants, gift shops, with some of the latter specializing in marine antiques, souvenirs, candies, fudge, handcrafted jewelry and pottery, wood and metal sculptures, designer and resort clothes, needle-work, t-shirts, and kites. Many tourists find that the 10 bars located on the Island are of necessity. Among historic and educational sites to visit in addition to Perry's Memorial, are the Village Blacksmith Shop (established 1905), the Perry Cave and Crystal Cave (a strontium geode), Heineman's Winery, the ruins of the Hotel Victory site at the State Park, the Viking Longhouse, the State Fish Hatchery, and the Lake Erie Islands Historical

Society (established 1985). Special weekend events during summers are Memorial Day, Founders Day, Fourth of July, Interlake Yacht Association Sail and Power Boat Races, and Wine Festivals in the fall. Other summertime forms of recreation are swimming, boating, sailing, fishing, golfing, biking, picnicking, and walking. In winter, ice fishing, snowmobiling, ice sailing, and special holiday events take place.

Chapter Thirteen continues with additional South Bass "Island Jottings" by Theresa Thorndale, Put-in-Bay's news correspondant to the *Sandusky Register*. Her "Lost Stories of Yesterday" are concerned with the Caves, Mail Service, and Graduation on the Island. The only "Story of Today" is an account of graduation for the Class of 1989, Put-in-Bay High School. This story presents the contrasts from the two graduation programs of 100 years previous as reported by Theresa Thorndale.

Prof. Moseley Studies Flora; Explores Caves

Theresa Thorndale

Sandusky Weekly Register,
6 June 1894, p. 7.

Prof. Edwin L. Moseley, of the Sandusky High School, with his class in botany arrived here Saturday on board the Steamer *Erie*. The party partook of a picnic dinner in the grove, and made wide incursions into the kingdom of flora, returning with large spoils in the way of plant specimens and wood flowers. The botanists also paid a visit to Green Island.

Sandusky Weekly Register,
16 March 1898, p. 4.

Among the passengers on the *American Eagle* on Friday, March 11 was Prof. Edwin L. Moseley of the Sandusky High School, accompanied by two members of his class. The party came equipped with electric lighting apparatus, scuff suits, and a variously assorted set of scientific instruments for a proposed exploration in Perry's Cave, and a contemplated trip through one of the subterranean canals that open into the Cove from nobody knows where. An examination of the strontian cave, and other geological features of interest will engross likewise the professor's attention while here. The party is quartered at Park Hotel.

Sketches and Stories of the Lake Erie Islands,
1898, pp. 348-350.

The caves of Put-in-Bay are a never ceasing wonder alike to the scientist and lover of adventure, both of whom seek from time to time to explore the mysteries and whole chapters might be written of the thrilling experiences in the Plutonian darkness of chambers and passages leading—nobody knows whither. All, or nearly all, of these caverns contain miniature lakes and channels of cold, clear water, connecting with Lake Erie and are generally conceded to be ancient water courses. The subterranean drainage of the Island is remarked in the caverns not only, but in the cellars and wells, the former becoming flooded when the wind is east

Edwin L. Moseley (1865-1948).

and the lake level high; the latter regularly rising and falling with the lake.

So far as revealed by exploration, Perry's Cave is the largest on the Island. This Cave is nearly forty feet below the surface. It is 200 feet long, 165 feet wide, and has an average height of seven feet. Though spanned by a single arch the interior has standing room upon its floors for 8,000 persons. The roof was formerly studded thick with stalactites, but these have nearly all been broken off and carried away by specimen collectors and vendors, but the stalagmite floor—formed by century droppings of water holding in solution *calcium carbonate*—forms a study of interest. At the further extremity, and extending back under cleft and caverned rocks, stretches a lake of crystal clearness and viewed by torchlight the scene at this point is weirdly beautiful. For a number of years Perry's Cave has been regularly opened each season to summer visitors, thousands of whom annually view it. An annex to this Cave is known as "Perry's Bedroom."

Sandusky Weekly Register,
13 July 1898, p. 3.

Perry's Cave is now dividing honors with Crystal Cave, recently opened to visitors. The latter lies at a short distance from the former and is reached by an island thoroughfare and the electric car line between. Crystal Cave is attracting the attention both of islanders and strangers from abroad. It is on the property of Gustav Heineman and was discovered in connection with the extensive strontia deposits recently unearthed and is pronounced a marvel of beauty and wonder. "I don't see how it has been kept so long in the dark," observed the oldest inhabitant after duly sizing up this natural curiosity. The Cave is 22 feet below the surface. It is descended by a broad stairway, and viewed by electric lights by which it is illuminated. The place resembles a "fairy grotto." The interior comprises several chambers and the sidewalls of each are solid strontia; dazzling, flashing in their polished crystalline whiteness. The ceilings are arched and high, as one visitor describes it--"with prismatically formed crystals emitting prismatic colors fascinatingly splendid with brilliancy, and radiance not unlike that of the clearest cut diamonds." The Cave is eligibly located near the electric car depot and will doubtless prove a fortune to its owner. Some beautiful specimens of strontia from Crystal Cave are exhibited at the Bay. This mineral is heavier than lead, and has a wonderful smoothness of polish and brilliancy.

Edwin L. Moseley and his student exploring Perry's Cave.

27. - PUT-IN-BAY (Ohio)
Group of Stalactites in Paradise Cave

Stalactites in Paradise Cave, 1905.

Anonymous

Sandusky Daily Star,
22 May 1902, p. 3.

All alumni of the Sandusky High School no matter when they graduated, are invited to take part in the excursion to Put-in- Bay, Saturday, May 24 and renew acquaintance with their classmates. The *Kirby* will leave the Big Four Dock at 7:30 a.m. and the *Arrow* will arrive at Columbus Avenue at about 7:30 p.m. The fare for the round trip is 25 cents. The manager of Daussa's Cave has kindly consented to admit those who come on this excursion without charge, and the manager of Crystal Cave will charge only five cents.

These caves have been open to the public only four or five years. Though small, they are very interesting. Crystal Cave is lined with crystals of celestite, a mineral consisting of strontium sulphate and named for its sky blue color. Nowhere else in the United States, it is believed, has been found a cavity of this size that shows so many large and beautiful crystals.

Daussa's Cave was explored by Mr. Moseley with the assistance of two pupils, George Feick and Frank Daniel. The entrance at that time resembled a wood-chuck hole. Its chief interest lies in the subterranean lake whose waters rise and fall with the influctuations in Lake Erie, nearly half a mile away. Life preservers and boards were passed down through the narrow entrance and made into a raft. On the floor of the lake were found many stalagmites which had been deposited long before from water that trickled down through crevices in the overhanging limestone arch. When they were formed the water must have drained off to a lower level, and this draining could have occurred only when Lake Erie was considerably lower than during the last half century. Some of the other caves on Put-in-Bay show submerged stalagmites or stalactites, but not so many as Daussa's.

Sandusky Weekly Register,
5 June 1895, p. 4.

Brown's Cave is located in a deep shaded grove of natural forest trees on the property of John Brown Jr. Its mouth is wide and high enough to admit a person entering it in an erect position, but it narrows away into dark mysterious passages unexplored save by cats of the neighborhood. During summer heat, the grove forms a favorite ground for campers, and tents of white canvas spread beneath dark foliaged trees, add romantic interest to the scene. The place is approached from the main road by a driveway bordered deep with red cedars. It is an ideal spot such as a man like its late proprietor would naturally choose in which to live and die. Captain Brown's home was a roomy, hospitable dwelling with its open veranda nestled deep amid native red cedars and orchard trees all in a glory of pink and white bloom. A tree clad, fenceless lawn stretched its green carpet to the Lake, edging a beach of shining sand and low, flat rock against which murmur the south channel waters. There is a fertile garden where succulent vegetables flourish in their season together with vineyard lands, and a deep shaded grove of natural forest trees.

Sandusky Weekly Register,
29 March 1899, p. 10.

Beyond a doubt the three caves of the Island will be leading attractions the coming season. Perry's Cave, the oldest and best known; will hold out extra inducements this summer in the way of amusements, which will increase its business phenomenally. We understand the Crystal Cave owners will have their buildings enlarged. The work of the new cave on the DeRivera estate is progressing finely. The work of clearing the lot and cleaning up has begun. Senor Traverso, a typical Spaniard, has been sent here by Dr. Deanson of New York and can be found at work near the aforesaid cave every day. He is a very pleasant gentleman and speaks the English language fluently. It is a pleasure to hold a conversation with him.

Edward Burch of Port Clinton was on the Island on the 24th. He came to look over the ground at the new cave with the intention of bidding on the work of laying the foundation for the dance hall which is to be erected near the cave entrance. While here he also looked over the park front with a view of sending in a bid to lay the new cement sidewalk. He also talked with the cannon committee and will give a bid on the mason work for the much-talked-of cannon. Mr. Burch was entertained at the Ward House by Landlord J. B. Ward.

Sandusky Weekly Register,
12 April 1899, p. 3.

F. H. Mollenhour, a Pittsburgh civil engineer, who has been engaged in exploring the caves in this vicinity, has made a partial report. He has discovered a subterranean cavern, about 500 feet long, underneath the Island.

This cave is divided into two large rooms, connected by a long passage. In one of them is a small lake, about seventy-five by forty feet, the water of which is as clear as crystal. The water is only about three feet deep and, rising from the lake's bottom, are innumerable stalagmites of exceptional beauty. The ceilings of both the rooms are studded with stalactites.

The cavern is almost 40 feet below the surface of the earth. It is level with the lake. There are two entrances, both on land owned by a Mr. Daussa of New York, who is a son-in-law of the late Jose DeRivera St. Jurgo., who owned the entire island at one time.

Theresa Thorndale

Sketches and Stories of the Lake Erie Islands,
1898, pp. 346-347, 352.

In the dim past, the Islands were alternately submerged or drained according to existing conditions of the earth's formative forces. Says Prof. John S. Newberry "We have evidence that the country about the Islands was once all dry land, and a large river [the Erigan] then flowed down the present bed of the lake and emptied near New York City." Prof. Moseley of Sandusky, who has thoroughly studied the lake region, deduces the theory that the lake bed is gradually becoming tilted, or elevated at its eastern extremity, causing a rise in the average level of its head waters and corresponding submergence as indicated. . . .In the caves on Put-in-Bay Island, the subterranean waters rise and fall with the Lake. Not only stalagmites, but also stalactites are attached to the floor and roofs of submerged caverns; the latter five feet below the present lake level. For these to form in water would be an impossibility and their position as indicated show, according to Prof. Moseley, a rise of the water, though other theorists might ascribe the circumstance to a shifting and settling of the honey combed rocks.

Large quantities of submerged timber in the extensive marshlands bordering the lake shores in the vicinity of the Islands likewise indicate a rise of at least eight feet, and the submerged channels of rivers and streams in the same vicinity show a rise of at least thirty-two feet. . . .If the above theory is correct, then instead of wearing away and draining Lake Erie to the compass of a stream,. . . Niagara Falls may become tilted to such a degree as to finally preclude the egress of the lake waters, which in consequence will continue rising and extending, submerging the lowlands along its shores and the Islands at its center until, filled to overflowing, they will form an outlet southward from the Lake Basin to the Valley of the Mississippi. This then seems the fate in store for both the Islands and mainland at the head of Lake Erie, unless averted by a change in the earth's structural program. However, in the event of such a calamity, it is safe to infer that the present inhabitants will not be there to suffer from the consequent drowning out.

Anonymous

Sandusky Weekly Star,
1 January 1903, p. 5.

Another cave has been discovered at Put-in-Bay which proves to a large degree, the theory of Prof. Moseley, of this city, that the waters of Lake Erie are rising. The new cave, named Paradise Cave, was discovered a few days ago in the front yard of the William Kindt property, located about 50 rods from the Crystal Cave, toward the Hotel Victory. The discovery was made quite accidentally and an investigation shows that one arm of the Cave extends a few feet under Kindt's cellar. There are two arms to the Cave diverging from the entrance in the yard. The Cave is from 200 to 250 feet in length and varies from 50 to 75 feet in width.

The cave is filled with stalactites, while there are some stalagmites. In one place the stalagmites are under water, thus indicating that the level of the lake water has raised as the formations were completed while above water.

The Island Mail Carrier

[Theresa Thorndale]

Sandusky Weekly Register,
6 February 1895, p. 11.

A more unenviable position can scarcely be imagined than has been that of the United States mail carrier on the island route during the past ten days of violent storm, severe cold, and precarious ice. Zero weather and high winds have been striving for the mastery on Lake Erie, and although the cold has been of an intensity sufficient to have congealed everything congealable for a distance of twenty miles around the archipelago, the violet gales sweeping up from every point of the compass, have kept the ice broken up between the islands and peninsula, giving the endless trouble, and rendering his trips to and for peculiarly hazardous. His contract binds him to dispatch and deliver three weekly mails--outgoing and incoming--and as a trip one way takes in Isle St. George [North Bass], Middle Bass, Put-in-Bay, Ottawa [Catawba], Port Clinton, and Sandusky, requires nearly a day--it requires two days usually--the period for the round trip. Uncle Sam's business being imperative, the carrier is forced to set out when the average man deems it unfit for a dog to be abroad, even upon land, and hugs hard the base burner, and studies the thermometer and weather bulletins. Each passage between Ottawa [Catawba] to the south shore of Put-in-Bay at Parker's Point made during the past week has been a matter of several hours of difficult and dangerous adventure on the carrier's part. With winds against which it was almost impossible to maintain an erect position, cutting the face and whirling snow prickling like needle points, and covering with drifts places of uncertainty; with intense cold and long exposure sufficient to freeze the warmest blood, the

U. S. Mail transport in wintertime from Catawba to Parker's Point.

indomitable carrier and his assistants have faced untold hardship and danger.

The strain of hard work in propelling the mail boat over rough, craggy surfaces where the ice held intact, and through the seething foam, and heavy running drift of the open water, probably kept these men from freezing, for they were ofttimes wet with dashing spray, which froze upon their garments, and with frequent immersions which they found impossible to avoid. In one trip the carrier reports having broken through the ice nearly two dozen times. In addition to the handling of the ironclad boat with mail pouches and heavy expressage, occasional passengers whom urgent business required to make the trip had to be looked after.

On one trip a young woman crossed from the Marblehead Peninsula. She had been employed in Toledo, and was summoned home by a cable dispatch announcing the sudden death of her father, the result of a frightful accident occurring at the Forest City ice houses. A casket intended for the victim of this accident was sent as far as Ottawa [Catawba]. There it halted, its transportation across being deemed impracticable. Times were set for the funeral, but on each occasion it was postponed for want of a casket; until it was finally proposed to have one made by some island mechanic, which though necessarily rude might answer the purpose. To this the widow would not assent, having ordered one costing $50, and wishing to have her husband buried with all dignity and respect. Thus the body was kept nearly a week when at last the casket arrived. There being no minister on the Island and none available from any other place at this time, the funeral service was conducted by a leading member of St. Paul's Episcopal church and the remains interred.

Blizzard Delays Island Mail

Theresa Thorndale

Sandusky Weekly Register,
21 February 1894, p. 4.

Carrier Michael Seitz of the island mail service received a large share of commiseration last Tuesday. It was given gratuitously, but did him little good, as Uncle Sam's business was too imperative to permit an appropriation thereof, and the mail was then twenty-four hours behind time, since during the blizzard no ordinary mortal could have crossed the island channels. His undertaking was indeed dangerous and difficult to a degree which would have intimidated any but the most courageous. The lake was packed full of scattered drift not sufficiently frozen to bear a man, and over the whole distance from Isle St. George and Middle Bass to Put-in-Bay, the carrier and his two assistants were obliged to break a passage for the mail boat. Reaching Webster's Cove, East Point, one of his iron clads left there which he had proposed transporting to Parker's Beach--to connect with Ottawa [Catawba]--had disappeared under a solid ridge of ice ten feet deep. The digging out would involve a long and arduous task, but the carrier insisted that he must have the boat if it took all day. Axes, picks, and shovels were procured at adjacent houses, and later in the day the boat was dragged forth, loaded with mail bags upon an islander's sled and hauled to the opposite side of the island, where the party again launched forth. Over the whole distance to Ottawa a passage for the boat had to be broken and forced with pike poles. The return trip on Wednesday was no better, ice having to be broken and dense drifts gotten over the entire route. It was late in the afternoon before the mail reached the Bay post office.

Mail Carrier Adrift in Fog

Theresa Thorndale

Sandusky Daily Register,
5 January 1897, p. 7.

In keeping with sad and regretful memories attending the passing of the old year was the gloom of mantling cloud and impenetrable fog which overhung and hid from view the nearest adjacent islands on the closing day of 1896. The atmosphere was charged with moisture which condensed upon and drearily dripped from grey roofs and naked branches. Not a breath ruffled the lake waters, an occasional stray ice floe lay white and misty on its surface, and a funeral-like silence brooded as if all the world were dead or dying with the year. So dense was the fog that the steamer American Eagle was unable to leave on her regular Sandusky run and lay all day at her dock.

Until twilight a crowd awaited at the post office the belated island mail, then about two hours overdue. It was then whispered about that perhaps the carrier and his son had got lost in the fog on the lake. Much anxiety became apparent and increased as the moments passed and as night approached with portend of stygian darkness and obscurity, though which no light could penetrate. The bell on the town hall was rang long and loud with the hope that if the carriers had gone astray on the open lake, its sonorous tones might guide them landward. They had indeed got befogged and lost and narrowly escaped missing land altogether. They had left the Catawba Peninsula at 1 p.m., and with a fair wind and plenty of sail had calculated to make the passage within an hour; but time passed, no land appeared, and they began to realize they had lost their reckonings. In addition to the carrier and his son, a passenger, John Brick, of Put-in-Bay, was with them, besides two young ladies, Misses Mary and Myrtle Vroman, on their way home from Detroit. The girls became chilled with the damp, cold air, and grew frightened at the ominous prospect. The party was provided with a compass, but the boat had drifted with the shifting ice far out of her course. Fortunately, at about 5 o'clock, they sighted through the gloaming the outlying shores of East Point and made land at that place. Had they missed the Point, the open lake, and night of fog and darkness would have confronted the party.

The island bells rang the old year out and the new in; whistles blew; a cannon sent its echoes abroad; and guns, pop guns, dinner horns, and trumpets took up the strain until 1897 was finally initiated. The neat, new calendars generously distributed by Postmaster Ingold went into effect.

Sandusky Weekly Register,
12 January 1898, p. 10.

Occasionally passengers arrive and depart with the mail. On Friday an island young man, Alex Herbster returned from a mainshore perigrenation bearing with him a newly found bride.

Sandusky Weekly Register,
21 February 1894, p. 4.

A representative of the class commonly known as "landlubbers" from a remote inland region of Ohio was a passenger to Put-in-Bay. The experience was to him entirely new, and had the electrical effect of causing his hair to stand erect. Before he had got very far, he would have given a good round sum to have been back once more in his own little town.

Commencement at High School

Theresa Thorndale

Sandusky Weekly Register,
26 June 1895, p. 4.

An event of prospective interest to island residents at this time is the first annual commencement of the Put-in-Bay high school to be held at the opera house Saturday evening, June 29, 1895, exercises beginning at 8 p.m. The program announced is as follows:

Music .... **Louisa Bohl**
Invocation .... **Rev. W. C. Sheppard**
Salutatory-Honesty is the Best Policy
.... **Mary M. Linskey**
Recitation-The Yosemite .... **Ollie J. Morrison**
Essay-Through Difficulties to Success
.... **Mamie Hinger**
Recitation-The Ancient Miner Story
.... **Carolyn Schmidt**
Music-Violin Solo .... **Frank Herbster**
Class History .... **Susie Brown**
Recitation-The Old Man Goes to Town
.... **Tina Herbster**
Essay-Handsome is That Handsome Does
.... **May Brady**
Recitation-Des Saenger's Flush .... **Anne Keimer**
Music-Piano Solo .... **Louisa Bohl**
Recitation-On Board the Cumberland
.... **Mina Bicksford**
The High School Journal
.. **Carl Oehschlager, editor Max Keimer, associate**
Recitation-The Death of Leonidas .... **Inez Dodge**
Music-Violin Solo .... **Frank Herbster**
Class Prophecy .... **Jay C. Idlor**
Oration-And Valedictory-Upward .. **Geo. J. Linskey**
Diploma Presentation .... **Supt. J. Calvin Oldt**
Benediction .... **Rev. W. C. Sheppard**
The Addenda .... **Lucy Rittman**
Ushers .... **Carl Schmidt, Wm. Gram and Ralph Jones**.

Patrons of the public schools, citizens in general, lovers of education and all are respectfully invited. Admission for adults, 25 cents,; reserved seats, 35 cents. Net proceeds to be used for benefit of public schools for the purchase of reference books, apparatus, or whatever the executive committee deem most needed in the schools.

Sandusky Weekly Register,
1 June 1898, p. 3

Members of the graduating class, Put-in-Bay High School, are getting ready for their debut. Creamy fabrics and filmy laces are now being considered, and graduating essays and other literary productions prepared.

Sandusky Weekly Register,
15 June 1898, p. 3

Of coming events, one of the most interesting and important is the fourth annual commencement of the Put-in-Bay High School to be held at the town hall Friday evening, June 17. The program of literary and other exercises will be as follows: The class address by Hon. Oscar T. Corson of Columbus will also form a feature of great interest, being known as one of the most prominent educational men of the state. Music will be given by the Put-in-Bay orchestra.

Sandusky Weekly Register,
22 June 1898, p. 3

An occasion of especial interest this week at Put-in-Bay was the commencement exercises of the Put-in-Bay high school held on Friday evening of June 17th at the town hall. The weather was propitious, and at an early hour the hall was filled by an expectant audience, representing not only people of Put-in-Bay, but also of Middle Bass who arrived on the evening steamer. When at 8 o'clock the curtain rose, an attractive scene was presented. The stage and entire hall were elaborately decorated with the National colors, flags, and ample lengths of bunting lavishly draping and festooning the walls, in varied styles of arrangement. Choice plants and brilliant illumination added also to the attractions of the scene. A motto, "Finished, but not begun," wrought of white daisies appeared above the stage and the air was heavy with the perfumes of flowers among which mingled roses of every variety.

The graduating class numbered seven members, and the fine young ladies forming its larger part were prettily costumed in white dotted Swiss, organdie, and other dainty fabrics with creamy sashes and bows and bouquets of choice selection, or in delicate pink with lace garniture and roses, and as "sweet girl graduates" filled the bill complete. They were something more than that, however, as the thoughtful, earnest, and able efforts seen in their literary productions abundantly proved, and the class as a whole gave evidence of the four years' training, culture, and study which under the careful tutilage of Prof. J. Calvin Oldt has been theirs. The exercises opened with a musical selection by the Put-in-Bay orchestra and invocation by Rev. Shepherd of Cleveland. The class program was as follows:

Salutatory. "America's Brightest Jewels," in which were woven many bright thoughts, by **Miss Annie Keimer**.

Essay. "Streams That Glide in Orient Plains," an interesting essay, **Miss Carolyn Schmidt**.

Essay. "Watched Rosebuds Open Slowly," **Miss Inez G. Dodge**, a rose-hued perspective of life; its duties, and toils.

Oration. "Finished, But Not Begun," a finished oration by **Gordon P. Ward**.

Essay. "The Outgrowth of Individual Effort," **Mary M. Quinskey**, was an exposition of earnest thought by an earnest worker.

Essay. "The Geology and History of Put-in-Bay," an essay with a scientific and historical trend, by **Miss Madge Connors**, attended especial attention by reason of the local and general interest attaching thereto.

Valedictory. **Carl E. Oelschlager**, Ignoti Nulla Cupido (No desire for the unknown) formed a fitting finale to a brilliant program.

Supplementing these presentations was rendered a selection by the orchestra, after which the Hon. Oscar T. Corson of Columbus, state commissioner of schools, who is known as one of the most prominent educational men of the state, occupied the platform. He was introduced, and favored the audience with an address such as has been seldom heard at this place. The speaker's observations were plain and practical as well as full of pith and point. His address to the audience was interrupted by frequent applause, and his remarks to members of the class were full of good advice and sound logic. The honorable gentlemen was a strenuous advocate of hard work, physical and mental, and deprecated the idea formed by so many fledgling scholars that an education would do away with the necessity of hard work.

The presentation of diplomas by Superintendent J. Calvin Oldt formed an interesting feature. The stage front was laden with floral offerings to the graduates, baskets and bouquets of roses and other floral tributes bowed with ribbons appearing. Altogether, the exercises were a pronounced success and the class, which is the largest ever graduated at Put-in-Bay, were loaded with congratulations.

High School Graduation: One Hundred Years Later

Kim Strosnider

Sandusky Register,
10 June 1989, p. A-3.
Quotations from Speaker Herdendorf's Typewritten Manuscript.

PUT-IN-BAY — The graduation of the eight-member Class of 1989 was doubly special for school secretary and board of education treasurer Martha Marquard: both her granddaughter and the last of her seven children graduated together in the Friday evening ceremony. "Yes, it'll be 32 years that I've signed report cards. . .and gotten vaccination shots, and now it all comes to an end," said Marquard as she waited in the town hall for the ceremony to begin.

Marquard's daughter Laura and granddaughter Suzanne Riddle graduated along with Nicole Booker, Megan Faris, Cinnamon Morris, David Ontko, Daniel Reitz, and Jennifer Robison. The eight seniors form one of the largest classes to graduate from the island school in recent years, according to administrator Kelly Faris.

Both salutatorian Megan Faris and valedictorian Jennifer Robison stressed the close bonds the eight students have developed. "Togetherness is probably one of the most important features of the Class of 1989," said Robison. "Without even one person not any of us would be the same." Faris compared the class to a community and enumerated the qualities she feels make each of her classmates unique: Nicole's sensitivity, Cinnamon's healing smile, David's lessons on standing up for yourself, Daniel's reminders that they are all still children, Suzanne's sense of humor, Jennifer's natural confidence, and Laura's growing independence.

As the classmates have grown and changed, so has their island home, Faris said. "We have worried about our quaint island losing its charm," she said, recalling business expansions, the selling of land, construction and the demise of days when a small child could walk safely through the village without holding an adult's hand. But though the island has changed, Faris said, "Every person has added to the community. With so many people loving and caring for their home, I don't think we never have to worry about it losing its natural charm and elegance."

The blue-and white-gowned graduates, sitting before a packed town hall, also were addressed by Dr. Charles E. Herdendorf, professor emeritus of The Ohio State University and former director of the Franz Theodore Stone Laboratory located on Gibraltar Island.

Herdendorf blended advice to the graduates with reflections on island ecology, saying:

> While human beings have long been drawn by the lure of the islands, we have failed over the ages to understand or appreciate their delicate nature. Limited in size, an island has less resiliency to adapt to the onslaught of a new and effective colonizer. Even unwittingly, humankind affects the ecology of an island by our very presence. Because the species of island life forms are few in number compared with those of the mainland, favorite food crops are planted and domestic animals are introduced, soon altering the island ecosystem. Today, islands are sought out by tourists in the hope that their isolation and less frenzied pace will bring temporary respite and solace. Arriving in increasing numbers, visitors take

Charles E. Herdendorf, Commencement Speaker.

little note of the natural island life they and their modern accommodations displace. Pressed by economic concerns, man eventually attempts to utilize every bit of island terrain. Thus, natural habitats are obliterated and the beauty of the island vanishes.

This situation does not have to be the story of Put-in-Bay and South Bass Island. Your challenge is to achieve that delicate balance between economic prosperity and the unique qualities of life that only an island can afford.

In addition to encouraging the graduates to keep abreast of new information in their chosen careers and to travel widely, Herdendorf pointed out to them the value of keeping a journal.

The great adventures that you will have throughout your life can come alive again and spark your memory through a journal. You may not write in it every day or even every week, but do record those special events and feelings whenever you can. Even though we cannot all be graphic artists, writing is a true art form that can paint the most vivid of pictures. Share these experiences and impressions in letters to your family and friends. (Not just notes that say, "Mom, send money.")

The ceremony, which could not be held at Perry's Victory and International Peace Memorial because of rain, concluded with the presentation of awards and diplomas. Robison, who will attend Miami University, was awarded the $1,000 four-year Ohio Academic Scholarship and the Presidential Academic Fitness Award. Faris, who plans to attend Bowling Green State University, was awarded a $200 four-year Gustav Heineman Award and a $1,250 four-year Lee Miller Scholarship. The $600, one-time Verhoff Scholarship was given to Morris, and Marquard received the $1,000 four-year Lonz-Island Scholarship.

In addition, the Kahler Family gave $100 in memory of John Kahler to seven of the graduates who plan to attend two- or four-year colleges. And, Lonz's Winery on Middle Bass Island gave each of the six graduates who applied for the Lonz-Island Scholarship a $1,000 one-time award.

The ceremony also served to promote six eighth graders into high school. They are Walter Duff, Jr., Nicholas Faris, Karen Goaziou, Rebecca Mandell, Elizabeth Schmidlin, and Kimberly Stoiber all of whom received certificates of promotion during the ceremony.

References:

Chapter Thirteen, South Bass "Island Jottings"
II. Caves, Mail Service, and Graduation

Cottingham, Kenneth. 1919. "The origin of the caves at Put-in-Bay, Ohio." *Ohio Journal of Science* 20: 38-42.

Herdendorf, Charles E. 1989. "Put-in-Bay High School Commencement Address - - June 9, 1989." Typewritten Manuscript, 3 pp.

Kraus, Edward H. 1905. "On the origin of the caves of the island of Put-in-Bay, Lake Erie." *American Geologist* 35: 167-171.

Langlois, Thomas H. 1951. "The caves on South Bass Island." *Inland Seas* 7: 113-117.

Moseley, E. L. 1898. "Lake Erie enlarging. The islands separated from the mainland in recent times." *The Lakeside Magazine* 1(9): 14-20.

Moseley, E. L. 1899. "Flora of the islands and its origin," pp. 10-32. *In Sandusky Flora. A catalogue of the flowering plants and ferns growing without cultivation, in Erie County, Ohio, and the peninsula and islands of Ottawa County*. Ohio State Academy of Science Special Papers No. 1. 167 pp.

Newell, Amy L. 1995. "The caves of Put-in-Bay." Lake Erie Originals, Put-in-Bay, Ohio. ix, 108 pp.

Stansbery, David H. 1965. "The indigenous minerals of South Bass in western Lake Erie." *Wheaton Club Bulletin* New Series 10: 18-21.

Verber, James L. and David H. Stansbery. 1953. "Caves in the Lake Erie islands." *Ohio Journal of Science* 53: 358-362.

White, George W. 1926. "Put-in-Bay caves," pp. 79-86 *In* "The limestone caves and caverns of Ohio." *Ohio Journal of Science* 26: 73-116.

Wright, G. Frederick. 1898. "A recently discovered cave of celestite crystals at Put-in-Bay, Ohio." *American Geologist* 22: 261. [Now known as Crystal Cave.]

Two Views of Capt. Walter Groves' Tombstone, in Crown Hill Cemetery. Circular Fountain, in DeRivera Park. The Put-in-Bay House.

News Notes Without Continuity:

CHAPTER FOURTEEN

A Potpourri of South Bass News "Joggings"

Theresa Thorndale

The Village Park

Sandusky Daily Register,
19 March 1889, p. 1.

Two acres of the Park, or Grove, [now named DeRivera Park] within the incorporated limits of Put-in-Bay village, which belong to the DeRivera estate, are to be sold during the year, it is said, unless bought by the Island and held as a body. The Park is liable therefore to be divided up and narrowed down to insignificant proportions and thus ruined as a resort for visitors and excursionists. A plan has been proposed for the purchase of the ground by the Island. What will be done remains to be seen.

Sandusky Weekly Register,
20 June 1894, p. 5.

Put-in-Bay has been receiving considerable attention. The grass under the trees has been smoothly shaven, some of the seats given lively coats of red paint and the tables and benches arranged for excursion parties.

Put-In-Bay House Hotel Ruins

Sandusky Daily Register,
3 April 1889, p. 2.

The spot upon which a few years ago went up in flame and smoke the glory of the once famous hotel known as the Put-in-Bay House, has long presented the appearance of a classical and picturesque ruin. The broken and dismantled walls, the sunken pavements, and the basins where fountains once played appear half hidden, half concealed by clumps of tall sumach, and tangles of wild vines and shrubbery, easily lead the imaginative visitor into fields of fancy where antiquities more remote than these stare him out of countenance by their solemnity and impressiveness. This poetic imagery, however, has recently taken wings and flown before the axe and mattock of the more realistic grubber. During the past week the grounds have been cleared up, the old weather beaten fence removed, and the handsomely carved posts of a new fence placed in line.

Edison's Phonograph

Sandusky Daily Register,
28 August 1889, p. 2.

Edison's great invention, known as the phonograph, recently exhibited at the Bay, attracted crowds of the curious. This delicate and wonderful instrument exhibited a proficiency at talking and singing, which astonished onlookers who had never before witnessed a similar performance.

Prospects of New Buildings

Sandusky Daily Register,
28 August 1889, p. 2.

It is stated by workmen on Hotel Victory that the foundations of the building will be completed this week. No fish hatchery this year, the preliminary legal measures of securing title to land, having taken up the greater part of the season. . . .Next year a big boom for Put-in-Bay, will include the building of the United States Fish Hatchery, the erection of the Perry Monument, the completion of Hotel Victory, the building of multitudinous cottages, and the establishment of a guest patronage that will make Saratoga and Long Branch little in comparison. This is the destiny which astrological calculators of Put-in-Bay are reading in the stars.

Sandusky Weekly Register,
18 April 1894, p. 4.

The prospective Lighthouse at Put-in-Bay for which Congress made recent appropriations, is to materialize this summer, say reports. It is to be located upon the south shore of the Island, and is to be a fine structure.

Big Chimney Falls in Storm

Sandusky Weekly Register,
21 February 1894, p. 4.

During the storm of February, the great chimney of the Put-in-Bay electric railroad power house near Hotel Victory fell with a stunning crash, breaking a hole through the roof of the building. No other damage is reported by Mr. Osborne, who has charge of the place.

Canoe Lands at East Point

Sandusky Daily Register,
28 August 1889, p. 2.

A canoe without paddle or paddler grounded its keel on Webster's Beach, East Point, last week. The waif had evidentially seen hard usage,and looked as worn and melancholy as if long moons agone it had parted from some Indian camp on the shores of far distant Superior and had since been aimlessly drifting from sea to sea at the sport of wind and tempest.

Jay Cooke Soon to Return

Sandusky Weekly Register,
2 May 1894, p. 9.

Gibraltar Island is being put in readiness for the reception of its distinguished owner and patron, Jay Cooke; expected early in May on his semi-annual visit. Viewed from a distance the Island is looking very beautiful in its early spring dress. The place is under the care and management of Fred Lemond. The entire Island has been thoroughly raked, and other improvements made.

Distinctive Tombstone Erected

Sandusky Weekly Register,
20 June 1894, p. 5.

A tombstone was recently erected in Crown Hill Cemetery to the memory of Capt. Walter Groves, the Put-in-Bay yachtsman, who died last autumn. The stone is a design representing a stump, surmounted by an anchor with name of deceased carved upon it.

The Daisy Her Favorite

Sandusky Weekly Register,
19 December 1894, p. 7. Seventy-third year.

The *Household Realm* published a symposium by well known women on the subject of Favorite Flowers. "Theresa Thorndale" The Register's Put-in-Bay correspondent wrote:

> So wide is the kingdom of Flora and so bewildering the beauty and brilliancy of its multitudinous productions, that to decide upon which individual flower to bestow preference, is to me a perplexing puzzle. So many claimants tempt and beguile by their prodigality of sweetness and color. But, if I were imprisoned and limited to the companionship of but a single blossom, I think that I should choose the daisy; because it is sweet, pretty and modest; because it is to me the personification of constancy and fidelity, blooming early and late, and outliving whole generations of flowers and more luxuriously brilliant; because it is a native of haunts which I most love, peeping from hedge rows, bordering wayside paths, and flecking hillside and meadows; and because it is suggestive of the sweet quietude and rest which lulls the heart of nature.—Lydia J. Ryall, "Theresa Thorndale."

Meat Supply Sold Out at Store

Sandusky Weekly Register,
6 February 1895, p. 11.

Bad ice has occasioned some distress among individuals who dote upon juicy steaks and tender pork cutlets. The latter gave out; then sirloin and porterhouse went by the board, followed by veal stew, mutton legs, "nacht wurst," and bologna, until the meat market was swept, and garnished, and now stands solitary with a look as melancholy as that of a bank which has suffered a "run," suspended payment, and closed its doors. Supplies are now on the way, however, and the hungry will soon be filled with meat and rejoicing.

Tent Camping Abandoned on East Point

Sandusky Weekly Register,
28 July 1897, p. 4.

Beautiful in their loneliness are the groves of East Point. In former years they were verbrant with the songs, shouts and laughter of gay parties tented there. So far the present season not a camper has spread his lodge, though seldom during the sultry month of July have the thick maples cast a shadow over sodden sweeps of fairer, fresher green. Further emphasized is the solitude of these sequestered haunts by the deserted and neglected houses adjacent falling into decrepitude and decay, and the voice of silence is touchingly eloquent with echoed sound from an unreturning past.

> Deserted is my own good hall,
> Its hearth is desolate;
> Wild weeds are gathering on the wall,
> And closed its oaken gate.

Byron describes it perfectly. However one of those old houses has renewed its youth. Though a stately dwelling with a French roof and an observatory, it stood for several years without an occupant, and only once annually were its doors and windows unbarred and its musty apartments opened to the air and sunlight. This occurrence was during the annual encampment of the Seventh O.V.I., the house being used as headquarters of commisary department and general storehouse for tents and camp equipments. That it should come to be whispered about that the dwelling was haunted was not surprising in view of the fact that an elderly woman—one of the last occupants—committed suicide by hanging herself in the adjacent stable. To further add to its gruesomeness, that bird of evil omen—a screech owl—was supposed there to rendevoux, making night hideous with its uncanny cries. Recently its owner of the house, Attorney McGuide of Detroit, resolved to give it a clearing out. Exercising all his powers of magice he succeeded in effectually exorcising all the ghosts, rats, bats, owls, and things. The regiment stores were moved to other quarters; the house itself was moved to another foundation, portions of it were remodelled and the whole given a coat of white paint, and the Seventh regiment people would hardly recognize the old house in its new dress. It is soon to receive its occupants.

Cycling Track added 1898 at front of Hotel Victory.

Natatorium added 1898 in Victory Park at Hotel Victory.

Natatorium and Cycling Track at Hotel Victory

Sandusky Weekly Register,
16 March 1898, p. 4.

Thomas W. McCreary of Toledo, general advertising agent for Hotel Victory, accompanied by Mr. Ryan of that city, arrived Friday, and were entertained over Sunday as guests at the Ward House. The object of this visit was the projection, and completion of plans for the improvement of the Victory. A new attraction the coming season will be a Natatorium, or swimming pool. It is to be located in the ravine fronting the Hotel. Its dimensions will be 30 x 66 feet with cement bottom, and a gradual depth of water from two to six feet. Wide platforms canopy covered, and furnished with comfortable seats will accommodate those who wish to view the bathers. In the evening the place will be lighted by electricity. A cycling track around the Hotel is contemplated, and negotiations are being made for a four-in-hand tally-ho for the use of guests. Mr. McCreary reports the prospects for Hotel Victory the coming season brighter than ever before.

Bakery Won't Pay at Put-In-Bay

Sandusky Weekly Register,
12 April 1899, p. 3.

The last few days a young man has been on the Island with a view of starting a bakery. If the young man has any money he had better keep it, as a bakery on the Island would be a bad investment.

Island Bicycle Race

Sandusky Weekly Register,
15 June 1898, p. 3.

The bicycle road race at this place last Thursday was a grand success and witnessed by an enormous crowd. The course covered was a distance of five miles, two and one half miles west of town and return on the Lake Shore road, which was very rough at the time. The number entering the race was 14, consisting of our own riders with the exception of two outsiders, one from Elyria and one from Wellington. The time prize was awarded to George Parsons of this place, he having covered the distance in 15 minutes and a quarter.

News Scarce at Put-in-Bay

Sandusky Weekly Register,
4 April 1898, p. 2; 1 June 1898, p. 3.

Real live news is just now a scarce article. While the islander is engaging with his wines, his nets, or his early cabbage garden; the housekeeper is rushing her spring sewing, carpet beating, house cleaning, and is too busy almost to be sociable. Nobody during the week—as far as heard from—has got married, maimed, or murdered; has eloped, embezzled, or abandoned. The Island seems practically destitute of even a possibly good sensation, and affairs move along in jog-trot fashion.

The resorts are all getting ready for an early opening, but aside from the bustle of preparation there is little doing. The islands are quiet and news of importance is scarce. Everybody keeps an eye on the bulletin board and the daily papers are more interested, apparently in news from abroad rather than at home.

Conventioner Put-Out with Put-In...

Anonymous

The Seneca Advertiser,
Tiffin, Ohio, 17 July 1902, p. 5.

"Put-in-Bay Island when the weather is hot is the hottest and most uncomfortable summer resort I ever visited," said an observing young Tiffin attorney in conversation with a friend last evening. "The hotel fare is inferior and the service only fair. The island attracts only conventions of average importance and excursionists. The insect known as the Canadian soldier is the only visitor who seems to be genuinely stuck on the island. Everybody else wants to go back on the next boat. There is no place like home for the real thing in rest and coolness. At home there are no forced amusements and minglings with people. A person need not dress up but can wear an ultra negligee outfit and lounge in the hammock during his leisure hours. I was considerably put out with Put-in."

A Pleasant Few Days with the Geese at Put-in-Bay

Joe Murray

Atlanta Journal,
18 November 1993.

Put-in-Bay, Ohio - The Canadian geese, on their way south to Chesapeake Bay for the winter, had flown in. I arrived by ferry. We had the place mostly to ourselves. The Dairy Queen had closed for the season.

Here on South Bass Island, three miles north of the Ohio mainland in Lake Erie, life goes on for the 500 permanent residents of Put-in-Bay after the tourists have gone away.

Winter's coming on. The ferry's closing down. After November, the only link with the mainland is by daily air service. Or, when its cold enough, you can skate across Lake Erie.

That's what they tell me. Once Lake Erie freezes over, folks have even been known to drive their cars across the ice. That's not to say they're desperate for something to do, I guess.

There's always ice fishing. Otherwise, the choices during the winter are limited. "You get divorced or you get pregnant."

That's according to Dave, a young man who meets the ferry in a golf cart. He rents golf carts to visitors who come over without their cars, just $15 a day, probably more during the season.

I'd stopped to ask Dave for directions to a hotel. I ended up renting his condo, just $40 a night, probably more during the season. Except for the geese, its nice and quiet.

From the balcony, I had a nice view of the sunrise across Lake Erie and of Perry's Victory and International Peace Memorial. Surely you've heard of Perry's Victory and International Peace Memorial. Well, neither had I.

But it's hard to miss, leastwise in Put-in-Bay. The lighthouse-like shaft of granite, soaring 353 feet high, was constructed during the centennial celebration of the War of 1812 to commemorate Commodore Perry's naval victory over the British.

If history had been otherwise, all of Put-in-Bay — territory of some 3 1/2 by 1 1/2 miles — would belong to Canada, as well as a half-dozen smaller, neighboring islands.

I'd also asked Dave to recommend a place to eat. The tourist guide listed more than 30 restaurants and snack shops. Dave had a short list — the one place still open this time of year.

The food was good and the dining area was not that crowded. The crowd, every time I stopped by was at the 30-foot-long bar. Along with getting divorced or pregnant, people get drunk here in winter.

That's what I was told at the police station across the way. Most of the crime of Put-in-Bay involves alcohol offences. Nobody could remember the last time they had a murder.

Not that the police have it easy — not in the spring and summer, when half a million tourists come and go.

The police force varies in size: five full-time personnel year around, and more than 30 during the season. One police chief quit after just two weeks, which included a Memorial Day weekend when 20,000 visitors crammed the island.

Put-in-Bay has its own school system, of course. Current enrollment, for kindergarten through 12th grade, is about 60. There's a high-school basketball team. Their record's not so good, I'm told, but at least it's something for the kids.

What we take for granted — malls, fast-food franchises, movie theaters — they don't have.

What they take for granted — a community without traffic, crime, or pollution problems — we don't have.

I stayed a day longer than I'd planned. The geese were still there when I left.

[And so it goes, yesterday and today at Put-in-Bay—RLS, editor].

Acknowledgements

As time passes, memory fades, if notes on projects are not recorded. After 30 years of work on this book, my faded recollections and paucity of notes may fail in acknowledging some individuals who may have had a part in making this book come into reality. In that regard, I express any necessary apologies.

I express sincere thanks to the following who have participated in the development of *Lost Stories*. Among the earliest individuals who were very helpful with this project were several librarians at the Sandusky Library, Sandusky, Ohio. They made possible my obtaining Theresa Thorndale's Put-in-Bay news stories from the microfilm copies of the *Sandusky Register* and other contemporary Sandusky newspapers. My former student W. Louis Phillips, C. G. obtained information on Lydia J. Ryall and her family from genealogical sources, including census records, obituaries, and death certificates. Mr. Phillips also made print copies of many of Theresa Thorndale's stories from the microfilm copies of the *Sandusky Register* owned by the Ohio Historical Society, Columbus, Ohio. In September 1973, I surveyed the Charles H. Frohman and Thomas H. Langlois collections at the Rutherford B. Hayes Presidential Center in Fremont, Ohio. Langlois' cards with biographical notes on residents of South Bass Island and his superb photographic images of the same area were quite valuable for this project.

Typing of the various portions of the manuscript involved several individuals at different time periods. Andrea Wilson (now Andrea Schlageter), while secretary for the F. T. Stone Laboratory on South Bass Island, first typed into the computer my originally planned content of the book based on my handwritten transcriptions from the microfilm of the *Sandusky Register*. J. Perry Edwards, while a student assistant, typed in additional stories from other sources and prepared a preliminary index of persons' names and geographical locations. After the book was in page format, Relda E. Niederhofer completed a final index. John W. Frederick did the initial word processing of the component parts for the Appendix, and Kathy Royer did the initial word processing for many of the short filler items added to the manuscript during the final phase of the book's page production. Charles E. Herdendorf has been a critical advisor and informant throughout the project providing valuable assistance on philosophy, style, and page development. Ricki C. Herdendorf deserves a special thanks for preparing the final word processed copy of the text and layout of the pages for the printing process.

Many of the illustrations used in the book are from my own extensive collection of post cards showing sites and scenes on the Lake Erie Islands, in addition to my own photographs. In the summer of 1985, I began to assemble photographs to illustrate individual stories. Many of these photographs are from the archives of the National Park Service at Perry's Victory and International Peace Memorial made available on loan to me by Superintendent Harry G. Myers of the Put-in-Bay office. Other photographs have been provided by The Franz Theodore Stone Laboratory, Put-in-Bay; and by former O. S. U. Stone Laboratory faculty, Drs. N. Wilson Britt, Charles E. Herdendorf, Loren S. Putnam, and David H. Stansbery. Most of these photographs, which were acquired through loan or gift from the above sources, were printed during the latter 1980's by A. E. Spreitzer, and these copies were retained until now for publication in this book. The sources of all photographs are acknowledged on the pages identified as "Credits for . . . Illustrations," beginning on page 201. Each photograph is identified by its page number in the book, and when known by its date, photographer, owner, or publication source.

Ronald L. Stuckey
18 October 2001

Andrea Wilson, Secretary (1982-1992) for the F. T. Stone Laboratory; in the office at Bayview House, July 1988.

Publication Notes

1. Special acknowledgement is extended to the various newspapers from which stories have been selected. The majority of the stories, having been written by Theresa Thorndale, came form the *Sandusky Register* and other Sandusky, Ohio, newspapers, including the *Clarion*, *Daily*, *Daily-Star*, *Enterprise*, *Star-Journal*, *Weekly*, and *Weekly-Star*. Other newspapers cited are the *Atlanta Journal* (Georgia), page 192; *Cleveland Plain Dealer*, pages 58 and 78; *Put-in-Bay Gazette*, pages 131 and 138; and *Seneca Advertiser* (Tiffin, Ohio), page 192.

2. The Archives for this book are to be deposited in the Manuscript Collection of the Library at the Hayes Presidential Center, Fremont, Ohio.

3. This book was composed in three styles of type: The stories are in Times; the introductions and summary portions for each chapter are in Helvetica; the headings are in New Century Schoolbook. The entire book was processed on a Power Macintosh 8500 Series Computer using Adobe PageMaker Version 6.5 software.

Chronology

A Chronology of Selected Major Events on South Bass Island Properties that Eventually Became Owned by the State of Ohio

10 September 1813	Commodore Oliver Hazard Perry defeated the British naval fleet in the Battle of Lake Erie, west of the islands in Lake Erie.
10 August 1821	Jay Cooke born near Sandusky, Ohio.
August 1850	Lydia J. Flint-Ryall born in Carlisle Township, Lorain County, Ohio.
1860 to about 1880	As a young lady, Lydia J. Flint-Ryall lived in Milton Township near the town of Ashland in Ashland County, Ohio.
1862	Capt. John Brown, Jr., son of the famed abolitionist, came to South Bass Island and became recognized as a community leader.
27 January 1864	Jay Cooke purchased Gibraltar Island from Jose de Rivera St. Jurgo.
1865	Jay Cooke erected a 15-room Victorian stone mansion for a summer home on Gibraltar Island; also a monument commemorating Perry's victory in the Battle of Lake Erie (September 1813).
Winter 1878-1879	Andrew Wehrle and Company, an ice harvesting company, was established on Peach Point.
1879-1880	Ice houses filled with ice for the first time.
Summer 1880	First ice shipped to Cleveland.
1882	Believed to be the year that Lydia J. Ryall arrived on South Bass Island.
about 1883	Forest City Ice Company of Cleveland, Ohio, purchased the Andrew Wehrle and Company.
6 February 1888	Put-in-Bay Hotel Company Inc. established by J. K. Tillosten, director and promoter, of Toledo, Ohio; plans made for a large hotel building designed by E. O. Fallis of Toledo.

May 1888	A. F. Rutherford hired to promote the large hotel.
Fall 1888	Construction of Hotel Victory began with part of the foundation laid.
2 March 1889	United States Congress approved legislation for construction of a fish hatchery in northern Ohio along shore of Lake Erie.
1 April 1889	Peach Point on South Bass Island selected as site for the United States Fish Hatchery; John Brown, Jr. appointed to survey and designate one-half acre of land on Peach Point for the building.
10 September 1889	Cornerstone of Hotel Victory laid (76th anniversary of Perry's Victory over the British).
12 October 1889	Contract to build United States Fish Hatchery awarded to George E. Gascoyne of Put-in-Bay.
1 July 1890	J. J. Stranahan appointed first superintendent of United States Fish Hatchery at Put-in-Bay.
1 July 1890	Construction of the building completed for the United States Fish Hatchery.
1891	An electric streetcar line between Hotel Victory and the village was organized and operated by the Put-in-Bay Water Works, Electric Light, and Railway Company.
29 June 1892	Hotel Victory opened for business.
10 July 1892	First trip made by the railway car to Hotel Victory.
10 July 1892	Henry Weaver became first manager of Hotel Victory.
12 July 1892	Official inaugural banquet held at Hotel Victory.
5 August 1892	Hotel Victory closed and was empty for 18 months.
10 September 1892	Hotel Victory went into receivership.
1893	J. K. Tillosten leased Hotel Victory from the receiver and opened for business.
9 August 1893	J. K. Tillosten closed Hotel Victory.
4 October 1893	Clubhouse of the Cincinnati Fishing Club opened on Oak Point.

Winter 1893-1894	Forest City Ice Company expanded into new large building next to the United States Fish Hatchery.
1894	United States Congress approved legislation for construction of a lighthouse on the south shore of South Bass Island.
20 February 1895	At sheriff's sale, Hotel Victory building sold to E. O. Fallis and Company, Toledo, Ohio; movable items also sold and moved from the premises.
2 May 1895	Capt. John Brown, Jr., Lydia Ryall's friend and neighbor, died at Put-in-Bay and was buried at Crown Hill Cemetery on South Bass Island.
20 June 1896	Hotel Victory reopened for business by General Manager H. A. Fisher.
1897	Hotel Victory property purchased by L. K. Parks, a Toledo, Ohio, attorney.
Summer 1897	South Bass Island Lighthouse built on Parker Point.
1898	Clubhouse of the Cincinnati Fishing Club sold to Captain Elliott J. Dodge, who operated the property as a hotel with John J. Day as proprietor.
Summer 1898	Natatorium opened in Victory Park in front of Hotel Victory.
July 1898	The book *Sketches and Stories of the Lake Erie Islands*, written by Lydia J. Ryall under the pseudonym of Theresa Thorndale, was published by the Sandusky Register Press, Sandusky, Ohio.
July 1898	The First Biological Survey of Lake Erie, directed by Jacob E. Reighard, who obtained financial support from the United States Commission for Fish and Fisheries, was begun in the United States Fish Hatchery at Put-in-Bay.
15 May 1899	C. W. and J. W. Ryan, brothers, Toledo hardware merchants purchased Hotel Victory from Parks.
15 May 1899	Thomas W. McCreary became manager of Hotel Victory. During his tenure, the Hotel was at the peak of its success and popularity. He died November 1907.
30 May 1899	Storehouse burned at United States Fish Hatchery.

Winter 1900-1901	Last winter that Forest City Ice Company stored ice on Peach Point (under name Columbia Ice Company).
Summer 1901	The First Biological Survey of Lake Erie, which began in 1898, concluded its investigations in the United States Fish Hatchery at Put-in-Bay.
1902	Peach Point purchased by Louis Schiele and John Hollway for 57 cottages.
5-7 August 1902	Superintendent J. J. Stranahan of the United States Fish Hatchery arranged for having the thirty-first annual meeting of the American Fisheries Society at Hotel Victory. Professors Jacob E. Reighard and Henry B. Ward were unable to present their research paper on the quantitative efficiency of plankton nets conducted in Put-in-Bay Harbor, because of an electrical failure at the Hotel Victory; their colored stereopticon illustrations could not be seen and the members present were disappointed.
March 1903	Congress appropriated funds to build a dwelling for the superintendent of the United States Fish Hatchery, now the Bayview House of the Franz Theodore Stone Laboratory.
1904	First cottage constructed on Peach Point; built by Ross Lewis at the tip of the Point.
26 October 1904	Jay Cooke left Gibraltar Island for the last time.
16 February 1905	Jay Cooke died at age 74 in Philadelphia.
Summer 1907	The Division of Fish and Game of the State of Ohio built a fish hatchery next to the United States Fish Hatchery at Put-in-Bay.
5 August 1907	Winged Victory Statue erected in Victory Park. Charles W. Fairbanks, vice-president of the United States, was speaker for dedication of the Statue.
November 1907	R. G. Diegle of Sandusky, formerly publicity director for Cedar Point Amusement Company, became manager of Hotel Victory.
1909	Because of lack of business, Hotel Victory closed and remained closed until 1918.
1913	The second edition of the book, *Sketches and Stories of the Lake Erie Islands*, written by Lydia J. Ryall, was published by the American Publishers Company, Norwalk, Ohio.

1 June 1914	State Fish Hatchery building at Put-in-Bay destroyed by fire.
1914-1915	New brick building constructed for a State Fish Hatchery at Put-in-Bay.
January 1916	Robert Mosbury of Toledo purchased Hotel Victory from the Ryan Brothers estate, but did not open the Hotel as announced.
1917	E. M. T. Automobile Company of Detroit purchased Hotel Victory from Robert Mosbury.
1917	The Oak Point House, formerly the Clubhouse of the Cincinnati Fishing Club, was purchased from Elliott J. Dodge by Arthur G. Smith.
late 1917	Walter E. Flanders Realty Company of Detroit purchased Hotel Victory from E. M. T. Automobile Company.
1918	Hotel Victory reopened for business.
May 1919	A Chicago syndicate purchased Hotel Victory from Flanders Realty Company; Harley J. Stoops became manager and opened the Hotel for summer business.
14 August 1919	Hotel Victory totally destroyed by fire.
30 June 1920	Lydia J. Ryall (Theresa Thorndale) died in Cleveland, Ohio, and was buried two days later in Crown Hill Cemetery on South Bass Island; no marker erected.
1925	Gibraltar Island, former summer home of Jay Cooke, was purchased by Julius F. Stone, Columbus businessman, and presented the Island to The Ohio State University as the permanent home of the University's field biological laboratory; named the Franz Theodore Stone Laboratory in memory of Stone's father (1813-1862).
Summer 1926	Classes first offered at the F. T. Stone Laboratory on Gibraltar Island.
1938	The Oak Point House was sold by Arthur G. Smith to the Ohio Division of Conservation, who leased it for 15 years to The Ohio State University for use as housing facility by the F. T. Stone Laboratory.

1938	The State of Ohio acquired 11 acres of the former Hotel Victory site.
Summer 1940	United States Fish Hatchery deeded to The Ohio State University for the Franz Theodore Stone Laboratory, in an authorization signed by President Franklin D. Roosevelt.
1946	The State of Ohio purchased 21 acres of the former Hotel Victory site, which together with the 11-acre site obtained in 1938, formed the South Bass Island State Park.
Winter 1956-1957	Oak Point House dismantled by the Ohio Department of Natural Resources and became the Oak Point Picnic Area.
31 October 1962	Light became automated in the South Bass Island Lighthouse; the last lightkeeper, Paul F. Prochnow, retired from service in the Coast Guard.
1967	South Bass Island Lighthouse leased for 30 years to The Ohio State University for use by The Franz Theodore Stone Laboratory.
September 1983	A meteorological station was installed on the United States Coast Guard steel tower at the South Bass Island Lighthouse by the National Oceanic and Atmospheric Administration (NOAA); personnel from the Stone Laboratory monitored the Station.
1997	South Bass Island Lighthouse became permanent property of The Ohio State University, for use by the Franz Theodore Stone Laboratory.
Winter 2002	OSU Stone Laboratory faculty member Ronald L. Stuckey, after 30 years of study, published his book, *Lost Stories: Yesterday and Today at Put-in-Bay; including Theresa Thorndale's "Island Jottings" of the 1890's.*

Credits for Black and White Illustrations

p. iv. 21 September 1991, *RLS, C45O-14.*

p. v. F. T. Stone Laboratory.

p. xiv. From Thomas Huxley Langlois and Maria Holmes Langlois. 1985. *The ice of Lake Erie around South Bass Island 1936-1964.* The Ohio State University, The Franz Theodore Stone Laboratory Contribution No. 14, p. 39. (CLEAR Technical Report 167; Sea Grant Book Series No. 4).

p. xv. Postcard, Studio C, Berlin, Wisconsin.

Chapter One: Lydia J. Ryall (Theresa Thorndale)

p. xvi. *Sketches* (Ryall, 1913, p. 546) (left); *Sketches* (Thorndale, 1898) (right).

p. 3. 14 September 1988, *RLS, C79-23A.*

p. 4. 14 September 1988, *RLS, C79-21A.*

p. 8. *Sketches* (Ryall, 1913).

p. 9. 11 July 2001, *RLS, C975-8A.*

Chapter Two: South Bass, "Island Jottings"

p. 10. 1910 map drawn by *RLS* from M. S. MacDiarmid. 1909-1910. "[Map of South Bass Island showing distribution of orchards and vineyards]." Survey of the northern and western lakes, West end of Lake Erie and the Bass Islands (upper left); *Thomas H. Langlois*, F. T. Stone Laboratory (lower); from an unknown source (upper right).

p. 15. 16 August 1974, *Thomas Duncan.*

p. 16. 1910 map (see citation for page 10); 1942 map redrawn by *RLS* from Bert Hudgins. 1943. "The South Bass Island Community." *Economic Geography* 19: 16-36, Fig. 12, p. 28; 1975 map drawn by *RLS* from literature studies and field observations of vineyards on South Bass Island.

p. 20. National Park Service, Perry's Victory Collection, Put-in-Bay Office.

p. 24. 16 March 1952, *Thomas H. Langlois 9788,* F. T. Stone Laboratory.

Chapter Three: The Hotel Victory

p. 28. Photo postcard, printer not identified (upper); *Sketches* (Ryall, 1913, pp. 108, 112) (lower).

p. 30. Photo postcard, printer not identified (upper); postcard, No. 36, printer not identified (lower).

p. 34. Postcard, H. L. Foltz, Put-in-Bay, Ohio (upper); *Sketches* (Ryall, 1913, p. 110) (lower).

p. 40. Postcard postmarked 1910, Alexander Mfg. Co., Sandusky, Ohio (upper); postcard, H. J. Foltz, Put-in-Bay, Ohio (lower).

p. 43. National Park Service, Perry's Victory Collection, Put-in-Bay Office.

p. 44. Postcard, Alexander Mfg Co., Sandusky, Ohio (upper); photo postcard, printer not identified (lower).

p. 47. Postcard postmarked 1901, Alexander Mfg. Co., Sandusky, Ohio. No. 3 (upper); postcard 1905, The Rotograph Co., New York City (lower).

p. 48. National Park Service, Perry's Victory Collection, Put-in-Bay Office (upper); from Earl L. Core. 1948. *The Flora of the Erie Islands.* The Ohio State University, Franz Theodore Stone Laboratory Contribution No. 9. p. 77, taken about 1940 by *N. Wilson Britt* (lower).

Chapter Four: The South Bass Island Lighthouse

p. 52. National Park Service, Perry's Victory Collection, Put-in-Bay Office.

p. 54. 1979. F. T. Stone Laboratory and Center for Lake Erie Area Research.

p. 55. 17 June 2001, *RLS, C971-OA.*

p. 60. United States Coast Guard and F. T. Stone Laboratory/ Ohio Sea Great College, The Ohio State University.

p. 61. About 1974, *Charles E. Herdendorf,* F. T. Stone Laboratory and Center for Lake Erie Area Research.

p. 62. About 1976, *Charles E. Herdendorf*, F. T. Stone Laboratory and Center for Lake Erie Area Research.
p. 65. July 1987, *Robert Boyce*, Photo Archives, The Ohio State University, Columbus.

Chapter Five: The Ice Companies on Peach Point

p. 68. F. T. Stone Laboratory (upper); National Park Service, Perry's Victory Collection, Put-in-Bay Office (lower).
p. 73. National Park Service, Perry's Victory Collection, Put-in-Bay Office.
pp. 76, 77. Postcard, H. A. Herbster, Put-in-Bay, Ohio.
p. 80. F. T. Stone Laboratory.

Chapter Six: The United States Fish Hatchery

p. 82. David H. Stansbery, Columbus, Ohio (upper); National Park Service, Perry's Victory Collection, Put-in-Bay Office (lower).
p. 89. National Park Service, Perry's Victory Collection, Put-in-Bay Office.
p. 91. Plate XIII, *Report of the [United States] Fish Commissioner for the Year Ending June 30, 1899.* Washington, D.C. 1900, opp. p. LXX.
p. 96. 1980, *Charles Piatt*, F. T. Stone Laboratory.
p. 97. 8 February 1949, *Thomas H. Langlois*, from Mary and Milton Trautman.

Chapter Seven: The Cincinnati Fishing Club on Oak Point

p. 100. 12 October 1893, *Sandusky Daily Register*, p. 4.
p. 104. National Park Service, Perry's Victory Collection, Put-in-Bay Office (upper); F. T. Stone Laboratory/ Ohio Sea Grant College, The Ohio State University (lower).
p. 106. About 1940, *Thomas H. Langlois*, F. T. Stone Laboratory (upper); 1 February 1950, *Thomas H. Langlois 7410*, F. T. Stone Laboratory (lower).

Chapter Eight: First Biological Survey of Lake Erie

p. 108. Negative No. 7476, Jacob E. Reighard Collection, Bentley Historical Library, The University of Michigan, Ann Arbor (upper); plate 6, *Report of the [United States] Fish Commissioner for the Year Ending June 30, 1896*. Washington, D.C. 1898, opp. p. 49, from *David H. Stansbery*, Columbus, Ohio (lower).
p. 110. Negative No. 7475, Jacob E. Reighard Collection, Bentley Historical Library, The University of Michigan, Ann Arbor (a, upper left); from the student yearbook, *Sombrero*, 1898, Archives, Library, University of Nebraska, Lincoln (b, upper right); collection 2322, negative 7018, the Ferdinard Hamburger Jr. Archives, Johns Hopkins University, Baltimore, Maryland (c, lower left); courtesy of the Hunt Institute for Botanical Documentation, Carnegie-Mellon University, Pittsburgh, Pennsylvania (c, lower right).
p. 111. Negative No. 7478, Jacob E. Reighard Collection, Bentley Historical Library, The University of Michigan, Ann Arbor.
p. 112. Henry B. Ward Collection, Archives, University of Illinois, Urbana-Champaign.
pp. 113, 114. Negative Nos. 7478, 7480, Jacob E. Reighard Collection, Bentley Historical Library, The University of Michigan, Ann Arbor.
p. 115. Henry B. Ward Collection, Archives, University of Illinois, Urbana-Champaign.

Chapter Nine: The State Fish Hatchery

p. 120. F. T. Stone Laboratory (upper); David H. Stansbery, Columbus, Ohio (lower).

p. 121 Various authors. 1986. *Put-in-Bay Yacht Club Yearbook, 100th Anniversary 1886-1986*. Put-in-Bay. Ohio. p. 106.

pp. 122, 124, 125. David H. Stansbery, Columbus, Ohio.

p. 126. National Park Service, Perry's Victory Collection, Put-in-Bay Office.

p. 128. *Thomas H. Langlois*, F. T. Stone Laboratory.

p. 130. From Bill Kah. *Ohio Conservation Bulletin* 21(8): 14. 1957. August (upper); from *The Ohio State University Bulletin* 42(13): 7. 7 March 1938 (lower).

Chapter Ten: Gibraltar Island: I. The Years Preceding Jay Cooke

p. 134. Postcard postmarked 1920, Alexander Mfg. Co., Sandusky, Ohio (upper); postcard, E. B. Ackley, Sandusky, Ohio. 29469-N (lower left); postcard, Alexander Mfg. Co., Sandusky, Ohio. C9389 (lower right).

p. 137. *Loren S. Putnam* (upper); F. T. Stone Laboratory (lower).

p. 139. Collection No. 2294, Negative No. SC1950, Ohio Historical Society, Columbus.

p. 141. Rutherford B. Hayes Presidential Center, Fremont, Ohio (upper); 17 June 2001, *RLS, C971-5A* (lower).

Chapter Eleven: Gibraltar Island: II. The Years During and Since Jay Cooke

p. 148. Rutherford B. Hayes Presidential Center, Fremont, Ohio (upper); F. T. Stone Laboratory (left and right lower).

p. 154. From Cooke Castle Update; in "Friends of Stone Laboratory," *Twineline* 23(4): 6. July/August 2001. F. T. Stone Laboratory/Ohio Sea Grant College, The Ohio State University.

p. 155. Modified from *Newsletter, Friends of Stone Laboratory*, Summer 1996, p. 4.

pp. 156, 158. F. T. Stone Laboratory.

Chapter Twelve: Adventures and Romance

p. 160. 14 September 1988, *RLS, B62-3A*.

p. 164. Postcard, The American News Co., New York. C175 (upper); National Park Service, Perry's Victory Collection, Put-in-Bay Office (lower).

Chapter Thirteen: South Bass, "Island Jottings" II.

p. 170. Postcard, Alexander Mfg. Co., Sandusky, Ohio 91030 (upper); National Park Service, Perry's Victory Collection, Put-in-Bay Office; postcard, H. A. Herbster, Put-in-Bay, Ohio 7134 (lower).

p. 173. Library Archives, Sandusky Library and Follett House Museum, Sandusky, Ohio.

p. 174. Souvenir-folder of historical Put-in-Bay. H. A. Herbster, Put-in-Bay, Ohio.

p. 178. From *Ohio Conservation Bulletin* 7(1):25. 1943. January; Lake Erie Islands Historical Society, Put-in-Bay, Ohio (upper); National Park Service, Perry's Victory Collection, Put-in-Bay Office (middle and lower).

p. 184. 4 May 1996, *RLS, C766-10*.

Chapter Fourteen: A Potpourri of South Bass News "Jottings"

p. 186. 14 September 1988, *RLS, B62-7A* (upper left, lower right); postcard postmarked 1911, The Rotograph Co., New York City (lower left); postcard, Kirkpatrick, Lakeside, Ohio, *K-25* (upper right).

p. 190. Postcard, Detroit Publishing Co., Detroit, Michigan.

p. 191. Postcard postmarked 1902, German-American Postal Card Co., Cleveland, Ohio.

p. 195. 18 July 1988, *RLS, B43-12*.

p. 221. August 1967, *Jane L. Forsyth,* F. T. Stone Laboratory.

Credits for Color Illustrations

Front Cover Illustrations:

Upper left: Sketch of Theresa Thorndale, *Sketches* (Ryall, 1913, p. 546).
Middle left: Fish Hatcheries and John A. Feick House, postcard, Schoor & Fuchs, Put-in-Bay, Ohio. *27356. N.*
Lower left: Hotel Victory, postcard, Alexander Mfg. Co., Sandusky, Ohio. *B568.*
Right: Jay Cooke's Mansion, Gibraltar Island, 17 June 2001, *RLS C971-16A.*

Back Cover Illustrations:

Upper left: Hotel Victory, postcard, A. C. Bosselman, New York City. *1172*
Middle left: Perry's Lookout and Needle's Eye, Gibraltar Island, postcard, E. B. Ackley, Sandusky, Ohio. *29469.*
Lower: Cottages on Peach Point, postcard, H. A. Herbster, Put-in-Bay, Ohio.
Upper middle: Clubhouse of the Cincinnati Fishing Club, Oak Point, about 1940, *Thomas H. Langlois*, F. T. Stone Laboratory.
Lower middle: Tombstone in the form of a tree stump for Captain Walter Groves, Crown Hill Cemetery, 14 September 1988, *RLS, C79-17A.*
Upper right: South Bass Island Lighthouse, about 1976, *Charles E. Herdendorf*, F. T. Stone Laboratory/Center for Lake Erie Area Research.
Middle right: Jay Cooke's Mansion, Gibraltar Island, 17 June 2001, *RLS,C971-7A.*

Frontispiece:

Loren and Mildred Putnam, August 1996, *Jeffrey M. Reutter*, F. T. Stone Laboratory/Ohio Sea Grant College, The Ohio State University.

Hotel Victory color postcards; insert between pages 48 and 49.

p. 48A. Main entrance, Chisholm Bros., Portland, Maine. *N-101.*
p. 48B. Upper: Main entrance, dining room building, cycling track, transportation car, H. C. Leighton Co., Portland, Maine. *N21688.*
Lower: Southwest portion of Hotel Victory, Detroit Publishing Co., Detroit, Michigan. *5102.*
p. 48C. Upper: Victory Park in front of Hotel Victory, copyright 1906, postmarked 1907, Detroit Publishing Co., Detroit, Michigan. *10609.*
Lower: Rustic Bridge at Victory Park, Alexander Mfg. Co., Sandusky, Ohio, *B526.*
p. 48D. Upper: Cliffs at Victory Park and Bay, postmarked 1908, H. C. Leighton Co., Portland, Maine. *N-4952.*
Lower: Sunset Rocks, Victory Park and Bay, postmarked 1908, Rotograph Co., New York City. *E20208.*

Writers of Articles

Anon.	Anonymous	33, 38, 42, 59, 60, 87, 88, 95, 96, 113, 123, 126, 131, 142, 152, 160, 175, 177, 192
C.H.B.	Charles H. Becker	102
C.E.H.	Charles E. Herdendorf	138
C.L.; E.S.P.	*Cleveland Leader; [Not identified] in Sandusky Daily Register*	36, 39
D.B.	Dwight Boyer	58
D.F.P.	*Detroit Free Press in Sandusky Clarion*	13
D.V.	David Vormelker *in Cleveland Plain Dealer*	78
Mrs. E.F.	Mrs. Ethan Fox	79
F.S.S.	Frank S. Snavely	57, 78
J.E.P.	James E. Pollard	157
J.B. Jr.	John Brown Jr.	70
J.M.	Joe Murray *in Atlanta Journal*	192
K.M.	Kim Strosnider	183
L.J.R.	Lydia J. Ryall	56, 122, 151
M.M.	Marshall McDonald	85
R.C.O.	Raymond C. Osburn	156
R.L.S.	Ronald L. Stuckey	1, 4, 7, 11, 25, 29, 49, 53, 61, 62, 64, 69, 77, 81, 83, 94, 97, 101, 107, 109, 114, 115, 121, 129, 132, 135, 136, 140, 142, 149, 150, 155, 161, 171
T.B.;.T.C.	*Toledo Blade; T. Commercial in Sandusky Weekly Register*	95; 37
T.H.L.	Thomas H. Langlois	127
T.T.	Theresa Thorndale	5, 14, 17, 31, 38, 42, 55, 71, 72, 84, 86, 87, 88, 89, 92, 105, 111, 151, 162, 166, 172, 176, 177, 179, 180, 181, 187

Index to Illustrations

Index to Names of Persons

D

E

F

G

H

I

J

K

L

R

S

T

Index to Topics*

The topics covered in this index pertain primarily to South Bass Island, the other islands in western Lake Erie, and the town of Sandusky in Erie County, Ohio.

* Numbers in bold-face type refer to pages with illustrations.

About the Author and Publisher

Ronald L. Stuckey, born 9 January 1938 in Bucyrus, Crawford County, Ohio, is a country farm boy who lived his first 18 years in Lykens Township. He graduated as valedictorian from Lykens High School (1956), earned a B.S. *cum laude* (1960) in Biology from Heidelberg College, Tiffin, Ohio, and an M.A. (1962) and Ph.D. (1965) in Botany from The University of Michigan, Ann Arbor.

From 1965-1991 he served as Professor of Botany in the Ohio State University, Columbus, where he taught courses in Local Flora, Aquatic Flowering Plants, and Plant Nomenclature. At the University's Stone Laboratory in Lake Erie, Stuckey enjoyed 25 summers (1966-1991) of teaching and research in field botany and vascular plants, and for eight of those summers he served as part-time administrator for the teaching program. Stuckey is an internationally recognized authority on the identification and, geographical distribution of aquatic and wetland plants in North America. He has also written extensively on the botanical history and exploration of eastern North America.

Stuckey is past president of the OSU Chapter of Sigma Xi, the Ohio Academy of Medical History, and The Ohio Academy of Science. The author of more than 100 scientific journal papers and several books, Stuckey has interests in bluegrass music, photography, geography, genealogy, and old books.

Ronald L. Stuckey
Stone Laboratory, 1967.

Your Memories of Put-in-Bay

Your Memories of Put-in-Bay

Ice covering vegetation and rock ledge along southwest shore of South Bass Island; taken by Thomas H. Langlois, Director of Stone Laboratory, 1938-1955.